Praise for *How Learning Works*, 2e

"Since the publication of the original *How Learning Works*, I have returned again and again to its thorough and readable summaries of the most important research on student learning. This second edition has become an even more essential resource for faculty, as the authors have infused the book's recommendations with greater awareness of the social, emotional, and cultural factors that impact student identity and development."

—**James Lang**, author of *Small Teaching*

"*How Learning Works* is a poignant and provocative book that engages meaningfully and intentionally with the intellectual and affective dimensions of teaching and learning that shape our complex and diverse higher education classrooms. Presenting a well-researched, relevant, and socially conscious range of cognitive and social principles and practices, the authors explore what it means to engage intentionally with students as whole beings, in a socially just, inclusive, and pedagogically responsible way."

—**Kasturi Behari-Leak**, dean of the Centre for
Higher Education Development, University of Cape Town

"The Second Edition of *How We Learn* is superb. I particularly admire its breadth of coverage, which includes socioemotional and cognitive components of learning. I highly recommend it for anyone at any level in education."

—**Henry L. Roediger, III**, James S. McDonnell Professor of Psychology;
Washington University in St. Louis; coauthor of *Make It Stick:
The Science of Successful Learning*

"*How Learning Works* is the essential book on teaching and learning in higher education. The new edition is even better than the original. Drawing deeply on recent research to outline eight principles of how learning works, the authors provide practical guidance to put those principles into action. This book is smart, useful, and inspiring!"

—**Peter Felten**, executive director, Center for Engaged Learning,
Elon University

"This book provides tremendous benefits to anyone who wants to engage students and facilitate learning in a higher education context. The authors have pruned the extensive research about how learning works into eight principles and their associated implications. Each chapter contains relatable challenges and offers evidence-based approaches for addressing them."

—**Bonni Stachowiak**, host + producer,
"Teaching in Higher Ed" Podcast

"*How Learning Works* is the perfect title for this excellent book. Drawing upon new research in psychology, education, and cognitive science, the authors have demystified a complex topic into clear explanations of eight powerful learning principles. Full of great ideas and practical suggestions, all based on solid research evidence, this book is essential reading for instructors at all levels who wish to improve their students' learning."

—**Barbara Gross Davis**, assistant vice chancellor for
educational development, University of California, Berkeley,
and author, *Tools for Teaching*

"As you read about each of the eight basic learning principles in this book, you will find advice that is grounded in learning theory, based on research evidence, relevant to college teaching, and easy to understand. The authors have extensive knowledge and experience in applying the science of learning to college teaching, and they graciously share it with you in this organized and readable book."

—**Richard E. Mayer**, professor of psychology,
University of California, Santa Barbara; coauthor,
e-Learning and the Science of Instruction; author, *Multimedia Learning*

How
Learning
Works

How Learning Works

8 Research-Based Principles for Smart Teaching

Second Edition

Marsha C. Lovett,
Michael W. Bridges,
Michele DiPietro,
Susan A. Ambrose,
Marie K. Norman

JB JOSSEY-BASS™
A Wiley Brand

Library of Congress Cataloging-in-Publication Data

Names: Lovett, Marsha C., author. | Bridges, Michael W., author. | DiPietro, Michele, author. | Ambrose A., Susan, 1958- author.| Norman, Marie K., author.
Title: How learning works : 8 research-based principles for smart teaching / Marsha C. Lovett, Michael W. Bridges, Michele DiPietro, Susan A. Ambrose, Marie K. Norman,
Description: Second edition. | Hoboken, New Jersey : Jossey-Bass, [2023] | Includes index.
Identifiers: LCCN 2022046789 (print) | LCCN 2022046790 (ebook) | ISBN 9781119861690 (cloth) | ISBN 9781119860150 (adobe pdf) | ISBN 9781119860143 (epub)
Subjects: LCSH: Effective teaching—Case studies. | Educational innovations—Case studies. | School improvement programs—Case studies. | Learning, Psychology of—Case studies. | Learning. | Teaching.
Classification: LCC LB1025.3 .B753 2023 (print) | LCC LB1025.3 (ebook) | DDC 371.102—dc23/eng/20221005
LC record available at https://lccn.loc.gov/2022046789
LC ebook record available at https://lccn.loc.gov/2022046790

Cover Design and Image: Judy Brooks

To faculty and instructors around the world,
whose dedication to student learning
continues to inspire us.

CONTENTS

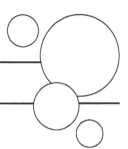

Appendices

LIST OF FIGURES, TABLES, AND EXHIBITS

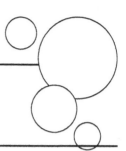

Figures

Tables

Exhibits

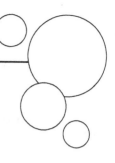

FOREWORD TO THE FIRST EDITION: APPLYING THE SCIENCE OF LEARNING TO COLLEGE TEACHING

In 1899, the famous American psychologist William James published a little book called *Talks to Teachers*, in which he sought to explain how to apply psychology to education—that is, he sought to use what he called "the science of the mind's workings" to generate practical advice for classroom teachers. At the time, the book was not much of a success, largely for two reasons: (1) there was a lack of research evidence on how learning works (i.e., the science of learning) and (2) there was a lack of research-based principles concerning how to help people learn (i.e., the science of instruction).

Much has happened in the learning sciences in the past 100 years, particularly in the last few decades. We finally have the makings of a research-based theory of how people learn that is educationally relevant (i.e., the science of learning) and a set of evidence-based principles for how to help people learn that is grounded in cognitive theory (i.e., the science of instruction). Indeed, these are exciting times if you are interested in fulfilling William James's mission of applying the science of learning to education.

The book you are holding—*How Learning Works: Seven Research-Based Principles for Smart Teaching*—is the latest advancement in the continuing task of applying the science of learning to education—particularly, college teaching. The authors are experts in helping college teachers understand how research in the science of learning can improve their teaching. If you are interested in what research in the science of learning and instruction has to say for you as a college teacher, then this book is for you.

The book is organized on seven learning principles—each a gem that is based on research evidence from the science of learning and the science of instruction.

The principles concern the role of the student's prior knowledge, motivation, and developmental level, as well as opportunities for the student to practice, receive feedback, and learn to become a self-directed learner. Each chapter focuses on one of the principles, such as "Students' prior knowledge can help or hinder learning." Each chapter begins with a concrete scenario in college teaching that exemplifies the principle being highlighted in the chapter, provides a clear statement and rationale for the principle, summarizes the underlying research and its implications, and offers specific advice on how to apply the principle.

Consider the following scenario: You are teaching a course in your field. Based on years of study and work, you are an expert in your field—but you are certainly not an expert in how to teach others about your field. In fact, you have almost no training in how to teach. Yet a fundamental part of your job involves college teaching. You have devised a teaching style that works for you, but you wonder whether there is any way to base what you are doing on scientific principles of learning and teaching. This description fits many college teachers.

The book you are holding is based on the idea that you wish to consider taking an evidence-based approach to college teaching—that is, you wish to inform your instructional decisions with research evidence and research-based theory. Why should you take an evidence-based approach? You could base your instructional choices on fads, ideology, opinions, expert advice, or habit—but these approaches may not be ideal if your goal is to be an effective teacher. Admittedly, advice from experts and your own personal experience can be useful aids to you in planning instruction, but they may be incomplete. In taking an evidence-based approach, you seek to add to your knowledge base by discovering what works and how it works. In short, it is helpful to understand what the science of learning has to offer you in your role as a college teacher.

Where should you look for help in improving your college teaching? Consider three common choices:

Sources that are too hard: You could try to digest research articles in the field of learning and instruction, but you might find them somewhat tedious and perhaps daunting. This approach is too hard because it focuses on scientific evidence without much focus on how to apply the evidence to teaching.

Sources that are too soft: You could read self-help guides that offer practical advice that is not necessarily based on research evidence or research-based theory. This approach is too soft because it focuses on practical advice without supporting evidence or theory to back up the advice.

Sources that are just right: You could read this book, which synthesizes empirical research evidence and research-based learning theory into practical advice for how to improve your college teaching. In short, the strength of this book is that it combines research evidence and practical advice to produce an evidence-based approach to improving your college teaching. If you are interested in what the science of learning has to contribute to your college teaching, then this book is for you.

What should you look for in this book? In reading this book, I suggest that you look to make sure that it meets four basic criteria for applying the science of learning to your college teaching:

Theory-grounded: the advice is grounded in a research-based theory of how people learn.
Evidence-based: the advice is supported by empirical research evidence showing how to help people learn.
Relevant: the advice has clear and practical implications for how to improve your teaching.
Clear: the advice is understandable, concrete, and concise.

As you read about each of the seven basic learning principles in this book, you will find advice that is grounded in learning theory, based on research evidence, relevant to college teaching, and easy to understand. The authors have extensive knowledge and experience in applying the science of learning to college teaching, and they graciously share it with you in this organized and readable book.

I congratulate you for your interest in improving your teaching and commend you for taking the important step of reading this book. If you want to improve your teaching, it is useful to understand what research says about how learning works and about how to foster learning. In light of these goals, I welcome you to the feast of evidence-based advice you will find in this volume.

Richard E. Mayer
University of California, Santa Barbara

ACKNOWLEDGMENTS

Creating the second edition of *How Learning Works* involved significant time and effort—not only on our part as coauthors but also from friends and colleagues who made extremely important contributions along the way. First, we would like to thank our educational development colleagues, Victoria Genetin (from the University of Michigan) as well as Phoebe Cook and Janet Lawler (from Carnegie Mellon University), for providing thoughtful and perceptive comments on our revised chapter drafts. The text was markedly improved as a result of their thorough reviews. We also thank Michelle Pierson for her assistance with copyediting the new manuscript and for the painstaking work of checking and properly formatting references.

Readers familiar with the original edition of *How Learning Works* are sure to have benefited from the conceptually helpful and visually attractive figures throughout the book (not to mention the striking cover). All of these visuals were created by our talented colleague Judy Brooks, who was willing to collaborate with us again on the second edition—creating new figures (for the new Chapter 1 and overhauled Chapter 7), enhancing several original figures to be more crisp and clear, and updating the full set to be stylistically coordinated. As ever, we are deeply grateful for Judy's expertise in design, her thoughtful approach to the learning principles at hand, and her artful creativity in depicting them so effectively. We also love the new cover—how it connects with but stands apart from the first edition's. And most of all, we appreciate the great conversations about the principles that were sparked by Judy's incisive questions and inspiring design ideas!

To the many friends and colleagues who contributed to the first edition, we reiterate our sincere thanks and acknowledge that the indelible mark of their comments, suggestions, and ideas are carried forward in the current edition. These thanks go to Anne Fay for her early contributions to the first edition, which shaped the principles and the research reported, to Aimee Kane for her thoughtful and reflective feedback later in that process, and to Lisa Ritter for careful attention and exacting standards as she served in the role of internal editor by copyediting the original manuscript. We are also thankful for an outstanding set of colleagues, at Carnegie Mellon and other universities in the United States and abroad, who were willing to take time from their busy schedules to read and provide insightful feedback on different chapters from the first edition. These colleagues include Vincent Aleven, Ryan Baker, Rebecca Freeland, Scott Kauffman, Edmund Ko, Ken Koedinger, Norma Ming, Matt Ouellett, Ido Roll, and Christian Schunn.

Finally, we would never have embarked on this entire endeavor in the first place if it were not for the thousands of faculty members and graduate students with whom we have worked over the years. We are humbled by your ongoing dedication to your students and by your willingness to share your stories and experiences, open up your courses to us, and reflect thoughtfully on and refine your teaching practice. We continue to learn and benefit from our interactions with you, and we hope this book provides something useful in return.

ABOUT
THE AUTHORS

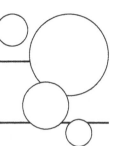

Marsha C. Lovett is vice provost for teaching and learning innovation at Carnegie Mellon University (CMU). In addition, she is director of CMU's Eberly Center for Teaching Excellence & Educational Innovation and a teaching professor in the Department of Psychology. Marsha leads a team of teaching consultants, learning engineers, designers, data scientists, and technologists to help instructors create meaningful and demonstrably effective educational experiences—for in-person, hybrid, and online learning. She received her doctorate in cognitive psychology from CMU and spent a year as a visiting scholar in the Graduate School of Education at the University of California, Berkeley. Marsha has taught a variety of courses—from introductory cognitive psychology to graduate research methods—and one of her favorite teaching memories is a seminar on human expertise that included students juggling, playing poker, and sharing cooking techniques. Marsha has studied learning in the laboratory and the classroom, leading to more than 50 articles on learning and instruction. She has presented workshops, keynotes, and invited talks across the United States and abroad. Marsha has also created several innovative, educational technologies to promote student learning and metacognition, and she has developed and/or evaluated online courses in the sciences, social sciences, and humanities. Marsha is happiest when she is working with educators to collect qualitative and quantitative data in their own courses and then leverage the results to enhance students' learning outcomes and sense of belonging.

Michael W. Bridges is executive director of the University Center for Teaching and Learning (UCTL) at the University of Pittsburgh. In this role, he leads the university's efforts to create exceptional and consequential learning experiences. Toward this goal he directs and works with a large team of instructional designers, teaching consultants, educational technologists, learning space designers, and assessment experts to support excellent teaching. Mike received his doctorate in social psychology from Carnegie Mellon University in 1997. His early career focused on understanding the role of psychosocial variables in recovery from coronary artery bypass surgery and breast cancer. He formerly served as the vice president for educational strategy and excellence at iCarnegie Global Learning, where he used the principles in this book to help instructors in Russia, Kazakhstan, India, Mexico, Colombia, and Qatar to design, develop, and deliver great courses. Mike has more than 30 years of teaching experience and still feels a mixture of anxiety and excitement on the first day of every class. His most recent interests focus on understanding the role of narratives in teaching and the unending quest for a recipe for perfect falafel.

Michele DiPietro is the executive director for faculty development, recognition, and the Center for Excellence in Teaching and Learning (CETL) and a professor in the School of Data Science and Analytics at Kennesaw State University. As executive director of CETL, Michele oversees university-wide faculty and graduate student development efforts, both in pedagogy and career and leadership development. They received their doctorate in statistics from Carnegie Mellon University in 2001. Their scholarly interests include the application of learning sciences to enhance college teaching, holistic faculty development, inclusion and justice in the classroom, teaching in times of tragedies, and more. Michele practices "shine theory," helping educators and administrators shine bright and find fulfillment in their work so that they might help their students shine. Michele has served as president of the POD Network in Higher Education, the premiere educational development organization in North America, and as a board member of the International Consortium for Educational Development. Their first year seminar "The Statistics of Sexual Orientation" has been featured in a variety of media, including *The Chronicle of Higher Education*. Michele is the recipient of the Bob Pierleoni Spirit of POD award, the highest award bestowed by the POD Network for professional achievement and legacy to the field.

Marie K. Norman is associate professor of medicine and clinical and translational science at the University of Pittsburgh. She is director of the Innovative Design for Education and Assessment (IDEA) Lab, where she leads hybrid and online educational initiatives for the Institute for Clinical Research Education (ICRE). She is also co-director of the Team Science Core of the Clinical and Translational Science Institute. Marie received her doctorate in cultural anthropology from the University of Pittsburgh and conducted her fieldwork in Nepal, funded by a Fulbright award. Her first love is teaching, and she is proud to have taught in higher education for more than 25 years, first in undergraduate and now in graduate education, teaching a wide range of courses, seminars, and workshops on topics from anthropology to leadership to team science to adult learning theory. She also brings experience from the business world, having served as director of intercultural education at iCarnegie Global Learning and senior director for educational excellence at Acatar, an educational technology start-up. Marie has been fortunate to work with educators in Colombia, Kazakhstan, Tatarstan, and Qatar, sharing the principles from this book and learning from their expertise. She has been closely involved in a number of diversity, equity, and inclusion initiatives, serving on the ICRE's Diversity Advisory Committee and helping to develop and administer the LEADS, PROMISED, Building Up, and TRANSFORM programs for scientists from underrepresented backgrounds. She is happiest working in collaboration with smart, curious, socially engaged people on projects at the intersections of teaching, learning, culture, technology, and design.

PREFACE TO THE
SECOND EDITION

When we wrote the first edition of this book, we all lived in the same mid-sized city in the Mid-Atlantic and worked at the same institution, a mid-sized university with a reputation for excellence in technical and creative fields. A lot of *mids*, in other words. Since then, a great deal has changed, not only in the world and in higher education but also in our own lives.

Michele became the director of a teaching center at a southern state university, considerably less resourced than what they had been used to, making strides in spite of those conditions but grappling with issues of salary compression and sometimes even salary inversion. The demographic makeup of the student body was much more diverse, with social attitudes spanning the full political spectrum. Class sizes were large and teaching assistants scarce, and faculty members struggled to put recommended teaching strategies into practice, simply because the administrative and grading burdens were too great. Michele encountered undocumented students and students living in poverty and began to better appreciate the precarity of their lives and its effect on their studies: students who had to skip class to avoid a police roadblock or make a court appearance, for instance. While the students were bright and dedicated, a few included veterans grappling with PTSD and students whose previous education was so insufficient they could not manage college classes. Through rapidly changing institutional leadership, Michele's campus made the national news multiple times over controversies about free speech and accusations of racism. A state law allowing guns in unrestricted areas of campus raised safety concerns for educators who taught controversial subjects. Long interested in yoga, Michele began to integrate their yoga practice into their work to foster a more compassionate, holistic, and radical approach to supporting faculty.

Marsha stayed at the university where we all first met, but she moved into new administrative roles and collaborations. Many of these collaborations focused on the intersections of learning and technology, specifically the uses of learning analytics. She developed several novel technologies to enhance students' learning and metacognition. At the same time, her personal experiences with faculty and students from different backgrounds shifted her outlook on teaching and learning. She encountered students who, despite attending an elite institution, regularly confronted food insecurity. She witnessed colleagues with disabilities, trans colleagues, and colleagues from minoritized groups navigating the entrenched hierarchies and rigid norms of institutions that were not designed for them, and in fact were sometimes openly rejecting. When she read the results of a qualitative study of students' experiences related to diversity and inclusion on her campus, she found the stories painful to read.

Meanwhile, Mike and Marie moved out of academia (temporarily) and into the business world, working together at a global education start-up. Their positions took them overseas to countries from Kazakhstan to India to Colombia and gave them a deep appreciation for the ways in which education and culture—not to mention politics and economics—are intertwined. Their work also introduced them to the fast-paced, competitive culture of business, which is so strikingly different from academia. In the process, they learned communication and marketing skills that are relevant to teaching and learning yet rarely part of academic training. Eventually, both found their way back to academia.

Marie joined the faculty in a school of medicine, coming to better appreciate the needs of adult learners in professional schools as well as the different forms of teaching that characterize clinical preceptorship, mentorship, and even team science. Her involvement in collaborations with Minority Serving Institutions and Hispanic and Native American Centers of Excellence disrupted her assumptions about how different institutions and institutional cultures operate and widened her understanding of the issues facing faculty members and students from different backgrounds. At the same time, she became deeply involved in online program development and the factors that make for engaging, rigorous, and creative online learning.

Mike returned to academia as an administrator, leading online education and faculty development initiatives at several universities, each with a distinctive institutional flavor. Guiding institutional strategy and working with a large, diverse staff widened his understanding of the roles and responsibilities of institutions of higher ed. At the same time, watching his own child progress through the school system and learn new skills, both academic and non-academic, has made him appreciate learning—and the learning principles featured in this book—in new ways.

At the same time, the world changed radically around us and higher education itself shifted in seismic ways. Demographic changes—a shrinking pool of college-aged students and population shifts to the southern and western parts of the country—left many institutions of higher education scrambling for students. To attract applicants, many doubled down in an arms race of campus amenities, sometimes to the detriment of academics. Some colleges and universities, unable to compete, folded. Greater ideological division in the country prompted more scrutiny of academic institutions through state boards of regents and other oversight agents. Declining state educational budgets led public institutions to tighten their belts, replacing tenure-track faculty with less-expensive adjuncts, increasing class sizes, and cutting programs. Competition from industry and alternate forms of training and credentialing forced academia to develop new business models and offerings, including "unbundled" degree programs, massive open online courses (MOOCs), micro-credentials, bootcamps, continuing and professional education units, and programs to engage alumni under the banner of "lifelong learning." New technologies entered (and left) the scene, changing the way instruction was delivered as well as the pressures on faculty. The rise of online programs brought new ways to reach students but with them a host of new challenges, both pedagogical and administrative.

And, of course, COVID-19 rocked higher education. As fears of the virus intensified, institutions closed their physical facilities and sent students home. Courses moved suddenly to remote delivery, only to move back to the physical classroom, then back online based on the shifting public health situation. Administrators, faculty members, and students learned to pivot quickly to keep up, developing more agility than they knew they had. But as students joined classes from home, universities struggled to justify their high cost and maintain relevance. A slew of questions arose: Would higher education remain online? What would this mean in terms of inclusion and access? Were physical campuses and in-person learning even necessary? What could universities offer that justified the increasingly high cost of a degree?

The murder of George Floyd, Breonna Taylor, and so many others at the hands of police brought to the surface a long overdue racial reckoning. The aftermath has left many institutions interrogating the role they should play in a modern democracy, and committing to dismantling structural bias and injustice more intentionally (and, one would hope, sincerely). Diversity, equity, and inclusion initiatives became more extensive and sophisticated. The #MeToo movement sparked deeper conversations about gender and power, and a nationwide explosion of interest in more fluid expressions of gender and sexual identity changed the conversation on college campuses—with a subsequent backlash. At the same time, the country saw the proliferation of misinformation, disinformation, and conspiracy theories. We saw verifiable facts discounted as "fake news," accuracy devalued in favor of personal opinion, and fabrications legitimized under the guise of free speech. As some legislatures capitalized on the confusion and fear of the moment to dictate what could and could not be taught in public universities, educators struggled with the assault on academic freedom and mourned what often felt like a loss of meaning in their work. Students and their families, for their part, have been buffeted by the turmoil, left with spiraling student debt from the rising cost of higher education, and a growing sense of cynicism about the cost of education relative to its value.

Throughout these social shifts—and sometimes in direct response to them—the research on learning evolved, providing empirical evidence where there were once just anecdotes and hunches, debunking long-standing assumptions about teaching and learning, and expanding into new areas of inquiry. The terminology of learning research—cognitive load, social presence, stereotype threat, growth mindset—moved into the mainstream, although many lessons from the learning sciences have yet to make their way into classroom practice.

The sum of these changes—in our own lives, the larger landscape, and the learning sciences—prompted our decision to rethink *How Learning Works*. To be clear, we are immensely proud of the first edition; however, we are not blind to its limitations. While we had aimed to be research-based, the research we referenced was, understandably, only in English. The studies we included were conducted largely with traditional-aged college students and not the broad population of students attending colleges and universities today. Our cases and strategies were predicated on our own experience teaching at an elite university. Indeed, the very definition of learning we used was steeped in Western thought and embedded in the cultural currents of the early 2000s. We were not fully cognizant then of how fully our perspectives were shaped and constrained by our cultural, linguistic, and institutional context. We are more so now.

So it is time for an update.

We have made significant changes in the second edition. Most notably, we have expanded from seven to eight principles, which has enabled us to delve more deeply into the social and emotional components of learning. A brand-new chapter (Chapter 1) explores individual differences among learners, and the intersections of identities and backgrounds that shape how students enter, respond to, and shape the learning environment. A reworked chapter (Chapter 7) investigates more fully the ways that instructors can shape the climate of their courses to make students feel included or marginalized—and the implications for learning and performance. Across all eight principles, we updated the research previously discussed while integrating new areas of research. Wherever possible, we applied a diversity, equity, and inclusion lens, exploring issues of power, identity, and belonging as they relate to teaching and learning. We have also referenced a broader range of institution types and student populations than in the previous edition and incorporated case studies and strategies relevant to emerging educational technologies and online and hybrid learning modalities.

As we have worked together, comparing notes from our experiences since writing the first edition, we have rediscovered how enduring the principles elaborated here are. They have proven to be as relevant in skill-oriented professional schools as they are in highly theoretical undergraduate courses, as applicable in large classes as in small, as important online as in person. Moreover, when we have presented the principles in our travels around the world, they have always resonated with our audiences. So much so, in fact, that *How Learning Works* has been translated into Arabic, Chinese, Japanese, Korean, Italian, and Spanish. We cherish the fact that our work is being used to spark conversations about teaching and learning around the world.

In closing . . . . .

One of the great joys of writing the second edition of this book was the opportunity for the four of us to reconnect with one another and reignite a collaboration we value deeply. Our original coauthor, Susan A. Ambrose has since retired and did not rejoin the effort. But the fun we had working together this time reminded us of the fun we had the first time.

We hope you enjoy the second edition of *How Learning Works* as much as we enjoyed writing it.

Marsha, Michele, Mike, and Marie

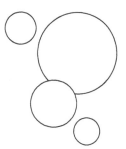

Introduction: Bridging Learning Research and Teaching Practice

Learning results from what the student does and thinks and only from what the student does and thinks. The teacher can advance learning only by influencing what the student does to learn.

HERBERT A. SIMON,[1] one of the founders of the field of cognitive science, Nobel Laureate, and university professor (deceased) at Carnegie Mellon University

Any conversation about effective teaching must begin with a consideration of how students learn. Yet instructors who want to investigate the mechanisms and conditions that promote student learning may find themselves caught between two kinds of resources: research articles with technical discussions of experimental designs and learning data or books and websites with concrete strategies for course design and classroom pedagogy. Texts of the first type focus on learning but are often inaccessible and lack clear application to the classroom, while texts of the second type are written in accessible language but often leave instructors without a clear sense of why (or even whether) particular strategies work. Neither of these genres offers what many instructors really need—a model of student learning that enables them to make sound teaching decisions. In other words, instructors need a bridge between research and practice, between teaching and learning.

We wrote this book to provide such a bridge. The book grew out of over 29 years of experience consulting with faculty colleagues about teaching and learning. In these consultations, we encountered a number of recurring problems that spanned disciplines, course types, and student skill levels. Many of these problems raised fundamental questions about student learning. For example: Why can't students apply what they have learned? Why do they cling so tightly to misconceptions? Why are they not more engaged by material I find so interesting? Why do they claim to know so much more than they actually know? Why do they continue to employ the same ineffective study strategies?

As we worked with faculty to explore the sources of these problems, we turned to the research on learning, and from this research we distilled seven principles, each of which crystallizes a key aspect of student learning. We expanded this to eight principles in the second edition, with the goal of exploring the social, emotional, and cultural dimensions of learning more deeply and grappling with inequality and marginalization more explicitly. These principles have become the foundation for our work. Not only have we found them indispensable in our own teaching and in our consultations with faculty but also, as we have talked and worked with thousands of faculty members from around the world, we have also found that the principles—and the research that informs them—resonate across disciplines, institution types, student populations, learning modalities, and cultures. In our experience, these principles provide instructors with an understanding of student learning that can help them (1) understand why certain teaching approaches are or are not supporting students' learning, (2) generate or refine teaching approaches and strategies that more effectively foster student learning in specific contexts, and (3) transfer and apply these principles to new courses, learners, and contexts.

In this book, we offer these principles of learning, along with a discussion of the research that supports them, their implications for teaching, and a set of instructional strategies targeting each principle. Before briefly summarizing the full set of principles and discussing the characteristics they share and some ways that this book can be used, we begin by discussing what we mean by *learning*.

WHAT IS LEARNING?

Any set of learning principles is predicated on a definition of learning. In this book, we define learning as a process that leads to change, which occurs as a result of experience and increases the potential for improved performance and future learning (adapted from Mayer, 2002). There are three critical components to this definition:

1. Learning is a process, not a product. However, because this process takes place in the mind, we can only infer that it has occurred from students' products or performances.
2. Learning involves change in knowledge, beliefs, behaviors, or attitudes. This change unfolds over time; it is not fleeting but rather has a lasting impact on how students think and act.
3. Learning is not something done to students, but rather something students themselves do. It is the direct result of how students interpret and respond to their experiences—conscious and unconscious, past and present.

OUR PRINCIPLES OF LEARNING

Our eight principles of learning come from a perspective that is developmental and holistic. In other words, we begin with the recognition that (1) learning is a developmental process that intersects with other developmental processes in a student's life and (2) students enter our classrooms not only with skills, knowledge, and abilities but also with social and emotional experiences that influence what they value, how they perceive themselves and others, and how they will engage in the learning process. Consistent with this holistic perspective, readers should understand that, although we address each principle individually to highlight particular issues pertaining to student learning, they are all at work simultaneously in real learning situations and are functionally inseparable.

In the following paragraphs, we briefly summarize each of the principles in the order in which they are discussed in the book.

Students differ from each other on multiple dimensions—for example, in their identities, stages of development, and personal histories—and these differences influence how they experience the world and, in turn, their learning and performance.

The starting point for all good teaching is this question: Who are my students? Because learning requires integrating new knowledge and skills with one's current worldview, the maturity, identities, and experiences students bring with them into our classroom affect their learning profoundly. Furthermore, these crucial components of learning are not static but rather evolve over one's life span. Consequently, teaching effectively requires close attention to individual differences among students as well as their social and intellectual development.

Students' prior knowledge can help or hinder learning.

Students come into our courses with knowledge, beliefs, and attitudes gained in other courses and through daily life. As students bring this knowledge to bear in our classrooms, it influences how they filter and interpret what they are learning. If students' prior knowledge is robust and accurate and activated at the appropriate time, it provides a strong foundation for building new knowledge. However, when knowledge is inert, insufficient for the task, activated inappropriately, or inaccurate, it can interfere with or impede new learning.

How students organize knowledge influences how they learn and apply what they know.

Students naturally make connections between pieces of knowledge. When those connections form knowledge structures that are accurately and meaningfully organized, students are better able to retrieve and apply their knowledge effectively and efficiently. By contrast, when knowledge is connected in inaccurate or random ways, students can fail to retrieve or apply it appropriately.

Students' motivation determines, directs, and sustains what they do to learn.

Students in higher education have considerable autonomy, so motivation plays a critical role in guiding the direction, intensity, persistence, and quality of the learning behaviors in which they engage. When students find positive value in a learning goal or activity, expect to successfully achieve a desired learning outcome, and perceive support from their environment, they are likely to be strongly motivated to learn.

> *To develop mastery, students must acquire component skills, practice integrating them, and know when to apply what they have learned.*

Mastery requires that students develop not only the component skills and knowledge necessary to perform complex tasks but also they must practice combining and integrating their skills and knowledge to develop greater fluency and automaticity. Finally, students must learn when and how to apply the skills and knowledge they learn. The process of helping students gain mastery is confounded by the fact that, because of their expertise, instructors may have lost conscious awareness of these elements.

> *Goal-directed practice coupled with targeted feedback enhances the quality of students' learning.*

Learning and performance are best fostered when students engage in practice that focuses on a specific goal or criterion, targets an appropriate level of challenge, and is of sufficient quantity and frequency to meet the performance criteria. Practice must be coupled with feedback that explicitly communicates about some aspect(s) of students' performance relative to specific target criteria, provides information to help students progress in meeting those criteria, and is given at a time and frequency that allows it to be useful.

> *The classroom environment we create can profoundly affect students' learning, positively or negatively.*

The social and emotional dimensions of the learning environment shape students' learning, engagement, achievement, and persistence in significant

5

ways. Thus, the classroom climates instructors establish are of critical importance. While a subtly or overtly alienating classroom climate can inhibit and derail learning, faculty members have the power to create classroom environments that are both intellectually challenging and welcoming to all students, enhancing learning in powerful ways. In particular, faculty members can use strategies that foster a sense of belonging, adopt course content that is deliberately inclusive, be thoughtful about the tone of documents and interactions, and cultivate a strong sense of instructor immediacy and presence, particularly online.

> *To become self-directed learners, students must learn to monitor and adjust their approaches to learning.*

Learners may engage in a variety of metacognitive processes to monitor and control their learning—assessing the task at hand, evaluating their own strengths and weaknesses, planning their approach, applying and monitoring various strategies, and reflecting on the degree to which their current approach is working. When students develop these metacognitive skills, they gain intellectual habits that not only improve their performance but also their effectiveness as learners.

WHAT MAKES THESE PRINCIPLES POWERFUL?

The principal strength of these eight principles is that they are based directly on research, drawing on literature from cognitive, developmental, and social psychology, anthropology, education, and diversity studies, and research targeting not only higher education but also K–12 education. Although this book does not provide an exhaustive literature review and any summary of research necessarily simplifies a host of complexities, we believe that our discussions of the research underlying each principle are faithful to the scholarship and describe features of learning about which there is widespread agreement. Indeed, several of our principles align with those that others have delineated (Pashler et al., 2007; Pittsburgh Science of Learning Center, 2009), a convergence that we believe attests to their salience.

Not only are our eight principles research-based but also, as we have shared them with colleagues over the years, we have found that they are

- *Domain-independent:* They apply equally well across all subject areas, from biology to design to history to robotics; the fundamental factors that affect the way students learn transcend disciplinary differences.
- *Experience-independent:* The principles apply to all educational levels and pedagogical situations. In other words, although the pedagogical implications of a principle will be somewhat different for first-year undergraduate students in a lab environment as opposed to graduate students in a studio environment, the principle still applies.
- *Cross-culturally relevant:* Although the research we discuss has been conducted primarily in the Western world, faculty colleagues in other countries have resonated with the principles, finding them relevant to their own classes and students. That said, it is important to bear in mind that culture can and does influence how the principles should be applied as instructors design and teach their courses.

INTENDED AUDIENCES

This book is intended for anyone interested in understanding more about how students learn and in applying that information to improve instruction. This includes—but is not limited to—faculty members, graduate students, faculty developers, instructional designers, and librarians. It also includes K–12 educators. In addition, the principles outlined here are valuable for instructors at all experience levels. They can help new and inexperienced instructors understand the components of effective course design and classroom pedagogy. They can help experienced instructors troubleshoot problems or adapt effective strategies to suit new courses, student populations, or modes of delivery. They can also help highly successful and experienced instructors reflect on what makes their approaches and methods effective. Finally, these principles can enable faculty members to better support student learning without having to rely on outside experts (a benefit that is particularly valuable for faculty at campuses without teaching and learning centers).

HOW TO READ THIS BOOK

Perhaps you are an instructor who has heard about best practices in teaching but do not understand why these practices work. Or maybe you know the research on learning but do not know how to put it into practice. We hope you will find this book a helpful bridge connecting research with practice in an approachable and feasible way.

Each chapter in this book begins with stories that represent teaching situations that we hope will strike readers as familiar. Although the instructors described in these stories are fictional, the scenarios are authentic, representing composites of real problems we have encountered over many years of consulting with faculty. We analyze these stories to identify the core problems or issues involved and use them to introduce the learning principle relevant to those problems. Then we discuss the principle in relation to the research that underlies it. Finally, we provide a set of strategies to help instructors design instruction with that principle in mind.

Because all of these principles combine to influence learning, no one principle stands alone. Consequently, the chapters can be read in any order.

NOTE

1. Herb Simon was a university professor at Carnegie Mellon University and had joint appointments in the departments of psychology and computer science. While at Carnegie Mellon, Herb played a major role in the development of the Graduate School of Industrial Administration (renamed the Tepper School of Business in 2004), the Department of Psychology, the School of Computer Science, and the College of Humanities and Social Sciences. He was one of the founding fathers of the fields of cognitive psychology and artificial intelligence, and won the Nobel Prize in Economics in 1978 and the National Medal of Science in 1986. For many years (until his death), Herb served as a member of the Advisory Committee to the Eberly Center for Teaching Excellence. He was often heard paraphrasing this quote from Elliott Dunlap Smith, a past president of Carnegie Mellon University.

CHAPTER 1

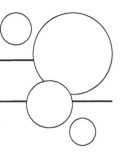

Why Do Students' Identities and Stages of Development Matter for Learning?

"End of Story"

Yesterday in my Economics class, we were discussing an article about the cost of illegal immigration to the US economy. The discussion was moving along at a brisk pace when one student, Gloria, began to intervene quite forcefully, saying the reading was biased and didn't represent the situation accurately. Another student, Danielle, responded: "Gloria, why do you always have to bring up race? Why can't we just discuss the figures in the articles without getting so defensive?" A third student, Kayla, who had been quiet up to this point in the semester, said that, as far as she was concerned, illegal immigrants should be arrested and deported, "end of story." Her grandparents were Polish immigrants, she continued, and had come to the US legally, worked hard, and made good lives for themselves, "but now even my dad says this country is getting sucked dry by Mexican illegals who have no right to be here, and it's just plain wrong." At that point, the rest of the class got really quiet, and I could see my three Hispanic students exchange furious, disbelieving looks. Annoyed, Gloria shot back: "Those 'illegals' you're talking about include some people very close to me, and you don't know anything about them." The whole thing erupted in an angry back-and-forth, with Gloria calling Kayla entitled and racist and Kayla looking close to tears. I tried to regain control of the class by asking Gloria to try to depersonalize the discussion and focus on the central economic issues, but when we returned to the discussion I couldn't get anyone to talk. Kayla and Gloria sat silently with their arms folded, looking down, and the rest of the class just looked uncomfortable. I know I didn't handle this situation well, but I really wish my students were mature enough to talk about these issues without being at each other's throats over secondary, unrelated points.

Professor Leandro Battaglia

Too Many Reasons

I used to think I was pretty good at getting students to participate in class, but lately I've been facing a "wall of silence." Knowing a few colleagues who do mid-semester feedback in their courses, I decided to give it a try and specifically asked my students why they don't participate more during class. Boy, did they give me an earful! One student wrote that, on top of a full course load, they are working late hours at two jobs. By the time they get to my class, they are too exhausted to think. One reported that she (I'm assuming it's a she) tried participating early in the semester but stopped when she didn't feel like her contributions were appreciated—like the time two male students made essentially her same points and were praised for the stolen ideas. Another disclosed that they are on the autism spectrum and have a hard time navigating social interactions, like when to jump into a discussion without being rude or weird, or how to disagree without sounding angry or condescending. . . . To avoid the uncertainty, they simply don't participate. Yet another mentioned feeling hurt when they were misgendered in class and, after that, they disengaged. And yet another wrote that professors, especially Southern ladies like me, don't really want to hear from their Black students. That stung. I try not to make assumptions about my students, but they seem to have no problem making assumptions about me. On and on it went. There were as many reasons for not participating as there were students. I tried to find some common theme that would point to one clear solution, but no. I want to help my students, I truly do. But each one seems to want something different from me, and I can't personalize my course for each individual student. Plus, now I'm even afraid I'll say the wrong thing and make it worse. What should I do?

Professor Charlotte Calhoun

WHAT IS GOING ON IN THESE TWO STORIES?

In both of these stories, students are bringing important aspects of their identities into the classroom, and these identities create a powerful lens for how they see and respond to the learning experience. Although Professor Battaglia has assigned a reading that touches on a controversial topic, he expects his students to be able to discuss the material in terms of economic principles rather than personal experience and ethnic identity, which in his mind are mutually exclusive. What begins with an intellectual discussion of the reading quickly devolves into a highly charged exchange about racial issues—in his mind, only marginally related to the course content—culminating in hurt feelings, discomfort, disengagement, and ultimately a complete collapse of the discussion. Professor Battaglia finds himself unable to rein in the chaos. The fracas that arises leaves him feeling helpless and wondering why students are unable to stay on topic or at least be civil about their disagreements.

If Professor Battaglia's discussion was derailed by vociferous conflict, Professor Calhoun's course is marred by silence and disengagement. Here is an educator who understands the value of course participation, tries her best, and uses best practices such as mid-semester feedback to assess her teaching, only to discover a seemingly endless list of explanations for non-participation. Some of the reasons are beyond her control, like the outside commitments some students have, and yet her course is suffering the consequences. Some responses would make many of us realize how much of our social interactions we take for granted, like in the case of the student on the spectrum, but again are way outside of Professor Calhoun's capacity to help. Some she likely didn't even realize until they were brought up, like the misgendering or the misattributing student contributions. And some are painful to read, like the student stating she doesn't care about Black students. It feels like an intractable predicament even for a well-meaning instructor, or as many intractable predicaments as there are students in her course. Either way, the learning experience for everybody is negatively affected.

WHAT PRINCIPLE OF LEARNING IS AT WORK HERE?

Even though the students in these stories were ostensibly part of the same learning environment, they were affected by it, and in turn affected their environment, in different ways. Their experiences were colored by their values and belief systems, their histories, identities, and other individual characteristics. In subsequent chapters, we will focus on processes that are common across all students. For instance, everybody needs to pay attention to learn something. Everybody needs practice opportunities and constructive feedback to develop skills, and so on. The strategies stemming from this approach will maximize our efficiency as educators, because they will apply to most of our students. But the uniqueness and individuality of our students also play a crucial role in the learning process, and we need to start there for an important reason.

The empirical evidence we rely on emerges from many studies involving tens of thousands of students in total, and the results are averaged across students to arrive at teaching and learning strategies that work for the average student. But as statisticians point out, often the average does not exist. Just like no family has exactly 2.3 children (the average number of children from the classic demographic studies of the 1960s), the average student loses any individuality that the actual students in those studies possessed, with an inevitable loss of information. In this trade-off, we give up a nuanced understanding of each student for a synthetic understanding of the average student, with definite advantages but also disadvantages. In particular, some researchers point out that most quantitative educational research in the United States is "essentially raceless" (Patton et al., 2015).

We will delve into the powerful results from this body of research in the next chapters, but we want to start by acknowledging that the uniqueness and individuality of our students, as well as the systems of power and inequity in which we are all situated, play a crucial role in the learning process. Accordingly, our first principle calls attention to the unique backgrounds and perspectives our students' bring to the learning environment (see Figure 1.1).

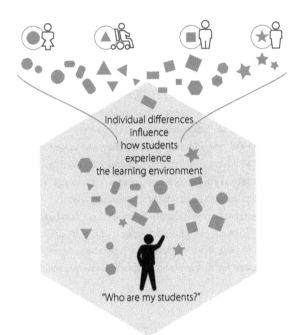

Figure 1.1. Students Bring Their Backgrounds and Lived Experiences into the Learning Context

Principle: *Students differ from each other on multiple dimensions—for example, in their identities, stages of development, and personal histories—and these differences influence how they experience the world and, in turn, their learning and performance.*

If learning was about filling empty brains with knowledge, there would be no need for this chapter. But learning also means integrating knowledge and skills into one's worldview; therefore, we need to unpack the role that developmental stage, identities, and experience play in learning. Furthermore, these crucial components of learning are not static, but they are evolving and developing through the life span, so it is important to examine some crucial insights from

13

developmental theory, particularly as related to social identity development and intellectual development.

The concept of life span development acknowledges that people face developmental challenges at every stage of life, but two considerations are important when dealing with college students. First, the college years are particularly important when it comes to developmental milestones. In fact, a preponderant body of research over decades documents that the developmental gains students make during college are considerably greater than the cognitive gains over the same span of time (Mayhew et al., 2016; Pascarella & Terenzini, 1991). Second, unresolved developmental challenges can derail our students' academic pursuits if they have not yet learned to channel them productively.

Ultimately, we have to teach the students we have at whatever developmental stage they occupy, not the enlightened version of the students we wish we had. But the good news is that if we understand how these variables influence the learning process, we can let this understanding inform our teaching.

WHAT DOES THE RESEARCH TELL US ABOUT INDIVIDUAL DIFFERENCES?

Just as the holistic movement in medicine calls for doctors to treat patients, not symptoms, student-centered teaching requires us to teach students, not content. Thus, it is important to recognize students as individuals who bring their unique combination of social, emotional, and intellectual characteristics to our courses. By considering "Who are my students?" along various dimensions of difference, we can better understand and support their learning needs.

This is an important part of making higher education more accessible and inclusive, and yet it is important to acknowledge that it can lead to several tensions. First, our natural inclination might be to treat all students the same, rather than giving different types or amounts of support to some. However, equal treatment would only advance student success if all of our students came to us with identical starting conditions. The concept of *equity* in education focuses on creating a learning environment that achieves *parity in the educational outcomes* experienced by groups of students who differ along dimensions such as race, gender, sexuality, and first-generation status (see Center for Urban Education, 2021; McNair et al., 2020). Preliminary steps to achieving equitable outcomes include recognizing where inequities currently exist and understanding what external factors likely contributed to underperformance (e.g., inadequate previous resources) so that they can be addressed. Research on dimensions of difference that have historically shown inequitable student outcomes can help us proactively make a positive difference for our students. This might require not treating all students the same (equality), but giving each student what they need (equity).

The second tension related to understanding and supporting our students' different learning needs is captured by this question: How could one course or faculty member ever tailor instructional supports to meet each student's unique social, emotional, and intellectual needs? This is precisely the question Professor Calhoun is asking. While differentiating instruction for each individual student may not be realistic, there are research-based strategies we can employ across situations to acknowledge, value, and leverage the diversity we find in our classes.

The third tension lies in the paradox between a common set of learning mechanisms that apply to all students—that is, the eight principles in this book—and the variety of ways those mechanisms unfold for individual students, based on the experiences and opportunities they have had. In other words, throughout the book we aim to strike a balance between describing general principles that hold across students and empowering instructors to apply those principles to their particular situations, contextualizing the relevant strategies accordingly. For this first principle on individual differences, there is an important implication. As instructors, when we observe different patterns of learning among our students, we should *not* interpret disparities in performance as inherent differences in the learning mechanisms or learning capabilities of students from particular groups (e.g., the mistaken interpretation that "those students just learn differently"). Instead, research demonstrates that many other factors explain these disparities including insufficient access to learning opportunities and resources, lack of positive societal expectations regarding students' success, history of being dismissed or mistreated, and more general societal influences such as racism, sexism, and classism. The good news is that, as teachers, the more we know about these factors, the more effectively we can mitigate them. Indeed, many examples highlight that when educators work to address these disparities in thoughtful and deliberate ways, they can be reduced and even eliminated (Maton et al., 2016; Treisman, 1992).

It is worth highlighting that one response to the desire to recognize observed differences in learning has been to hypothesize that students have different "learning styles"—that individuals differ with regard to what mode of instruction or study is most effective for them (e.g., "visual learners" versus "auditory learners") and so tailoring instruction to match students' learning styles will enhance learning outcomes. While many learners may have a preferred mode in which they like to learn or in which they believe they learn better, out of the many studies that have investigated possible impacts of learning styles, there is virtually no evidence that students actually learn better when instruction is matched to their learning style (Pashler et al., 2008; Stahl, 1999). Unfortunately, myths about learning styles persist, perhaps because learners' expressed preferences are so strongly felt and/or because individuals can differ in their aptitudes for processing particular types of information. However, the very robust result from the literature is that changing instruction to align with students' learning style does *not* have an impact on learning. Indeed, this is an example of how research on individual differences can tell us that we need *not* adjust our instruction to address learning styles or preferences as a way of enhancing outcomes.

By looking to other individual differences—including more visible (e.g., race, age) as well as less visible ones (e.g., socioeconomic status, sexual orientation, social identity, and intellectual development)—where the research does show interventions can have a positive effect, we can focus our efforts where they will make a difference. The remainder of this section thus delves into several areas of research that offer actionable insights for improving teaching and learning. We begin with identity characteristics, including intersectional identities. Then we turn to students' different levels of development, first focusing on social identity development and then on intellectual development. Next, we highlight research that seeks to leverage the differences among students as an asset, demonstrating the advantages that diversity can create. Finally, we summarize the implications of this research and make additional connections back to the stories from Professors Battaglia and Calhoun.

Identity Characteristics

We already posed the crucial question in this chapter—Who are my students? Subsequent chapters will help us explore this question further in recognition of the fact that our students possess different prior knowledge, singular motivation profiles and beliefs about their personal agency, distinctive skill sets, and a multitude of goals and hopes for the future. Here, however, we will consider a set of variables related to students' visible and invisible social identities, in other words, race, gender, sexual orientation, ability, age, socioeconomic status, religious beliefs, and so on. Why do we need to consider these variables? In a neutral world, we might not need to, but in the world we live in these variables predict achievement to a considerable degree. Research has consistently shown that students from different racial groups have different outcomes when it comes to enrollment, grade point average, retention, and graduation (Chen, 2013; NASEM, 2016; Reardon, 2011). These differences are systematic, not random. Other identity variables beyond race have been shown to affect achievement as well (e.g., Gonyea & Moore, 2007; Rankin et al., 2010), including first-generation status and transfer status.

We want to be very clear about an important point. As we said, the learning mechanisms in the brain are similar across students. There are no biological variables that would predict lower achievement on the basis of demographic variables alone. When scholars talk about addressing racial disparities, they are really talking about addressing the consequences of structural racism and other *isms*. For instance, even today, despite all the progress that has been made, we live in a society where children are raised differently according to their identities. As just one example, cisgender women are socialized to be less assertive and to speak accordingly. Often, the prevailing attitude with cisgender men is that of "boys will be boys," which shapes their risk-taking and boundary-pushing attitudes and behaviors. These forces have obvious implications for learning and performance. Gender non-conforming children face pressures to conform and many end up expending considerable energy concealing and repressing their natural reactions (DiPietro, 2012). Similarly, Black and Hispanic students face pressures to conform in their speech, attire, and behaviors, resulting in mental energy expended in *code-switching* between their culture and the normative culture and documented consequences on performance (Terry et al., 2010). Higher education has taken heed of these statistics, and many universities have launched initiatives to address these disparities, such as the statewide African American Male initiative in the University System of Georgia (USG, 2011); the Meyerhoff Scholars Program at University of Maryland, Baltimore County (Maton et al., 2016); and Women@SCS at Carnegie Mellon University (Blum, 2004). That these initiatives even exist is proof of the need, and also a demonstration that, when student identities are centered, it is possible to bridge these gaps.

If we posit an encyclopedic knowledge of all the research on all these different student characteristics as a required foundation for effective teaching, we will effectively paint ourselves into a corner, as Professor Calhoun quickly realized. The purpose of research is to understand in detail, which leads to specialization. This idea suffers from the "curse of dimensionality" (Bellman, 1957), as there are simply too many variables to corral. For instance, the research on trans people identifies over 30 possible developmental milestones, depending on whether they identify as binary or nonbinary, decide to transition or not, do it through hormones or surgeries, decide to disclose their identity to others or not, and so on (Beemyn & Rankin, 2011). For educators, it would be ineffective and inappropriate to speculate, or downright ask, which students have had what surgeries. Instead, we need an approach that enables us to take into account the particulars of student characteristics in ways that point to sound and actionable pedagogical principles. One way in which these variables affect student learning and performance is that they can affect students' sense of belonging to the institution. Chapter 7 elaborates on the construct of social and academic belonging and its implications for student learning. For now, suffice it to say that fitting in and feeling welcomed into one's environment influences students' ability to succeed (Braxton, 2012; Tinto, 2012).

Another mechanism that influences student learning and success is their physical and psychological health and well-being. For instance, we know that health and well-being can influence class attendance, perceived competence, and concentration (NCMHC, 1999), as well as GPA and graduation (Eisenberg et al., 2009). Furthermore, we know that some of these variables intersect with students' identities as in the documented case of lesbian, gay, bisexual, and transgender (LGBTQ+) students being more likely to skip classes they perceive as negatively influencing their mental well-being, for instance, when the instructor makes casual or intentional homophobic comments (Rankin et al., 2010).

Not all of the identities and demographic characteristics of every single student are salient in every educational environment, but it is important to remember the intersectionality of multiple identities (Crenshaw, 1989). Intersectionality here refers not only to the fact that each student comes with a unique *profile* of identities, but that one identity can trouble our understanding of how another identity can play out in certain contexts. For instance, the discourse about women in the classroom has centered from the very beginning on the erasure and invisibility of women (Hall & Sandler, 1982). Women students are more often ignored when they ask questions, not given credit for their contributions in discussions, assigned menial roles in group projects such as notetakers, and so on (Babcock et al., 2022; Hall & Sandler, 1982). When we turn our attention to Black women in the classroom, however, some of them experience the same invisibility, but many others report being called on frequently, to provide "the Black perspective." Even though the Black women in this predicament are only acknowledged as one-dimensional members of a group and not in all of their complexity as human beings, they nevertheless find themselves in a position of hypervisibility, with every word they utter scrutinized as representative of an entire race (Stewart, 2018).

For many students, their identities influence how they have been seen and treated in the world, including in pivotal educational experiences that have shaped their experience. Chapter 2 discusses the ways in which prior knowledge affects learning, focusing on content knowledge. But we need to realize that knowledge beyond what is covered in our courses can shape our students' learning experience. Many students, in ways that are very real to them, "know" whose opinions matter in their courses. They know who is expected to succeed or fail. They know which students are assumed to be bright, or lazy, or cheaters. In fact, many instructors unconsciously make assumptions about students' experiences or knowledge, abilities, and identities and viewpoints, and these assumptions shape the attributions they make such as whose request for an extension is justified, or which paper with an unusual sentence is worth investigating for plagiarism. DiPietro (2007) has organized some of the assumptions under each of the three categories, and that checklist is reproduced in Appendix A as a set of reflective questions. These assumptions are influenced by students' visible, assumed, or disclosed identities, or even by things as trivial as clothing (Morris et al., 1996). When the anonymous student commented on Professor Calhoun's evaluations that professors don't want to hear from Black students, that assertion was likely coming from previous experiences that have convinced the student this is the case. We all might envision the ideal scenario: When a student raises their hand, they would be called on, time permitting; when a student makes a comment, that comment would be acknowledged and incorporated in the discussion or redirected if the comment was factually inaccurate; when a student doesn't understand something, the instructor would diagnose where comprehension broke down and offer an alternative explanation. Unfortunately, our educational system has not always lived up to this ideal. Many students report being routinely ignored by their professors when they raise their hands or having their comments unacknowledged. Sometimes, their comments are credited to other students if they volunteer them later in the discussion. And even more discouragingly, some students see their lack of understanding attributed to one of their identities, as in the case of the women who have been told by their professors that they will never excel at math because of their gender. As this last example starts to illustrate, these micro-inequities (Hall & Sandler, 1982) cluster within certain social groups. Scholars call this phenomenon *privilege* (McIntosh, 2003), meaning that what should be the standard for all students ends up becoming a privilege only for certain groups. It is not difficult to see the implications of this fact. Professor Calhoun's students opted to not engage in discussions. Others might have to expend emotional labor to suppress their immediate responses or risk being labeled confrontational and problematic, like Gloria. Students will, in general, find coping strategies, but they are not necessarily conducive to learning and academic success.

Considering these individual differences is therefore crucial, especially at a time when university demographics have shifted greatly. The gender distribution of college students has shifted to a female majority (Belkin, 2021). The racial mix of students is more diverse than ever, with White students being the minority despite White people being the majority in the general population (National Center for Education Statistics, 2019). Students who identify as members of the LGBTQ+ community are also overrepresented in higher education (Association of American Universities, 2020). One student in five reports having a disability (National Center for Education Statistics, 2021). More than half of college students are first in their family to go to college (RTI International, 2019), and 2% are undocumented (Feldblum et al., 2020). Nontraditional students (over 25 years of age, who also hold a job) make up a staggering 75% of the student body (National Center for Education Statistics, 2020). Beyond these identities, 9% of students suffer from post-traumatic stress disorder (Read et al., 2011), often brought on by physical or sexual violence. And finally, a worrisome percentage of college students display basic needs insecurity, including 39% of students who have experienced food insecurity and 17% of students who were unhoused in the previous year (Baker-Smith et al., 2020).

As humans, we default to prototypes in our thinking (Rosch, 1973), but the prototypical image of a college student in our brain does not resemble most of today's students. If we don't check our perceptions, we risk planning courses with only a small percentage of our actual audience in mind, the percentage who is ready to learn, has no reasons to distrust the educational system, and can devote all its energies to our courses. In the words of McClusky (1963), these students have ample *margin* for learning. He defines margin as power divided by load. Traditional students have considerable power in many forms—physical (energy, health), social (strong connections from being part of a cohort straight out of high school), mental (reasoning capacity), and economic (family support). Likewise, their load is rather small, as being a college student is their main task. By contrast, many other students experience considerable load, both external, such as job and family demands, and internal (experiences that have made them feel marginalized and distrustful of the educational system), and they can experience their power as restricted—physically if they are older, economically if they are financially insecure, and so on. As the ratio of power to load shifts, their margin shrinks and they are less able to devote energies to learning. These students can still succeed, as long as they are supported with strategies that increase their power or lessen their load.

Levels of Development: Social Identity Development and Intellectual Development

Students, and indeed humans, are always developing. A classic model of student development by Chickering (1969) articulates seven "vectors" along which 17- to 22-year-old students develop as they go through college. These vectors include developing competence (in intellectual, physical, and interpersonal skills), autonomy (from parents to relying more on peers and finally toward personal autonomy), identity (through establishing a sense of self and comfort with one's own body and appearance, gender and sexual orientation, and racial and ethnic heritage), and purpose (via nurturing specific interests and committing to a particular profession and/or lifestyle). It is easy to see how these dimensions can have consequences for learning and performance. For instance, a student who does not need to rely on their parents to be woken up in the morning and not miss class has developed an autonomy that will serve them well in college and in life.

Other models acknowledge and study the process of development as it unfolds for individuals beyond 17 to 22 years of age. For example, based on a longitudinal study that followed a subgroup of former students into their twenties and thirties, Baxter-Magolda (2001, 2008) developed a stage model for how people transition into *self-authorship*—moving from doing what is expected of them to experiencing conflict between external sources of authority and their internal interests and then to choosing their own belief system that they can use to navigate life's challenges, choose relationships, and build a strong sense of self. As an example, Gloria from Professor Battaglia's course seems to have progressed to a stage where she is not interested in other people's approval and does not

21

hesitate to speak for something she believes is right. In the final stage of Baxter-Magolda's self-authorship theory, individuals leverage a belief system that is strong but not rigid; it takes into account the ambiguity and uncertainty of life such that one does not need other people to agree with them or to validate their opinions. In that sense, perhaps none of the students in Professor Battaglia's course have fully achieved this stage and its associated equanimity.

Finally, Knowles (1984) developed a model of *andragogy* that highlights several characteristics that are distinctive to adult learners and that continue to develop over time. For example, as adults mature, they accumulate experiences that become an increasing resource for learning. Additionally, adult learners (more than younger learners) need to know the reason for learning, seek immediate application, and are oriented to problems rather than content. From these characteristics, it is clear that an individuals' stage of development and stage of life make a difference in their learning.

Among all the dimensions in which students develop, we believe two of them have direct implications for learning and performance: social identity development and intellectual development. So far, we have discussed the general importance of student identities. But identities are constructed rather than static, and so it is important to understand how students come to understand their membership in certain groups as part of their social identities (Tajfel, 1978). In addition, students' intellectual maturity is also developing. As they deepen their understanding of what it means to know something, their capacity to grapple with instructional material also grows.

Most developmental models share a basic conceptual framework, so we can start there. Typically, development is described as a response to intellectual, social, or emotional challenges that catalyze students' growth. It should be understood, though, that developmental models depict student development in the aggregate (i.e., in broad brushstrokes) and do not necessarily describe the development of individual students. In fact, individual students do not necessarily develop at exactly the same pace relative to other students, or even relative to other areas of their own self. A student can be highly developed in one area (say, intellectual maturity) and less developed in another area (say, moral maturity). Furthermore, movement is not always in a forward direction. That is, under some circumstances, a student might regress or foreclose further development altogether. In many models this movement is described as stages, but research points out that life is not a video game where the character levels up and never has to revisit lower levels. For this reason, some models describe development as the reworking of certain key themes through the life span across multiple pathways (Beemyn & Rankin, 2011; Erikson & Erikson, 1997). A complete review of the student development literature is beyond the scope of this book. Rather, we wish to highlight some insights from that body of research that can illuminate the challenges Professors Calhoun and Battaglia are facing. For a broader treatment of student development models, we recommend the excellent treatise of Patton et al. (2016).

Social Identity Development As we have seen in the opening stories, students bring all of who they are to the learning environment. As much as we wish we could just focus on the content and bracket everything else out of our courses, that is simply impossible. Students' identities inform how they look at the world, including our content. Indeed, believing that the "normal" way to teach and learn a topic is to only focus on the content, undisturbed by extraneous elements, as Professor Battaglia wishes, might too be an expression of our identities (Collins, 2018). Therefore, understanding how identity, and in particular social identity, develops is a solid investment in our pedagogical growth. Identity development models are usually psychosocial, meaning they describe both the psychological changes people experience as their self evolves as well as how these changes affect their behaviors (such as social interactions), including those in the classroom. The basic premise of identity theory is that identity is not a given; instead, it needs to be achieved and continually negotiated as individuals try to balance developmental tensions and tasks throughout their lives (Erikson & Erikson, 1997). For students, much of the work of identity development happens as they begin to question values and assumptions inculcated by parents and society and start to develop their own values and priorities (Marcia, 1966).

One aspect of student identity development that is particularly salient for college students is that of social identity—the extent and nature of their identification with certain social groups, especially those groups that are often targets of prejudice and discrimination. Social identity has been studied extensively in relation to race/ethnicity, for example, the development of Black identity (Cross, 1995), Asian American identity (Kim, 2012), Latino and Latina identity (Gallegos & Ferdman, 2012), Indigenous people's identity (Choney et al., 1995), and Jewish identity (Kandel, 1986). Sexual identity has also been investigated, for instance, gay and lesbian identity (Cass, 1979) and bisexual identity (Gómez & Arenas, 2019). In addition, research has investigated gender identity, particularly for transgender individuals (Beemyn & Rankin, 2011), as well as the development of individuals with disabilities (Forber-Pratt & Aragon, 2013; Gibson 2006;

Gibson et al., 2018) and religious identity development, such as faith identity development (Fowler, 1981), Muslim identity development (Peek, 2005), and atheist identity development (Smith, 2011). Unfortunately, space does not allow for an extensive treatment of all this research, but we wish to highlight some fundamental insights from social identity development theory. We are keenly aware of the tension of generalizing across so many categories in a chapter dedicated to individual differences, and we do so with care. What we hope to transmit is the sense that this is just the beginning of a larger conversation. One does not need to become a social psychologist in order to teach effectively, but some key insights from this literature can have a positive impact on our teaching.

Many social identity development models describe similar trajectories, which culminate with the establishment of a positive social identity as a member of a specific group (Adams et al., 2007). At the same time, other models reject the idea of a unified trajectory and underscore how people in the same social group can have radically different perspectives on the world, each of them valid in and of itself and not as a precursor to a "more developed" stage (Choney et al., 1995; Gallegos & Ferdman, 2012). In our treatment, we will start from a generalized trajectory and then delve into some of the unique aspects of key models.

Hardiman and Jackson (1992) have proposed a social identity development model that describes two developmental paths, one for minority groups and one for dominant groups. This model pulls the threads together from other models, highlighting the similar stages members of minority groups go through, but underscores the fact that for any given stage, members of majority groups have to deal with complementary developmental challenges. Therefore, we will use this model as the point of departure.

The first stage of the Hardiman-Jackson model corresponds to early childhood, where individuals start out in a *naive* stage, devoid of any preconception or prejudice. They see differences in the people they observe, such as skin color, but they do not attach value to those. It is only in a second stage that, through persistent and systematic societal reinforcement, conscious or unconscious *acceptance* of certain messages about different groups sets in—the socially constructed ideas about which groups are healthy, normal, beautiful, lazy, smart, sinful, and so on. For example, Kayla's perception that immigrants are "sucking this country dry" might come from this stage. Both dominant and minority groups at this second stage accept broader societal attitudes. For minority students, this can have several results. They may have negative attitudes about themselves—in other words, internalized racism, homophobia, sexism, and so on—and behave so as to conform to the dominant image. For example, gay students at this stage may use homophobic language and try to act "straight."

Many students stop here, unless their worldviews are challenged by more information, different perspectives, recognition of injustice, or meaningful work with people from different groups. If they are challenged, it can move them forward to a stage of *resistance*. In this stage, students are acutely aware of the ways in which *isms* affect their life and the world. In addition, members of dominant groups usually experience shame and guilt about the privilege resulting from their own membership in it. Conversely, members of minority groups tend to experience pride in their own identity, often valuing their group more than the socially dominant one, which is sometimes seen as the source of societal evils. These students tend to go through a phase of *immersion* (Cross, 1995), in which they prefer to socialize with members of their own group and withdraw from other groups. Fries-Britt (2000) documents the struggles of high-ability Black students who are torn between identification with their academics and identification with their racial group, which might view their academic excellence as "acting White." In her book *Why Are All the Black Kids Sitting Together in the Cafeteria?* Beverly Daniel Tatum (2017) lucidly analyzes such racial dynamics. Moreover, she points out that racial minority students are usually aggressively questioning societal racism at the same developmental juncture when White students are feeling overwhelmed by the same accusations, a stage that Helms (1993) calls *disintegration*. The first story portrays one such tension. Gloria is very conscious of the racial subtext underpinning immigration debates, but Danielle sees it only as Gloria's pet peeve. Kayla's highly emotional reaction can be seen as an example of disintegration. In this emotionally fraught situation, they are unable to move forward with a productive discussion.

Unique phenomena are experienced by other groups in these stages. For lesbian, gay, and bisexual students, a crucial step toward positive self-identity is coming out. D'Augelli (1994) points out that adopting a lesbian, gay, or bisexual identity necessitates abandoning an implied heterosexual identity, with the consequent loss of all its attendant privileges. This underscores the point that many of our students' identities will not be directly visible to us, yet students will still be processing their experiences through those identity lenses. Rankin (2003) documents the feelings of LGBT students who, in response to marginalization experienced in their courses on the basis of their sexual and gender identity, report spending all their free time at the LGBT center on campus as a way to experience a positive environment for themselves, even at the cost of not spending enough time studying and struggling in those courses. Professor Calhoun's student who stopped participating after being misgendered might be adopting a similar stance, disengaging from a situation they do not see as affirming of their identity, even as they realize the academic cost of such behavior. In the case of students with disabilities, including students on the spectrum, Gibson (2006) points out that they go through a stage called *realization,* where they come to see themselves as having a disability and realize that this affects how they are treated. One of the features of this stage is varied attempts at managing this concern. The student who disengaged from Professor Calhoun's class might be seeking to minimize the likelihood of being labeled by their classmates as weird and different in response to previous attempts at participation.

If students successfully move through this stage, they arrive at more sophisticated stages, those of *redefinition* and *internalization*. In these stages, students redefine their sense of self, moving beyond the dominant–minority dichotomy. These identities become one part of their makeup but not the defining feature. They no longer experience guilt or anger, but they might commit to work for justice in their spheres of influence.

Intellectual Development Intellectual development in the college years has been studied since the 1950s. Although the formulation presented here is that of Perry (1968), it is extended in the work of later researchers who have found very similar developmental trajectories (Baxter-Magolda, 1992; Belenky et al., 1986). Even though these models contain different numbers of stages, all of them describe a student's trajectory from simplistic to more sophisticated ways of thinking. A student's movement forward is usually propelled by a challenge that reveals the inadequacies of the current stage.

In the earlier stages, students' reasoning is characterized by a basic *duality* in which knowledge can easily be divided into right and wrong statements, with little to no room for ambiguity and shades of gray. Kayla's exclamation—"It's just plain wrong!"—exemplifies this way of thinking. Students at this stage of intellectual development believe that knowledge is something absolute, that it is handed down from authorities (the teacher, the textbook), and that the role of students is to receive it and give it back when asked. This is a quantitative view of knowledge, with education seen as a process of amassing piles of "right" facts. The implicit assumption is that all that is knowable is known, and great instructors have the answers to any question. Students start at this stage because most of their prior instruction has been delivered in this way, focusing on the right answer and the right way of thinking about a topic. Freire (2000) challenges this pedagogy, which he terms the "banking model of education," where instructors make little incremental deposits of knowledge in the students' brains. He points out they still "own" the knowledge and can demand it back at will, on the test, or on a pop quiz. When professor Battaglia's readings are challenged by Gloria, he has choices. If he sticks to his plan, he is unconsciously employing the banking model, and communicating to the students that the right way, indeed the only way to think about immigration, is as a cost. Freire points out that the banking model reinforces the very societal inequalities education is supposed to tackle. When students are taught in this manner, they initially do not recognize different perspectives and are not likely to see discussions as a legitimate way of gaining knowledge about an issue.

Challenged with a sufficient number of questions where the answers are yet unknown, or with issues for which there is no clear right answer, students move forward to a stage of *multiplicity*. Knowledge now becomes a matter of opinions, and anybody can have an opinion on an issue. Students at a multiplistic stage view evaluation as very subjective and can become frustrated if their opinion does not score them a good grade. At this point they have difficulty seeing how to differentiate among different opinions, as they all seem valid. The instructor might no longer be seen as an authority but only as another perspective among all the possible ones. At first it might be hard to see how this stage represents a move forward, but two important things have happened in this stage. First, students are now more open to differences of opinions because they are no longer fixated on the "right one." This crucial transition is foundational for all further development in later stages. Second, learning can now become personal. They, too, are entitled to their own opinion and can legitimately dialogue and disagree with the instructor or the textbook, which means they can start to construct their own knowledge. Gloria's claim that the readings are biased could not have come from a student in an earlier developmental stage.

With enough insistence that opinions need to be justified with evidence, students progress to stages characterized by *relativism*. Students with this worldview realize that opinions are not all equal and that indeed their pros and cons can be understood and evaluated according to general and discipline-specific rules of evidence. This transition marks a shift from a quantitative to a qualitative view of knowledge. Instructors become guides and facilitators, expected to provide good models of how to interact with the content in a critical way, which is how the role of the student is now understood. As students hone their analytic and critical skills, they find the empowerment inherent in this stage, but they might also experience some frustration as they realize that all theories are necessarily imperfect or incomplete.

Students who successfully navigate this challenge move to the last set of stages, which are characterized by a sense of *commitment*. While it is true that all theories have pros and cons, learners realize they must provisionally commit to one as a foundation to build on, refining it as they go. In a sense, they have come full circle, as they now choose one theory or approach over the others, but unlike in the dualistic stage, their choice is now nuanced and informed. It is easy to see how this sense of commitment might apply to moral issues as well as cognitive ones. In fact, Kohlberg (1976) and Gilligan (1977) have formulated moral development theories that echo Perry's, in which students move from strongly held but unexamined views about right and wrong to more nuanced, responsible ethical positions where actions are evaluated in context according to a variety of factors. One of the lessons from their work is that moral development cannot be divorced from learning. For example, both Kayla's and Gloria's positions on immigration are indeed as much moral as they are intellectual.

Other developmental researchers have expanded Perry's work to focus on gender differences in the various stages. For example, Baxter-Magolda (1992) has found that, in dualistic stages, men might prefer to engage in a game of displaying their knowledge in front of their peers whereas women might focus on helping each other master the material. In their study of women's intellectual development, Belenky and others (1986) found two parallel ways of knowing. For some women, studying something means isolating the issue from its context and focusing on deep analysis of one feature—which the researchers term *separate* knowing. For other women, studying something means asking questions such as "What does this mean for me? What are the implications for the community?"— which they term *connected* knowing. We should reiterate that these empirical differences in ways of knowing and learning do not mean that women learn differently but that they have been socialized to focus on community and care. And, of course, both ways of knowing can be found among men as well. Danielle, who is very comfortable limiting the discussion to only the figures in the readings, is an example of separate knowing, whereas Gloria, who cannot divorce the readings from her firsthand knowledge of undocumented immigrants, is an example of connected knowing.

The research underlying these models clearly indicates that intellectual development takes time—it does not happen overnight and cannot be forced.

Given the kind of development involved in the later stages, it is perhaps not surprising that Baxter-Magolda's research also shows many students leave college still in multiplistic stages, and that their development toward relativistic and committed stages continues well beyond college. This is good news if we consider that people who do not go to college tend to stay in dualistic stages, but it is also below the expectations that most instructors have for their students. Instructors, therefore, must make sure their expectations are reasonable given students' current level of intellectual development: what is reasonable for a graduating senior may not be for a first-year student, and vice versa. However, although development cannot be forced, it can be nurtured and encouraged by posing appropriate challenges and providing the support necessary to foster intellectual growth (Vygotsky, 1978). The strategies at the end of the chapter provide some suggestions in this direction.

Asset-Based Approaches

While understanding and navigating the differences among students may feel like a task that is added to our teaching activities, it is important to remember that, in addition to helping to create more just and equitable educational experiences, cultivating diversity in groups has tangible benefits and should thus be considered an asset. Research supports the notion that heterogeneous groups often perform better than homogeneous ones. For example, in studies of diversity in various industry settings, a consistent finding is that more diverse groups produce more innovations (e.g., Díaz-García et al., 2013; Nathan & Lee, 2013). One explanation for diversity's benefits is that people working in diverse teams are better at considering multiple perspectives and using a broader lens when solving problems (e.g., Hong & Page, 2004). For example, in his book *The Difference*, Page notes that when groups of intelligent individuals are working to solve hard problems, the diversity of the problem-solvers matters more than their individual ability (Page, 2008). For example, in one study conducted with sorority and fraternity members, temporary teams of three were composed of members from a single sorority/fraternity and assigned to solve a murder mystery. When a fourth member was added to each team from either the same sorority/fraternity or not, the "mixed" teams' solutions were more likely to identify the correct suspect (Phillips et al., 2008). These results suggest that as educators we can cultivate and disseminate the benefits of diversity in our classrooms by reminding students that their individual differences are important and helpful—in the

29

sense of enhancing their overall capacity for solving problems and learning together.

Research on gender diversity in teams supports the related hypothesis that heterogeneous groups engage in better processes that, in turn, can lead to better outcomes (e.g., Bear & Woolley, 2011; Nielsen et al., 2017; Woolley & Malone, 2011). Across numerous studies, Woolley and colleagues have shown that having more women in a group leads to more evenly distributed contributions from team members and hence more varied information and ideas shared. Thus, if we consider our class of students as members of a collaborative team, research supports the idea that diversity is a strength for the group's processes and outcomes.

In addition to these benefits, students who are learning in contexts with diverse others have greater opportunities to become aware of their own biases and learn to see things from other perspectives, especially when they are explicitly encouraged to engage meaningfully with each other as individuals. We cannot expect this to happen on its own—just because a student is in a group with diverse others—but rather we can foster interactions where students get to know each other and learn about their different backgrounds and experiences. For example, first-year college students who were exposed to such collaborative learning activities experienced a greater frequency of interacting with diverse others, and, in turn, demonstrated greater openness to diversity (Loes et al., 2018). Given that our students' future careers will more and more likely involve working with diverse others and being expected to engage effectively in diverse teams, supporting students to develop these positive skills and attitudes in our courses will serve them well during their studies and beyond.

Implications of This Research

Even though some of us might wish to conceptualize our classrooms as culturally neutral or might choose to ignore the cultural dimensions, students cannot check their sociocultural identities at the door, nor can they instantly transcend their current level of development. Professor Battaglia knows that immigration is a loaded topic, but he thought students could consider the economic aspects alone. In fact, Gloria's and Kayla's identities as Hispanic and Polish American, respectively, as well as their level of intellectual development and preferred ways of knowing, obviously influence their approach to the course topic, what aspects of the readings they focus on, how they make sense of the material, and what stances they take as a result. Similarly, Professor Calhoun's students' decisions to participate or not during discussions is shaped by their identities and circumstances. Therefore, it is important that the pedagogical strategies we employ in the classroom enable multiple ways to engage and reflect an understanding of social identity and intellectual development so that we can anticipate the tensions that might occur in the classroom and be proactive about them. The strategies in this chapter explicitly link pedagogy, individual differences, and developmental considerations.

WHAT STRATEGIES DOES THE RESEARCH SUGGEST?

Here are a number of strategies that may help you support your students' different identities and encourage student development. Note that these strategies do not require tailoring your teaching to meet every individual student's needs. Instead, they provide various ways instructors can be more aware of student differences, communicate the value of and leverage diversity among students, and be more deliberate and transparent in fostering student development.

Strategies to Address Awareness and Self-Reflection

Examine Your Assumptions About Students Because assumptions influence the way we interact with our students, and those interactions in turn affect their learning, we need to uncover—and at times question—those assumptions. It is common for instructors to assume that students share our background and frames of reference (e.g., historical or literary references). It is equally common to make assumptions about students' ability (e.g., Asian students will do better in math), identity and viewpoint (e.g., students share your sexual orientation or political affiliation), and attributions (e.g., tentative language indicates intellectual weakness). These assumptions can result in behaviors that are unintentionally alienating and can affect climate and students' developing sense of identity. Setting aside time to probe for such possible assumptions can create opportunities to consider how they might arise in your teaching actions and where you might want to make adjustments.

Consider Your Own Intersectional Identities An activity called the Social Identity Wheel (e.g., University of Michigan, 2022) invites us to identify and reflect on our own social identities (e.g., race, gender, ability disability, sexual orientation, etc.). Specifically, this activity asks which identities matter most in our self-perception and which matter most in others' perception of us. Focusing on how our different identities are more or less keenly felt in different contexts can help us recognize that privilege operates to normalize some identities (the ones we don't experience as salient) over others. For example, someone who speaks English as their first language can reflect on why they rarely need to think about their language as an aspect of their identity, whereas those who identify language as a key aspect of their identity may feel this dimension very keenly in the classroom. Engaging in this activity fosters personal reflection that can help educators become more aware of and more sensitive to the impact that different identities have on all of us. (Note: the Social Identity Wheel can also be used effectively as an activity that students complete as a prompt for them to engage in this same kind of reflection.)

Educate Yourself About Identities Other Than Your Own It is natural to have much greater knowledge and experience about the identities we inhabit, but as this chapter highlights, it is critical to recognize that "our students are not us," and we likely have a knowledge gap about their different identities. Rather than burdening students from marginalized groups to "teach" us, we should take on the responsibility to learn more ourselves, cultivating humility and curiosity as we do so. A concrete way to approach this might involve leveraging resources (books, articles, podcasts), especially those created by individuals representing marginalized identities, for professional (and even personal) development. These could be from the popular press, as many such reading/listening guides have been created in recent years, and/or they could include more scholarly resources (see, for example, the references for this chapter).

Anticipate and Prepare for Potentially Sensitive Issues We usually know from our own or our colleagues' past experiences what issues seem to be "hot topics" for some of our students. Preparing students to learn from these opportunities requires careful framing (e.g., an acknowledgment that the topic can have personal significance for many students and also an articulation of the expectations for the tone of the discussion), an explanation for why the course is dealing with the issue (e.g., the necessity to hear all sides of the debate to arrive at a multifaceted understanding), and ground rules that ensure a civil discussion (see Appendix B on ground rules). In addition, many teaching center websites have sample documents (e.g., ground rules, discussion norms, or invitations) and specific suggestions regarding process (e.g., how to engage students in coauthorship and co-implementation of ground rules).

Strategies to Address Students' Identities

Use Multiple and Diverse Examples Using examples is a great way to help students understand that theories and concepts can operate in a variety of contents and conditions *as long as* students can understand—and, ideally, relate to—those examples. When you are leveraging an example, think about how it could be more relevant and meaningful to your particular students and how more than one example could increase the likelihood of students relating. Some helpful tips in this regard involve identifying and using examples that can work across cultures and relate to people with different gender identities, sexual orientations, socioeconomic statuses, and ages. For example, using gender neutral terms and seeking applied contexts that students might naturally encounter on campus (as shared experience) can help. This simple strategy can help students feel connected to the content as well as a sense of belonging in the course or field, and it can reinforce their developing sense of competence and purpose.

Encourage Learners to Bring Their Own Experiences and Backgrounds to Bear As with prior knowledge, inviting students to connect their past experiences and backgrounds with the course material supports enhanced learning. There are many ways to do this. For example, you can ask students to relate course concepts to something from their own experience or ask them to share aspects of their culture(s) that provide a particular lens for interpreting a reading. Many faculty members find that when they leverage their students' diversity in this way, everyone (instructor included) can learn from the variety of perspectives in a given class.

Broaden the Curriculum Consider the readings, authors, and theories from which you typically draw. Do they include traditionally underrepresented voices and perspectives? How might your course and syllabus design incorporate a broader set of perspectives? Likewise, consider expanding your learning objectives in ways that could highlight knowledge, skills, and dispositions associated with diversity, equity, and inclusion.

Avoid Deficit Thinking When seeking to support students' different identities, stereotypes or other assumptions focused on dysfunction or shortcomings may come to mind. Rather than looking at differences as deficits, explicitly work to reframe your thinking: cultivate an asset-based approach in which your default assumption is that all of your students are capable of succeeding and each student brings distinctive strengths. Then be sure to translate that asset-based thinking into your language and in your pedagogical choices. For example, instead of making the well-intentioned comment that certain students are underprepared, recognize that these students likely bring unique experiences that, if capitalized on, can enrich the learning environment. In addition, recognize that other students may actually be *over*-prepared given various enrichment opportunities they have had the privilege to enjoy.

Convey High Standards Plus Assurance When Providing Feedback Given historical as well as students' personal experiences, students with marginalized identities may feel stigmatized or stereotyped when they receive criticism. To offset these effects, Claude Steele recommends in his book *Whistling Vivaldi* (2010) to accompany your feedback with explicit acknowledgment of what is motivating your feedback and an explicit assurance that you believe the student can achieve the standards you have set, with appropriate strategies and effort. For example, some sample language might draw on the approach used in research on this topic: "It's obvious to me that you've taken this task seriously, and I'm going to do likewise by giving you some straightforward, honest feedback. . . . Judging by the standards of the assignment, here are some comments that I hope you find helpful. . . . Remember, I wouldn't go to the trouble of giving you this feedback if I didn't think that you are capable. . . ."

Acknowledge and Grapple with the Larger Sociopolitical Context Particular political issues and national or global events have a greater impact on some students than others, making for an uneven playing field. Rather than ignore how societal issues might be weighing on your students' minds, acknowledge that they may be grappling with difficulties as a result. Also, be proactive in connecting students to university resources for support, for example, campus food pantry, veterans affinity groups, office of disability resources. Many faculty members share information on these resources in their syllabus or course home page and offer reminders throughout the semester.

Think About Students as Individuals People often treat another culture as monolithic even while treating their own as multifaceted. This is likely a result of the greater familiarity and exposure we have to our own culture, not a reality about the other culture. Remember that each student is just one individual and should not be presumed to represent their broader group identity, let alone reflect any general trends given they are a unique individual. Be on the lookout for this group-based thinking. One way to help prevent it is to focus on your students as unique individuals, for example, "How is <insert specific name> experiencing my class, given his/her/their unique set of experiences and identities?"

Discuss Communication Styles Explicitly Students' comments often reveal the communication style they have been socialized into. For instance, a student might say, "This is probably a stupid question, but . . ." Another student might change the intonation of their comment at the end to make it sound like a question. We can treat these comments as opportunities, and explicitly discuss how they work to self-sabotage the speaker and make them seem less confident.

Vary Teaching Methods and Provide Choice in Assignments By incorporating a variety of methods in your instruction and assessment, you are giving students greater opportunity to show what they know in ways that work best for them. In addition, giving students choice in assignments, when appropriate, allows students to have more agency over their own learning and to address topics that are culturally relevant to them. For example, if your course has a project or paper, you might allow students to choose the topic or format (e.g., oral presentation, recorded podcast, or written report). Incorporating students' voices and choices regarding topics of discussion and learning can even come into instruction. For example, you could reserve some time at the beginning of the semester and poll your students about what they would like to learn.

Consider the Impact of Trauma and the Value of Trigger Warnings Trauma is defined as an event that overwhelms our capacity to cope with it and therefore produces symptoms. Some of the material we teach is meant to challenge the students, but for students who have been already traumatized, exposing them to triggering content unexpectedly or without allowing them to regulate their exposure in some way can have a deleterious impact, particularly when we teach about rape, racism, violence, and so on. The conversation on the value of trigger warnings is not settled, but it behooves all of us to consider how specific types of content affect our more vulnerable students and how we can best prepare them for it.

Incorporate Universal Design for Learning Universal design for learning (UDL) leverages the flexibility of digital technologies to offer options and provide accessibility for diverse learner needs. More important, this approach starts with diverse learner needs and builds that into the design process, acknowledging that such designs can be beneficial to all learners regardless of their particular needs. Some strategies for UDL include providing multiple means of representation of the material—including visual, text, audio, and video—and ensuring that information is accessible to all learners (e.g., by using accessible language, clear organization of content, and digitally accessible formats for students with visual, auditory, or physical disabilities). Digital accessibility is a component of UDL that involves many aspects, from font size, screen-reader compatibility, transcripts for audio, and more. Many institutions provide digital accessibility support that you can draw on, and there are online resources available for all (e.g., see udloncampus.cast.org/).

Strategies to Address Developmental Stages

Make Uncertainty Safe For those students who are comfortable in black-and-white worldviews, there can be an emotional resistance to intellectual development, and it can be helpful to support students in dealing with ambiguity. There are various ways to do this. Validate different viewpoints, even unpopular ones. Explicitly express to students that part of critical thinking is embracing complexity rather than oversimplifying matters. Explain that even though it might seem frustrating, the point of classroom discussions is not always to reach consensus but rather to enrich everybody's thinking. Finally, model this attitude in your own actions and comments as it applies to your disciplinary context.

Resist a Single Right Answer Textbooks present information very linearly, but knowledge is generated and contested over time. If you want students to be in dialogue with the texts in your discipline, create a structure that can support it. You can ask students to generate multiple approaches to a problem or debate a devil's advocate position. Ask them to articulate their perspectives before you volunteer yours so as not to bias them. When appropriate, use assignments with multiple correct solutions, and highlight how a range of responses are appropriate.

Incorporate Evidence into Performance and Grading Criteria If you want students to support their opinions with evidence, use rubrics and other tools to scaffold this practice. You can educate students to use a rubric by modeling how it is applied to a sample piece of work and by asking students to read each other's work and circle the pieces of evidence to highlight them visually (see Appendix E). Incorporating evidence in your grading scheme will also reduce "grade grubbing" based on the notion that personal opinions are subjective and cannot be graded fairly.

Explain the Importance of Stretching Outside One's Comfort Zone Despite the lack of empirical evidence, the discourse about learning styles proliferates. Many students treat their learning preference as an identity, and this can foreclose development. Some instructors preface the content by explicitly discussing the fact that multiple learning preferences are present in any given course. They add that their duty as the instructor is to use the way of presenting the material that best fits the content, and that when multiple ways are possible they will vary their teaching methods to reach all students in the classroom. Therefore, approaching the material only in one way will lead to missing key aspects. They go on to explain the plasticity of the brain and reassure the students that once they start stretching outside of their comfort zone, unfamiliar ways of reasoning will gradually become more approachable.

Strategies to Address Margin, Power, and Load

Increase the Power We can't easily affect student's economic power, but we can work on their mental power by discussing better ways of reasoning and strategies for time management. We can also increase their social power by building social connections in our courses. For instance, on the first day of class some instructors direct all students to turn to their left and their right and exchange contact information with the two closest students, explaining that everybody at some point will have to miss class due to illness or emergencies and it will be important to feel comfortable reaching out to fellow students to catch up.

Decrease the Load One way to increase the margin for learning is to lessen the load. The strategy of connecting students to campus resources such as the food pantry can help decrease the external load, but we can also help our students to let go of some internal load in the form of self-sabotaging habits and behaviors, such as perfectionism, procrastination, or others.

Reflect on the Impact of Our Pedagogical Choices on Power and Load Sometimes, well-meaning instructors include tasks in their courses with the purpose of increasing their students' power, but the impact might not be uniform on all students. For instance, these instructors might include group work outside of class to enable students to tackle real-world rather than rote problems, thus increasing their power. However, the effect might be the opposite for some students. Students with jobs and family commitments who have to squeeze in group meetings at inconvenient times might find their load increased, unless the work

37

can be done asynchronously. As instructors, we should be sure to look at our assignments and activities from a range of perspectives to avoid unintentionally exacerbating load and/or reducing power.

SUMMARY

In this chapter, we have argued that we need to consider students holistically as intellectual, social, and emotional beings with unique identities and experiences that influence their learning and their performance. We have reviewed the research that documents how students are still developing in many areas, particularly in their sense of identity and epistemological processes, and we have documented how their level of development too can influence learning and performance. We have advocated that this diversity of experiences, identities, and developmental stages not be treated as a problem to fix but a benefit to our courses that can enrich the learning experience for everybody when leveraged appropriately. We have suggested strategies to examine our assumptions and our own identity as educators as those, too, influence the learning environment, as well as concrete techniques to try out in our courses. Each of the next chapters will focus on specific aspects of the learning process and the pedagogical strategies that it suggests.

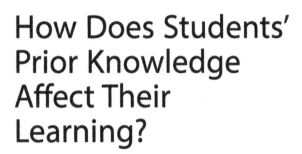

CHAPTER 2

How Does Students' Prior Knowledge Affect Their Learning?

Lies, Damn Lies, and Statistics!

I teach an online section of research methods, and, in my experience, students can name and perform simple tests and arrive at p-values, but many struggle with the conceptual framework underpinning hypothesis testing. I asked my students to list the statistical tests they were familiar with, and, as I expected, they mentioned T-tests, chi-square, and ANOVA. With that foundation in place, I decided to do a synchronous exercise to illustrate the concepts of Type I and Type II errors. To help them understand the concept, I used the analogy of false positives and false negatives in a COVID test. I figured everybody would relate to the topic, some even from a personal or family experience, and the connection would help them learn the concepts better. I thought my assignment was pitched at the appropriate level; it simply required that students take a data set that I provided, select and apply the appropriate statistical test from those they had already learned, analyze the data, and interpret the results. I was shocked at what some students turned in. I expected them to be able to do the calculations by rote at the very least. Instead, some students chose a completely inappropriate test while others chose the right test but did not have the foggiest idea how to apply it. Still others could not interpret the results. One student even tried to derail the whole activity by regurgitating conspiracy theories about COVID and brushing the exercise off with the old saw "Lies, damn lies, and statistics!" He had been fine with statistics up until now, but the moment it challenged his beliefs, he was ready to jettison it! I can't reconcile this mindset.

Professor Soo Yon Won

Why Is This So Hard for Them to Understand?

Every year in my introductory psychology class I teach my students about classic learning theory, particularly the concepts of positive and negative reinforcement. I know that these can be tough concepts for students to grasp, so I spell out very clearly that *reinforcement* always refers to increasing a behavior and *punishment* always refers to decreasing a behavior. I also emphasize that, contrary to what they might assume, *negative reinforcement* does not mean punishment; it means removing something aversive to increase a desired behavior. I also provide a number of concrete examples to illustrate what I mean. But it seems that no matter how much I explain the concept, students continue to think of negative reinforcement as punishment. In fact, when I asked about negative reinforcement on a recent exam, almost 60% of the class got it wrong. Why is this so hard for students to understand?

Professor Anatole Dione

WHAT IS GOING ON IN THESE TWO STORIES?

The instructors in these stories seem to be doing all the right things. Professor Won takes the time to gauge students' knowledge of statistical tests so that she can pitch her own instruction at the appropriate level. Professor Dione carefully explains a difficult concept, provides concrete examples, and even gives an explicit warning about a common misconception. Yet neither instructor's strategy is having the desired effect on students' learning and performance. To understand why, it is helpful to consider the effect of students' prior knowledge on new learning.

Professor Won assumes that students have learned and retained basic statistical skills in their prerequisite course, an assumption that is confirmed by the students' self-report. In actuality, although students have some knowledge—they are able to identify and describe a variety of statistical tests—it may not be sufficient for Professor Won's assignment, which requires them to determine when particular tests are appropriate, apply the right test for the problem, and then interpret the results. Here Professor Won's predicament stems from a mismatch between the knowledge students have and the knowledge their instructor expects and needs them to have to function effectively in her course.

In Professor Dione's case it is not what students do *not* know that hurts them but rather what they *do* know. His students, like many of us, have come to associate positive with "good" and negative with "bad," an association that is appropriate in many contexts, but not in this one. When students are introduced to the concept of negative reinforcement in relation to classic learning theory, their prior understanding of "negative" may interfere with their ability to absorb the technical definition. Instead of grasping that the "negative" in negative reinforcement involves removing something to get a positive change (an example would be a mother who promises to quit nagging if her son will clean his room), students interpret the word *negative* to imply a negative response, or punishment. In other words, their prior knowledge triggers an inappropriate association that ultimately intrudes on and distorts the incoming knowledge.

WHAT PRINCIPLE OF LEARNING IS AT WORK HERE?

As we teach, we often try to enhance our students' understanding of the course content by connecting it to their knowledge and experiences from earlier in the same course, from previous courses, or from everyday life. But sometimes—like Professor Won—we overestimate students' prior knowledge and thus build new knowledge on a shaky foundation. Or we find—like Professor Dione—that our students are bringing prior knowledge to bear that is not appropriate to the context and that is distorting their comprehension. Similarly, we may uncover misconceptions and inaccuracies in students' prior knowledge that are actively interfering with their ability to learn the new material. Although, as instructors, we can and should build on students' prior knowledge, it is also important to recognize that not all prior knowledge provides an equally solid foundation for new learning.

Principle: *Students' prior knowledge can help or hinder learning.*

Students do not come into our courses as blank slates but rather with knowledge gained in other courses and through daily life. This knowledge consists of an amalgam of facts, concepts, models, perceptions, beliefs, values, and attitudes, some of which are accurate, complete, and appropriate for the context, some of which are inaccurate, insufficient for the learning requirements of the course, or simply inappropriate for the context. As students bring this knowledge to bear in our classrooms, it influences how they filter and interpret incoming information.

Ideally, students build on a foundation of robust and accurate prior knowledge, forging links between previously acquired and new knowledge that help them construct increasingly complex and robust knowledge structures (see Chapter 3 on organization of knowledge). However, students may not make connections to relevant prior knowledge spontaneously. If they do not draw on relevant prior knowledge—in other words, if that knowledge is *inactive*—it may not facilitate the integration of new knowledge. Moreover, if students' prior knowledge is *insufficient* for a task or learning situation, it may fail to support new knowledge, whereas if it is *inappropriate* for the context or *inaccurate*, it may actively distort or impede new learning. This is illustrated in Figure 2.1.

Understanding what students know—or think they know—coming into our courses can help us design our instruction more appropriately. It enables us not only to leverage their accurate knowledge more effectively to promote learning but also to identify and fill gaps, recognize when students are applying what they know inappropriately, and actively work to correct misconceptions.

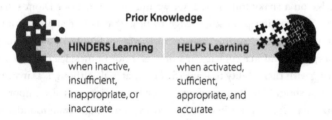

Figure 2.1. Qualities of Prior Knowledge That Help or Hinder Learning

WHAT DOES THE RESEARCH TELL US ABOUT PRIOR KNOWLEDGE?

Students connect what they learn to what they already know, interpreting incoming information, and even sensory perception, through the lens of their existing knowledge, beliefs, and assumptions (National Research Council, 2000; Vygotsky, 1978). In fact, there is widespread agreement among researchers that students *must* connect new knowledge to previous knowledge in order to learn (Bransford & Johnson, 1972; Resnick, 1983). However, the extent to which students are able to draw on prior knowledge to *effectively* construct new knowledge depends on the nature of their prior knowledge, as well as the instructor's ability to harness it. In the following sections, we discuss research that investigates the effects of various kinds of prior knowledge on student learning and explore its implications for teaching.

Activating Prior Knowledge

When students can connect what they are learning to accurate and relevant prior knowledge, they learn and retain more. In essence, new knowledge "sticks" better when it has prior knowledge to stick to. In one study focused on recall, for example, participants with variable knowledge of soccer were presented with scores from different soccer matches and their recall was tested. People with more prior knowledge of soccer recalled more scores (Morris et al., 1981). Similarly, research conducted by Kole and Healy (2007) showed that college students who were presented with unfamiliar facts about well-known individuals demonstrated twice the capacity to learn and retain those facts as students who were presented with the same number of facts about unfamiliar individuals. Both these studies illustrate how prior knowledge of a topic can help students integrate new information.

However, students may not spontaneously bring their prior knowledge to bear on new learning situations (see the discussion of transfer in Chapter 5). Thus, it is important to help students activate prior knowledge so they can build on it productively. Indeed, research suggests that even small instructional interventions can activate students' relevant prior knowledge to positive effect. For instance, in one famous study by Gick and Holyoak (1980), college students were presented with two problems that required them to apply the concept of convergence. The researchers found that even when the students knew the solution to the first problem, the vast majority did not think to apply an analogous solution to the second problem. However, when the instructor suggested to students that they think about the second problem in relation to the first, 80% of the student participants were able to solve it. In other words, with minor prompts and simple reminders, instructors can activate relevant prior knowledge so that students draw on it more effectively (Bransford & Johnson, 1972; Dooling & Lachman, 1971).

Research also suggests that asking students questions specifically designed to trigger recall can help them use prior knowledge to aid the integration and retention of new information (Woloshyn et al., 1994). For example, Martin and Pressley (1991) asked Canadian adults to read about events that had occurred in various Canadian provinces. Prior to any instructional intervention, the researchers found that study participants often failed to use their relevant prior knowledge to logically situate events in the provinces where they occurred, and thus they had difficulty remembering specific facts. However, when the researchers asked a set of why questions (e.g., "Why would Ontario have been the first place baseball was played?"), participants were forced to draw on their prior knowledge of Canadian history and relate it logically to the new information. The researchers found that this intervention, which they called *elaborative interrogation*, improved learning and retention significantly.

Researchers have also found that if students are asked to generate relevant knowledge from previous courses or their own lives, it can help to facilitate their integration of new material (Peeck et al., 1982). For example, Garfield and her colleagues (2007) designed an instructional study in a college statistics course that focused on the concept of variability—a notoriously difficult concept to grasp. The instructors first collected baseline data on students' understanding of variability at the end of a traditionally taught course. The following semester, they redesigned the course so that students were asked to generate examples of activities in their own lives that had either high or low variability, represent them graphically, and draw on them as they reasoned about various aspects of variability. While both groups of students continued to struggle with the concept, post-tests showed that students who had generated relevant prior knowledge outperformed students in the baseline class two to one.

When professor Won asked students what tests they were familiar with, she was helping them activate their prior knowledge. Exercises to generate prior knowledge can be a double-edged sword, however, if the knowledge students generate is inaccurate or inappropriate for the context (Alvermann et al., 1985). Problems involving inaccurate and inappropriate prior knowledge will be addressed in the next two sections.

Implications of This Research

In conclusion, we know that students learn more readily when they can connect what they are learning to what they already know. However, instructors should not assume that students will immediately or naturally draw on relevant prior knowledge. Instead, they should deliberately activate students' prior knowledge to help them forge robust links to new knowledge.

Accurate But Insufficient Prior Knowledge

Even when students' prior knowledge is accurate and activated, it may not be sufficient to support subsequent learning or a desired level of performance. Indeed, when students possess *some* relevant knowledge, it can lead both students and instructors to assume that students are better prepared than they truly are for a particular task or level of instruction.

In fact, there are many different types of knowledge, as evidenced by a number of typologies of knowledge (e.g., Alexander et al., 1991; Anderson, 2016; Anderson et al., 2001; DeJong & Ferguson-Hessler, 1996). One kind of knowledge that appears across many of these typologies is *declarative knowledge*, or the knowledge of facts and concepts that can be stated or declared. Declarative knowledge can be thought of as "knowing what." The ability to name the parts of the circulatory system, describe the characteristics of hunter-gatherer social structure, or explain Newton's third law are examples of declarative knowledge. A second type of knowledge is often referred to as *procedural knowledge*, because it involves knowing how and knowing when to apply various procedures, methods, theories, styles, or approaches. The ability to calculate integrals, draw with 3D perspective, and calibrate lab equipment—as well as the knowledge of when these skills are and are not applicable—fall into the category of procedural knowledge.

Declarative and procedural knowledge are not the same, nor do they enable the same kinds of performance. Studies have shown that students can often

45

perform procedural tasks without being able to articulate a clear understanding of what they are doing or why (Berry & Broadbent, 1988; Reber & Kotovsky, 1997; Sun et al., 2001). For example, business students may be able to apply formulas to solve finance problems but not to explain their logic or the principles underlying their solutions. Similarly, design students may know how to execute a particular design without being able to explain or justify the choices they have made. These students may have sufficient procedural knowledge to function effectively in specific contexts, yet lack the declarative knowledge of deep features and principles that would enable them both to adapt to different contexts (see discussion of transfer in Chapter 5) and explain themselves to others. This is exactly what professor Won was expecting in her research methods course based on previous years.

This year, however, she faced the fact that some of her students know *what* various statistical tests are, but this knowledge is insufficient for the task she has assigned, which requires them to know *why* specific tests are appropriate for a given data set and *how* to execute them properly and interpret the results. This is also not uncommon. In fact, research on science learning demonstrates that even when students can state scientific facts (e.g., "Force equals mass times acceleration"), they are often weak at applying those facts to solve problems, interpret data, and draw conclusions (Clement, 1982). As we can see, declarative and procedural knowledge are two distinct components of expertise, and neither translates into the other.

Implications of This Research

Because *knowing what* is a very different kind of knowledge than *knowing how* or *knowing when*, it is especially important that, as instructors, we are clear in our own minds about the knowledge requirements of different tasks and that we not assume that because our students have one kind of knowledge that they have another. Instead, it is critical to assess both the amount and nature of students' prior knowledge so that we can design our instruction appropriately.

Inappropriate Prior Knowledge

Under some circumstances, students draw on prior knowledge that is inappropriate for the learning context. Although this knowledge is not necessarily inaccurate, it can skew their comprehension of new material. One situation in which prior knowledge can distort learning and performance is when students import everyday meanings into technical contexts. Several studies in statistics, for example, show how commonplace definitions of terms such as *random* and *spread* intrude in technical contexts, distorting students' understandings of statistical concepts (Del Mas & Liu, 2007; Kaplan et al., 2009). This seems to be the problem for Professor Dione's students, whose everyday associations with the terms *positive* and *negative* may have skewed their understanding of *negative reinforcement*.

Another situation in which inappropriate prior knowledge can impede new learning is if students analogize from one situation to another without recognizing the limitations of the analogy. For the most part, analogies serve an important pedagogical function, enabling instructors to build on what students already know to help them understand complex, abstract, or unfamiliar concepts. However, problems can arise when students do not recognize where the analogy breaks down or fail to see the limitations of a simple analogy for describing a complex phenomenon. For example, skeletal muscles and cardiac muscles share some traits; hence, drawing analogies between them makes sense to a point. However, the differences in how these two types of muscles function are substantial and vital to understanding their normal operation, as well as for determining how to effectively intervene in a health crisis. In fact, Spiro and colleagues (1989) found that many medical students possess a misconception about a potential cause of heart failure that can be traced to their failure to recognize the limitations of the skeletal muscle–cardiac muscle analogy.

Knowledge from one disciplinary context, moreover, may obstruct learning and performance in another disciplinary context if students apply it inappropriately. According to Beaufort (2007), college composition courses sometimes contribute to this phenomenon by teaching a generic approach to writing that leaves students ill-prepared to write well in particular domains. Because students come to think of writing as a "one-size-fits-all" skill, they misapply conventions and styles from their general writing classes to disciplinary contexts in which they are not appropriate. For example, they might apply the conventions of a personal narrative or an opinion piece to writing an analytical paper or a lab report. Beaufort argues that without remediation, this intrusion of inappropriate knowledge can affect not only students' performance but also their ability to internalize the rhetorical conventions and strategies of the new discipline.

Furthermore, learning can also be impeded when linguistic knowledge is applied to contexts where it is inappropriate (Bartlett, 1995). For example, when many of us are learning a foreign language, we apply the grammatical structure we know from our native language to the new language. This can impede learning when the new language operates according to fundamentally different grammatical rules, such as a subject-object-verb configuration as opposed to a subject-verb-object structure (Thonis, 2005).

Similarly, misapplication of cultural knowledge can—and often does—lead to erroneous assumptions. For example, when Westerners draw on their own cultural knowledge to interpret practices such as veiling in the Muslim world, they may misinterpret the meaning of the veil to the women who wear it. For instance, Westerners may assume that veiling is a practice imposed by men on unwilling women or that Muslim women who veil do so to hide their beauty. In fact, neither of these conclusions is necessarily accurate; for instance, some Muslim women voluntarily choose to cover—sometimes against the wishes of male family members—as a statement of modern religious and political identity (Ahmed, 1993; El Guindi, 1999). By the same token, some women think of the veil as a way to accentuate, not conceal, beauty (Wikan, 1982). Yet if Westerners interpret these practices through the lens of their own prior cultural knowledge and assumptions, they may emerge with a distorted understanding that can impede further learning.

Research suggests that if students are explicitly taught the conditions and contexts in which knowledge is applicable (and inapplicable), it can help them avoid applying prior knowledge inappropriately. Moreover, if students learn abstract principles to guide the application of their knowledge and are presented with multiple examples and contexts in which to practice applying those principles, it not only helps them recognize when their prior knowledge is relevant to a particular context (see Chapter 5 on mastery) but also helps them avoid misapplying knowledge in the wrong contexts (Schwartz et al., 1999). Researchers also observe that making students explicitly aware of the limitations of a given analogy can help them learn not to approach analogies uncritically or stretch a simple analogy too far (Spiro et al., 1989).

Another way to help students avoid making inappropriate associations or applying prior knowledge in the wrong contexts is to deliberately activate their relevant prior knowledge (Minstrell, 1989, 1992). If we recall Professor Dione's course from the story at the beginning of the chapter, we can imagine a potential application for this idea. When presented with the counterintuitive concept of negative reinforcement, Professor Dione's students drew on associations (of positive as desirable and negative as undesirable) that were interfering with their comprehension. However, if Professor Dione had tried activating a different set of associations—namely of positive as adding and negative as subtracting—he may have been able to leverage those associations to help his students understand that positive reinforcement involves adding something to a situation to increase a desired behavior whereas negative reinforcement involves subtracting something to increase a desired behavior.

Implications of This Research

When learning new material, students may draw on knowledge (from everyday contexts, from incomplete analogies, from other disciplinary contexts, and from their own cultural or linguistic backgrounds) that is inappropriate for the context and that can distort their interpretation of new material or impede new learning. To help students learn where their prior knowledge is and is not applicable, it is important for instructors to (1) clearly explain the conditions and contexts of applicability; (2) teach abstract principles but also provide multiple examples and contexts; (3) point out differences, as well as similarities, when employing analogies; and (4) deliberately activate relevant prior knowledge to strengthen appropriate associations.

Inaccurate Prior Knowledge

We have seen in this chapter that prior knowledge will not support new learning if it is insufficient or inappropriate for the task at hand. But what if it is downright wrong? Research indicates that inaccurate prior knowledge (in other words, flawed ideas, beliefs, models, or theories) can distort new knowledge by predisposing students to ignore, discount, or resist evidence that conflicts with what they believe to be true (Alvermann et al., 1985; Brewer & Lambert, 2001; Chinn & Malhotra, 2002; Dunbar et al., 2007; Fiske & Taylor, 2017). Some psychologists explain this distortion as a result of our striving for internal consistency. For example, Vosniadou and Brewer (1987) found that children reconcile their perception that the earth is flat with formal instruction stating that the earth is round by conceiving of the earth as a pancake: circular but with a flat surface. In other words, children—like all learners—try to make sense of what they are learning by fitting it into what they already know or believe.

This phenomenon highlights an interesting tension. As professionals, we might feel a responsibility to our field to represent it properly and to quickly dispel inaccurate knowledge. But, from a learning standpoint, this process of progressive adaptation cannot be altogether bypassed for all inaccurate knowledge. Researchers have identified different types of inaccurate prior knowledge. It is helpful to delve into the typology because the levels of complexity of inaccurate knowledge correlate with how challenging it is for students to embrace more accurate knowledge.

Inaccurate prior knowledge can be corrected fairly easily if it consists of relatively isolated ideas or beliefs that are not embedded in larger conceptual models (e.g., the belief that we only use 10% of our brain or that the heart oxygenates blood). Research indicates that these proposition-level beliefs (Chi & Roscoe, 2002) respond to refutation; in other words, students will generally revise them when they are explicitly confronted with contradictory explanations and evidence (Broughton et al., 2007; Chi, 2008; Guzetti et al., 1993).

The next level of inaccuracy is that of ontological miscategorizations (Chi, 2008). As an example, some students have trouble reasoning about electric current in circuits. Educators report that in problems where a circuit branches off in two directions, these students answer questions as if each branch of the circuit receives only half of the voltage (Mazur, 1996). That is, they effectively liken electricity flowing in a circuit to water flowing through a pipe system. Water does indeed split at a junction, with only half of the water going each way, but electricity is in a different ontological category than water. Water is a physical object that can only be in one place at a given time, but electricity is a process that affects all of the circuit at all times. These miscategorizations may respond to refutation over time if the individual inaccuracies they contain are refuted systematically (Chi & Roscoe, 2002).

However, some kinds of inaccurate prior knowledge—called *misconceptions*—are remarkably resistant to correction. Misconceptions are models or theories that are deeply embedded in students' thinking. Many examples have been documented in the literature, including naive theories in physics (such as the notion that objects of different masses fall at different rates), "folk psychology" myths (e.g., that blind people have more sensitive hearing than sighted people or that a good hypnotist can command total obedience), and stereotypes about groups of people (Brown, 1983; Kaiser et al., 1986; McCloskey, 1983; Taylor & Kowalski, 2004).

Misconceptions are difficult to refute for a number of reasons. First, many of them have been reinforced over time and across multiple contexts. Moreover, because they often include accurate—as well as inaccurate—elements, students may not recognize their flaws. Finally, in many cases, misconceptions may allow for successful explanations and predictions in a number of everyday circumstances. For example, although stereotypes are dangerous oversimplifications, they are difficult to change in part because they fit aspects of our perceived reality and serve an adaptive human need to generalize and categorize (Allport, 1954; Brewer, 1988; Fiske & Taylor, 2017).

Research has shown that deeply held misconceptions often persist despite direct instructional interventions (Confrey, 1990; Gardner & Dalsing, 1986; Gutman, 1979; Ram et al., 1997). For example, Stein and Dunbar conducted a study (described in Dunbar et al., 2007) in which they asked college students to write about why the seasons changed, and then they assessed their relevant knowledge via a multiple-choice test. After finding that 94% of the students in their study had misconceptions (including the belief that the shape of the earth's orbit was responsible for the seasons), the researchers showed students a video that clearly explained that the tilt of the earth's axis, not the shape of the earth's orbit, was responsible for seasonal change. Yet in spite of the video, when students were asked to revise their essays, their explanations for the seasons did not fundamentally change. Similarly, McCloskey et al. (1980) found that other deeply held misconceptions about the physical world persist even when they are refuted through formal instruction.

In recent years we have seen the emergence of a particularly stubborn set of misconceptions, impervious to logic and reason, that put to the test students' capacity to reason about them and eventually embrace more accurate knowledge. Distrust of vaccines or beliefs about the efficacy of improbable alternative treatments seem to fall in this category, and the student who was rejecting Professor Won's COVID analogy might hold such misconceptions. Throwing data and facts at these misconceptions, or at those who hold them, backfires spectacularly, to the point that this has been documented in the literature as the backfire effect (Nyhan & Reifler, 2010). Even what data and empirical evidence have a corrective effect, this effect decays quickly (Nyhan, 2021) and people revert to comforting, if inaccurate, beliefs. For this reason, some have dubbed misconceptions and conspiracy theories that keep coming back despite having been debunked several times as "zombie beliefs" (Krugman, 2020). For instance, in recent years, some people have called into question the whole scientific enterprise in their effort to hold on to inaccurate beliefs, using a rhetorical move that has been termed the "scientific impotence excuse" (Munro, 2010). They might call into question scientific consensus by referencing outlier opinions, claim

51

that science cannot be trusted because it changes constantly, or in the case of Professor Won's student dismiss statistics as simply a way of lying with data. And so on.

Indeed, sensemaking theory (Weick, 1995) underscores that people generally favor plausibility over accuracy when attempting to make sense of a phenomenon. But what makes demonstrably false statements more plausible than the truth? Psychologists have been puzzling over that question for decades. Benson (2016) synthesizes available research by noting that our brains are faced with impossible tasks daily. There is too much information in the world to process it all. Even if we tried, the task of making meaning out of so much information would be impossibly energy-intensive and time-consuming. Moreover, the cognitive resources required to commit all this information and meaning to memory for long-term retention would be prohibitive. To cope with these impossibilities, the brain has no choice but to come up with strategies to filter information, create stories, and jump to conclusions. These strategies, which in essence are biases, are both a blessing and a curse. Over 200 cognitive biases have been identified. One of the most studied ones is the confirmation bias (Wason, 1960), which documents the phenomenon that people tend to pay more attention to information that confirms their beliefs and to disregard information that does not confirm their beliefs. Cognitive dissonance theory (Festinger, 1957) suggests that we have an inner drive to hold our beliefs in internal harmony. When new information upsets this harmony, it creates cognitive dissonance, and we typically move in the direction of reducing the dissonance to reestablish balance.

For some, reducing cognitive dissonance might mean simply disregarding new information that disrupts established mental models. But the phenomenon is not exclusively cognitive in nature. If we take a psychosocial approach to knowledge resistance, as Klintman (2019) does, then we realize that many such misconceptions have been held and rehearsed in the brain for a long time, which has reinforced their salience. They have likely been connected to other important beliefs, including those that make up a person's morality and worldview (see the importance of making connections in the brain for knowledge retention in Chapter 3). Many of these beliefs have been taught by respected and trusted authority figures. They are shared beliefs in the individual's social sphere, which makes them normative and creates a sense of in-group/out-group ("we" all believe this way, and "they" don't). This means there are social benefits within the group for holding and espousing such beliefs and social costs for renouncing them.

In turn, that means that challenging these beliefs can arouse emotions, another powerful lever in the brain. In other words, these beliefs have become tied to individuals' social identities, and we have seen in the previous chapter how identities can shape our learning.

Results like these are sobering. Yet the picture is not altogether gloomy. To begin with, it is important to recognize that conceptual change often occurs gradually and may not be immediately visible. Thus, students may be moving in the direction of more accurate knowledge even when it is not yet apparent in their performance (Alibali, 1999; Chi & Roscoe, 2002). Moreover, even when students retain inaccurate beliefs, they can learn to inhibit and override those beliefs and draw on accurate knowledge instead. Research indicates, for instance, that when people are sufficiently motivated to do so, they can consciously suppress stereotypical judgments and learn to rely on rational analysis more and stereotypes less (Monteith & Mark, 2005; Monteith et al., 1998). Moreover, since consciously overcoming misconceptions requires more cognitive energy than simply falling back on intuitive, familiar modes of thinking, there is research to suggest that when distractions and time pressures are minimized, students will be more likely to think rationally and avoid applying misconceptions and flawed assumptions (Finucane et al., 2000; Kahnemann & Frederick, 2002).

In addition, carefully designed instruction can help wean students away from misconceptions through a process called *bridging* (Brown, 1992; Brown & Clement, 1989; Clement, 1993). For example, Clement observed that students often had trouble believing that a table exerts force on a book placed on its surface. To help students grasp this somewhat counterintuitive concept, he designed an instructional intervention for high school physics students that started from students' accurate prior knowledge. Because students did believe that a compressed spring exerted force, the researchers were able to analogize from the spring to foam, then to pliable wood, and finally to a solid table. The intermediate objects served to bridge the difference between a spring and the table and enabled the students to extend their accurate prior knowledge to new contexts. Using this approach, Clement obtained significantly greater pre- to posttest gains compared to traditional classroom instruction. In a similar vein, Minstrell's research (1989) shows that students can be guided away from misconceptions through a process of reasoning that helps them build on the accurate facets of their knowledge as they gradually revise the inaccurate facets.

53

Implications of This Research

It is important for instructors to address inaccurate prior knowledge that might otherwise distort or impede learning. In some cases, inaccuracies can be corrected simply by exposing students to accurate information and evidence that conflicts with flawed beliefs and models. However, it is important for instructors to recognize that a single correction or refutation is unlikely to be enough to help students revise deeply held misconceptions. Instead, guiding students through a process of conceptual change is likely to take time, patience, and creativity.

WHAT STRATEGIES DOES THE RESEARCH SUGGEST?

In this section we offer (1) a set of strategies to help instructors determine the extent and quality of students' prior knowledge relative to the learning requirements of a course. We then provide strategies instructors can employ to (2) activate students' relevant prior knowledge, (3) address gaps in students' prior knowledge, (4) help students avoid applying prior knowledge in the wrong contexts, and (5) help students revise and rethink inaccurate knowledge.

Strategies to Gauge the Extent and Nature of Students' Prior Knowledge

Talk to Colleagues As a starting point for finding out what prior knowledge students bring to your course, talk to colleagues who teach prerequisite courses or ask to see their syllabi and assignments. This can give you a quick sense of what material was covered and in what depth. It can also alert you to differences in approach, emphasis, terminology, and notation so that you can address potential gaps or discrepancies. Remember, though, that just because the material was taught does not mean that students necessarily learned it. To get a better sense of students' knowledge, as well as their ability to apply it, you might also ask your colleagues about students' proficiencies: for example, what concepts and skills did students seem to master easily? Which ones did they struggle with? Did students seem to hold any systematic and pervasive misconceptions? This kind of information from colleagues can help you design your instructional activities so they effectively connect to, support, extend, and, if needed, correct students' prior knowledge.

Administer a Diagnostic Assessment To find out what relevant knowledge students possess coming into your course, consider assigning a short, low-stakes assessment, such as a quiz or an essay, at the beginning of the semester. Students' performance on this assignment can give you a sense of their knowledge of prerequisite facts and concepts or their competence in various skills. For example, if your course requires knowledge of technical vocabulary and basic calculus skills, you could create a short quiz asking students to define terms and solve calculus problems. You can mark these assignments individually to get a sense of the skill and knowledge of particular students or simply look them over as a set to get a feel for students' overall level of preparedness. Another way to expose students' prior knowledge is by administering a concept inventory. Concept inventories are ungraded tests, typically in a multiple-choice format, that are designed to include incorrect answers that help reveal common misconceptions. Developing a concept inventory of your own can be time-intensive, so check the internet to see whether there are inventories already available in your discipline that would suit your needs. A number of concept inventories have been widely used and have high validity and reliability.

Have Students Assess Their Own Prior Knowledge In some fields and at some levels of expertise, having students assess their own knowledge and skills can be a quick and effective—though not necessarily foolproof—way to diagnose missing or insufficient prior knowledge. One way to have students self-assess is to create a list of concepts and skills that you expect them to have coming into your course, as well as some concepts and skills you expect them to acquire during the semester. Ask students to assess their level of competence for each concept or skill using a scale that ranges from cursory familiarity ("I have heard of the term") to factual knowledge ("I could define it") to conceptual knowledge ("I could explain it to someone else") to application ("I can use it to solve problems"). Examine the data for the class as a whole in order to identify areas in which your students have either less knowledge than you expect or more. In either case, this information can help you recalibrate your instruction to better meet student needs. See Appendix C for more information about student self-assessments.

Use Brainstorming to Reveal Prior Knowledge One way to expose students' prior knowledge is to conduct a group brainstorming session. Brainstorming can be used to uncover beliefs, associations, and assumptions (e.g., with questions such as "What do you think of when you hear the word *evangelical*?"). It can also

55

be used to expose factual or conceptual knowledge ("What were some of the key historical events in the Gilded Age?" or "What comes to mind when you think about environmental ethics?"), procedural knowledge ("If you were going to do a research project on the Farm Bill, where would you begin?"), or contextual knowledge ("What are some methodologies you could use to research this question?"). Bear in mind that brainstorming does not provide a systematic gauge of students' prior knowledge. Also, be prepared to differentiate accurate and appropriately applied knowledge from knowledge that is inaccurate or inappropriately applied.

Assign a Concept Map Activity To gain insights into what your students know about a given subject, ask them to construct a concept map representing everything that they know about the topic. You can ask students to create a concept map (see Appendix D on concept maps), representing what they know about an entire disciplinary domain (e.g., social psychology), a particular concept (e.g., Newton's third law), or a question (e.g., "What are the ethical issues with stem cell research?"). Some students may be familiar with concept maps, but others may not be, so be sure to explain what they are and how to create them (circles for concepts, lines between concepts to show how they relate). There are a number of ways to construct concept maps, so you should give some thought to what you are trying to ascertain. For instance, if you are interested in gauging students' knowledge of concepts as well as their ability to articulate the connections among them, you can ask students to generate both concepts and links. But if you are primarily interested in students' ability to articulate the connections, you can provide the list of concepts and ask students to arrange and connect them, labeling the links. If there are particular kinds of information you are looking for (e.g., causal relationships, examples, theoretical orientations) be sure to specify what you want. Review the concept maps your students create to try to determine gaps in their knowledge, inappropriate links, and the intrusion of lay terms and ideas that may indicate the presence of naive theories or preconceptions.

Look for Patterns of Error in Student Work Students' misconceptions tend to be shared and produce a consistent pattern of errors. You (or your TAs or graders) can often identify these misconceptions simply by looking at students' errors on homework assignments, quizzes, or exams and noting commonalities across the class. You can also keep track of the kinds of problems and errors that students reveal when they come to office hours or as they raise or answer questions during class. Paying attention to these patterns of error can alert you to common problems and help you target instruction to correct misconceptions or fill gaps in understanding. Some instructors use classroom response systems (also called *clickers*) to quickly collect students' answers to concept questions posed in class. Clickers provide an instant histogram of students' answers and can alert instructors to areas of misunderstanding that might stem from insufficient prior knowledge.

Strategies to Activate Accurate Prior Knowledge

Use Exercises to Generate Students' Prior Knowledge Because students learn most effectively when they connect new knowledge to prior knowledge, it can be helpful to begin a lesson by asking students what they already know about the topic in question. This can be done any number of ways, such as by asking students to brainstorm associations or create a concept map. Once students have activated relevant prior knowledge in their heads, they are likely to be able to integrate new knowledge more successfully. However, since activities like this can generate inaccurate and inappropriate as well as accurate and relevant knowledge, you should be prepared to help students distinguish between them.

Explicitly Link New Material to Knowledge from Previous Courses Students tend to compartmentalize knowledge by course, semester, professor, or discipline. As a result, they may not recognize the relevance of knowledge from a previous course to a new learning situation. For example, students who have learned about the concept of variability in a statistics course often do not bring that knowledge to bear on the concept of volatility in a finance course both because of the difference in terminology and because they do not see the link between the two contexts. However, if you make the connection between variability and volatility explicit, it enables students to tap into that prior knowledge and build on it productively.

Explicitly Link New Material to Prior Knowledge from Your Own Course Although we often expect students to automatically link what they are learning to knowledge gained earlier in the same course, they may not do so automatically. Thus, it is important for instructors to highlight these connections. Instructors can help students activate relevant prior knowledge by framing particular lectures, discussions, or readings in relation to material learned previously in the semester. For example, in a literary theory course, the professor might begin class by saying, "In Unit 2 we discussed feminist theory. Today we are going to talk about a school of

57

thought that grew out of feminist theory." Sometimes all it takes to activate students' relevant prior knowledge is a slight prompt, such as "Think back to the research design Johnson used in the article from last week" or "Where have we seen this phenomenon before?" Students can also be encouraged to look for connections within course materials in other ways. For example, the instructor can ask students to write reflection papers that connect each reading to other readings and to larger themes in the course. Also, discussions provide an ideal opportunity to elicit students' knowledge from earlier in the semester and to link it to new material.

Use Analogies and Examples That Connect to Students' Everyday Knowledge Examples or analogies that draw on students' everyday lives and the wider world make new material more understandable and create more robust knowledge representations in students' minds. For example, an instructor could draw on students' memories from childhood and experiences with younger siblings to help them understand concepts in child development. Similarly, an instructor could use students' experiences with the physical world to introduce concepts such as force and acceleration. Analogies are also useful for connecting new knowledge to prior knowledge. For example, students' experience with cooking can be enlisted to help them understand scientific processes such as chemical synthesis (just as in cooking, when you mix or heat chemicals, you need to know when precision is and is not critical). Students often show more sophisticated reasoning when working in familiar contexts, and we can build on their knowledge from these contexts as we explore new material. As we have seen in Chapter 1, however, student experiences and identities can vary widely, and we need to be mindful about what we assume constitutes a shared context.

Ask Students to Reason on the Basis of Relevant Prior Knowledge Often students have prior knowledge that could help them reason about new material and learn it more deeply. Thus, it can be useful to ask students questions that require them to use their prior knowledge to make predictions about new information before they actually encounter it. For example, before asking students to read an article from the 1970s, you might ask them what was going on historically at the time that might have informed the author's perspective. Or when presenting students with a design problem, you might ask them how a famous designer, whose work they know, might have approached the problem. This requires students not only to draw on their prior knowledge but also to use it to reason about new knowledge.

Strategies to Address Insufficient Prior Knowledge

Identify the Prior Knowledge You Expect Students to Have The first step toward addressing gaps in students' prior knowledge is recognizing where those gaps are. This requires identifying in your own mind the knowledge students will need to have to perform effectively in your course. To identify what the prior knowledge requirements are for your class, you might want to begin by thinking about your assignments, and ask yourself, "What do students need to know to be able to do this?" Often instructors stop short of identifying all the background knowledge students need, so be sure to continue asking the question until you have fully identified the knowledge requirements for the tasks you have assigned. Be sure to differentiate declarative (knowing what and knowing why) from procedural knowledge (knowing how and knowing when), recognizing that just because students know facts or concepts does not mean they will know how to use them, and just because students know how to perform procedures does not mean that they understand what they are doing or why (see "Strategies to Expose and Reinforce Component Skills" in Chapter 5).

Remediate Insufficient Prerequisite Knowledge If prior knowledge assessments (as discussed in previous strategies) indicate critical gaps in students' prior knowledge relative to the learning requirements of your course, there are a number of possible responses depending on the scale of the problem and the resources and options available to you and to your students. If only a few students lack important prerequisite knowledge, one option that might be open to you is simply to advise them against taking the course until they have the necessary background. Alternatively, if a few students lack prerequisite knowledge but seem capable of acquiring it on their own, you might consider providing these students with a list of terms they should know and skills they should have and letting them fill in the gaps on their own time. If a larger number of students lack sufficient prior knowledge in a key area, you might decide to devote one or two classes to a review of important prerequisite material or (if it is applicable) ask your teaching assistant to run a review session outside class time. If a sizable proportion of your class lacks knowledge that is a critical foundation for the material you planned to cover, you may need to revise your course altogether so that it is properly aligned with your students' knowledge and skills. Of course, if your course is a prerequisite for other courses, such fundamental revisions may have broader implications, which may need to be addressed at a departmental level through a discussion of objectives and course sequencing.

Strategies to Help Students Recognize Inappropriate Prior Knowledge

Highlight Conditions of Applicability It is important to help students see when it is and is not appropriate to apply prior knowledge. For example, a statistics instructor might explain that a regression analysis can be used for quantitative variables but not for qualitative variables, or a biology instructor might instruct students to save their expressive writing for other courses and instead write lab reports that focus on conciseness and accuracy. If there are no strict rules about when prior knowledge is applicable, another strategy is to present students with a range of problems and contexts and ask them to identify whether or not a given skill or concept is applicable and to explain their reasoning.

Provide Heuristics to Help Students Avoid Inappropriate Application of Knowledge One strategy to help students avoid applying their prior knowledge inappropriately is to provide them with some rules of thumb to help them determine whether their knowledge is or is not relevant. For example, when students are encountering different cultural practices and might be tempted to assess them according to their own cultural norms, you might encourage them to ask themselves questions such as "Am I making assumptions based on my own cultural knowledge that may not be appropriate here? If so, what are those assumptions, and where do they come from?" By the same token, if you know of situations in which students frequently get confused by the intrusion of prior knowledge (e.g., students' understanding of negative reinforcement in the second story at the beginning of this chapter), you might want to provide them with a rule of thumb to help them avoid that pitfall. For example, an instructor teaching classical learning theory could advise his students, "When you see 'negative' in the context of negative reinforcement, think of subtraction."

Explicitly Identify Discipline-Specific Conventions It is important to clearly identify the conventions and expectations of your discipline so that students do not mistakenly apply the conventions of other domains about which they know more. For example, students may have experience with writing from a science course (lab reports), from a history course (analytical paper), or from an English course (personal narrative), so when they take a public policy course they may not know which set of knowledge and skills is the appropriate one to build on. It is important to explicitly identify the norms you expect them to follow. Without explicit guidance, students may analogize from other experiences or fields that they feel most competent in, regardless of whether the experiences are appropriate in the current context.

Show Where Analogies Break Down Analogies can help students learn complex or abstract concepts. However, they can be problematic if students do not recognize their limits. Thus, it is important to help students recognize the limitations of a given analogy by explicitly identifying (or asking students to identify) where the analogy breaks down. For example, you might point out that although the digestive system is similar to plumbing in that it involves tube-like organs and various kinds of valves, it is far more complex and sensitive than any ordinary plumbing system.

Strategies to Correct Inaccurate Knowledge

Be Realistic Before we get into actual strategies to work on dispelling misconceptions, it is important to set realistic expectations. Some inaccurate knowledge can be dispelled fairly easily, but deeply embedded misconceptions are harder to unlearn. What can be reasonably accomplished in 14 weeks of a semester or 10 weeks of a quarter? It might be that the first encounter with challenging truths only begins to chip away at the inaccuracies, and, for some, the psychological cost of admitting having been wrong all along might outweigh other considerations. There will likely be other opportunities down the road for students to hear that message reinforced over and over.

Ask Students to Make and Test Predictions To help students revise inaccurate beliefs and flawed mental models, we can ask them to make predictions based on those beliefs and give them the opportunity to test those predictions. For example, physics students with an inaccurate understanding of force could be asked to make predictions about how forces will act on stationary versus moving objects. Being confronted with evidence that contradicts students' beliefs and expectations can help them see where their knowledge or beliefs are incorrect or inadequate, while motivating them to seek knowledge that accounts for what they have seen. Predictions can be tested in experiments, in or outside a laboratory environment, or through the use of computer simulations.

Ask Students to Justify Their Reasoning One strategy to guide students away from inaccurate knowledge is to ask them to reason on the basis of what they believe to be true. When students' reasoning reveals internal contradictions, it can bring them to the point where they seek accurate knowledge. A caveat to this approach is that students may not necessarily see those internal contradictions.

Moreover, if their attitudes and beliefs are very deeply held (e.g., religious beliefs that defy logical argument), these contradictions may have little effect.

Anticipate Predictable Moves Some of the misconceptions students bring are predictable. If the learning objectives of the course include challenging those misconceptions, it is helpful to learn the objections and rhetorical moves that commonly surface in defense of the flawed mental models. For instance, many of those who believe that vaccines cause autism are aware that the original paper to make this claim has been exposed as fabrication and its author discredited. But the goalpost has been moved and new objections keep being added. Staying abreast of those will help us address misconceptions in a systematic way.

Describe the View from the Other Side When the misconceptions are tied up in students' identities, it might be helpful to reassure them that our goal is not for them to embrace a new religion or a new political affiliation. But, as educated people and future leaders, they need to be able to understand those with opposite views. Assignments that ask students, say, to explain how somebody who accepts the theory of evolution would explain a specific phenomenon still test whether students understand the basic mechanisms of the theory, but reduce the threat to students' identity.

Discuss Epistemology Upfront In courses that routinely engage misconceptions, it might be helpful to have an overarching discussion about epistemology in the beginning. How do we know what we know? What counts as evidence? Is it okay to change our mind and under what circumstances? What are the hallmarks of an open mind and of a closed mind? If students are able to come to consensus on these theoretical issues, then it will be that much easier to remind them when confronting specific misconceptions.

Teach Information Literacy Skills Given that most of our students' information comes from the free web, it is crucial that they learn how to evaluate the knowledge and the sources. Those are skills that can only be mastered when taught and practiced, so it is important to make time for information literacy. Most colleges and universities have resources to support this skill. In fact, most librarians would be delighted to be invited into courses to explain how to evaluate information from the web.

Provide Multiple Opportunities for Students to Use Accurate Knowledge Misconceptions can be hard to correct in part because they have been reinforced through repeated exposure. Thus, replacing inaccurate knowledge with accurate knowledge requires not just introducing accurate knowledge but also providing multiple opportunities for students to use it. Repeated opportunities to apply accurate knowledge can help counteract the persistence of even deeply held misconceptions.

Allow Sufficient Time It is easier for students to fall back on deeply held misconceptions than to employ the reasoning necessary to overcome them. Therefore, when you are asking students to use new knowledge that requires a revision or rethinking of their prior knowledge, it can be helpful to minimize distractions and allow a little extra time. This can help students enlist the cognitive resources necessary to identify flaws in their knowledge or reasoning and instead to consciously employ more thoughtful, critical thinking.

Differentiate Instruction Many of these strategies might be unnecessary for the majority of our students, who are quite ready and willing to unlearn inaccurate knowledge and learn actual verified facts. It might be helpful to differentiate instruction and create additional resources for students who struggle with specific concepts so the rest of the class can move forward without repetition they don't really need.

SUMMARY

In this chapter we have examined the critical role of prior knowledge in laying the groundwork for new learning. We have seen that if students' prior knowledge has gaps and insufficiencies it may not adequately support new knowledge. Moreover, if prior knowledge is applied in the wrong context, it may lead students to make faulty assumptions or draw inappropriate parallels. In addition, inaccurate prior knowledge—some of which can be surprisingly difficult to correct—can both distort students' understanding and interfere with incoming information. Consequently, a critical task for us as instructors is to assess what students know and believe so we can build on knowledge that is accurate and relevant, fill in gaps and insufficiencies where they exist, help students recognize when they are applying prior knowledge inappropriately, and help students revise inaccurate knowledge and form more accurate and robust mental models.

CHAPTER 3

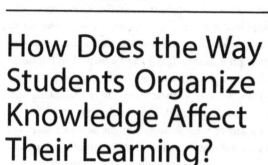

How Does the Way Students Organize Knowledge Affect Their Learning?

That Didn't Work Out the Way I Anticipated

For the past 12 years, I've taught our department's introductory art history course. I present the material using a standard approach. That is, I begin with an introductory description of key terms and concepts, including a discussion of the basic visual elements (line, color, light, form, composition, space). Then, for each of the remaining 40 class sessions, I show slides of important works, progressing chronologically from prehistoric Europe to rather recent pieces. As I go, I identify important features that characterize each piece and point out associations among various movements, schools, and periods. I give a midterm and a final exam during which I present slides and ask students to identify the title of the work, the artist, the school, and the period in which it was produced. While the students seem to enjoy the class sessions, they complain about the amount of material they must memorize for the exams. I know there are a lot of individual pieces, but they naturally cluster by period, school, and technique. Once you categorize a work according to those groupings, it should be fairly easy to remember. Nevertheless, the students seem to be having a lot of difficulty in my exams identifying even some of the most important pieces.

Professor Rachel Rothman

There Must Be a Better Way!

Anatomy and physiology is one of the core courses required for our nursing, premed, and pharmacy students. The course is organized on the major systems of the body and requires students to identify and describe the location and function of the major organs, bones, muscles, and tissues in the body. On the whole, students attend the lectures and labs consistently, and most of them appear to work really hard. Indeed, I often find them in the student lounge poring over their notes or quizzing each other in order to memorize all the individual structures. With a lot of work, they learn to identify most of the parts of the human body and can describe the role of each part in its body system. However, when asked to explain the relationships among parts or higher-order principles that cut across systems, the students often fall apart. For example, on the last exam I asked them to identify and describe all the structures involved in the regulation of blood pressure. To my surprise, most of the students were unable to answer the question correctly. I just don't get it—they know all the parts, but when it comes to how those parts fit together, they have a really difficult time.

Professor Anand Patel

WHAT IS GOING ON IN THESE TWO STORIES?

Although the content of the courses in these two stories differs substantially, the two instructors have similar goals. They want their students to develop a deep, functional understanding of a multifaceted, complex domain. In the first story, the domain is the accumulated corpus of artistic expression created by humans over the past 30,000 years. In the second story, the domain is the complex array of organs, systems, and interacting parts that make up the human body. Each domain comprises many individual elements, and each element—be it a bone in the wrist or Picasso's *Guernica*—is related to other elements in important ways. Knowing about these elements, but also having a meaningful picture of how they are related to each other, is critical to deep understanding. In each of the stories, however, the students appear to lack a sufficiently coherent, organized representation of the material, which impedes their learning and performance.

In the first story, Professor Rothman provides her students with the concepts and vocabulary to analyze the visual elements in works of art and to make

65

connections across various artists, schools, and periods. Then, for the rest of the semester she presents works of art in chronological order, referring to the key features of each piece of art she presents. It appears, however, that mentioning these features in relation to individual works was not sufficient to enable her students to see deeper relationships and make broader connections among clusters of works. That is, while these relationships and comparisons are natural to Professor Rothman, providing her with an easy way to group and organize the factual information, her students may not have made the same connections. Instead, they may have latched onto chronology as the prominent organizing principle for the material and hence organized their knowledge along a time line. Because this chronological structure for organizing knowledge entails remembering a great number of isolated facts, without any other overarching organizational structure to facilitate information retrieval and use, these students may be struggling (and largely failing) to memorize what they need to know for the exam.

In the second story, Professor Patel's students have knowledge of the individual parts of the human body, but this knowledge does not translate into an understanding of how those parts are functionally related to one another. One reason for this may be that students have organized their knowledge much the same way as a standard anatomy and physiology textbook: according to the major body systems (e.g., the skeletal system, the digestive system, the circulatory system). If Professor Patel's students have organized their knowledge on discrete parts of the body, it could have several effects on their ability to use this information. If these students were asked to name the major bones of the hand or the function of the pancreas, they would probably have little difficulty, since such questions mesh well with how they have organized the information. However, to answer Professor Patel's question about how various structures work together to regulate blood pressure, these students would need an alternative way to organize their knowledge—one including the functional relationships that cut across multiple systems, not simply the parts in isolation. In other words, the way these students have organized their knowledge facilitates one kind of use, but it is not sufficiently flexible to support the demands of all the tasks they face.

WHAT PRINCIPLE OF LEARNING IS AT WORK HERE?

As experts in our fields, we create and maintain, often unconsciously, a complex network that connects the important facts, concepts, procedures, and other elements within our domain. Moreover, we organize our domain knowledge on meaningful features and abstract principles. By contrast, most of our students have not yet developed such connected or meaningful ways of organizing the information they encounter in our courses. And yet, how they organize their knowledge has profound implications for their learning, a point that is highlighted in our next principle.

Principle: *How students organize knowledge influences how they learn and apply what they know.*

When we talk about the ways people organize their knowledge (or, for the sake of simplicity, their *knowledge organizations*), we are not focusing on particular pieces of knowledge, but rather how those pieces are arranged and connected in an individual's mind. Knowledge can be organized in ways that either do or do not facilitate learning, performance, and retention.

As an illustration, consider two students who are asked to identify the date when the British defeated the Spanish Armada (National Research Council, 2001). The first student tells us that the battle happened in 1588, and the second says that they cannot remember the precise date but thinks it must be about 1590. Given that 1588 is the correct answer for this historical date, the first student appears to have more accurate knowledge. Suppose, however, that we probe the students further and ask how they arrived at their answers. The first student simply says that they memorized the correct date from a book. By contrast, the second student says that they based their answer on the knowledge that the British colonized Virginia just after 1600 and the inference that the British would not dare organize massive overseas voyages for colonization until navigation was considered safe. Figuring that it took about ten years for maritime traffic to be properly organized, the second student arrived at the answer of "about 1590."

These students' follow-up answers reveal knowledge organizations of different quality. The first student has learned an isolated fact about the Spanish Armada, apparently unconnected in their mind to any related historical knowledge. By contrast, the second student seems to have organized their knowledge in a much more interconnected (and causal) way that enabled them to reason about the situation in order to answer the question. The first student's sparse knowledge organization would likely not offer much support for future learning, whereas the second student's knowledge organization would provide a more robust foundation for subsequent learning.

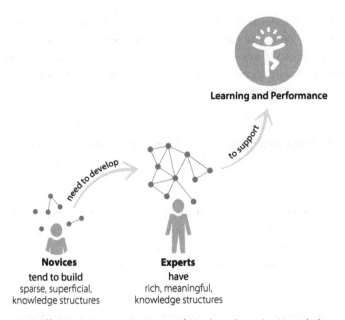

Figure 3.1. Differences in How Experts and Novices Organize Knowledge

Although the two students in this example are both relative novices, the differences in their knowledge organizations correspond, in very rough terms, to the differences between novices and experts. As illustrated in Figure 3.1, novice and expert knowledge organizations tend to differ in two key ways: the degree to which knowledge is sparsely versus richly connected and the extent to which those connections are superficial versus meaningful. Although students often begin with knowledge organizations that are sparse and superficial, effective instruction can help them develop more connected and meaningful knowledge organizations that better support their learning and performance. Indeed, the second student in the preceding example shows progression in this direction.

WHAT DOES THE RESEARCH TELL US ABOUT KNOWLEDGE ORGANIZATION?

As a starting point for understanding how knowledge organizations differ and the consequences of those differences, it helps to consider how knowledge organizations develop. This is addressed in the next section. The remaining sections then elaborate on two important ways that experts' and novices' knowledge organizations differ and review research that suggests how novices can develop knowledge organizations that better facilitate learning.

Knowledge Organization: Form Fits Function

People naturally make associations based on patterns they experience in the world. For instance, we tend to build associations between events that occur in temporal contiguity (e.g., a causal relationship between flipping the switch and a light turning on), between ideas that share meaning (e.g., a conceptual relationship between fairness and equality), and between objects that have perceptual similarities (e.g., a category-member relationship between a ball and a globe). As these associations build up over time, larger and more complex structures emerge that reflect how entire bodies of knowledge are organized in a person's mind.

The way people organize their knowledge tends to vary as a function of their experience, the nature of their knowledge, and the role that that knowledge plays in their lives. As a case in point, consider how people in different cultures classify family members. The terms they use provide a window into how a culture organizes standard kinship knowledge. In the United States, for example, we typically employ different terms to distinguish our parents from their siblings (in other words, *mother* and *father* are distinguished from *uncle* and *aunt*). This linguistic distinction—which seems natural and inevitable to many of us—corresponds to the special role of the nuclear family in US society. However, in a number of cultures that are organized on extended families, mother/aunt and father/uncle share the same kinship term (Levi-Strauss, 1969; Stone, 2000). This is because mothers and aunts (and similarly, fathers and uncles) occupy similar functional roles in these children's lives. As an example in the other direction, notice that most people in the United States do not use different kinship terms for paternal versus maternal uncles (and aunts). Because these categories of family members do not have functionally distinct roles in family life, there is no need to distinguish them linguistically. However, in some cultures maternal and paternal uncles and aunts have divergent roles (e.g., the disciplinarian paternal uncle versus the indulgent maternal uncle), and in those cases a linguistic distinction is made, indicating these relatives are in functionally different categories. As this example suggests, in cultures that need to distinguish among particular categories of family members, the language—and, by inference, typical knowledge organizations—will reflect that need for differentiation. This points to the fact that knowledge organizations develop in the context of use, thus providing ways of grouping and classifying knowledge that serve practical functions.

This example of kinship terminology highlights the point that no organizational structure is necessarily better or more "correct" than another. Instead, it is more appropriate to think of knowledge organizations as well or poorly matched to a given situation. After all, a system of organizing kinship that collapses father and uncle into a single category would be potentially confusing in a society in which the difference between these types of family members mattered, but reasonable in a society in which the difference was unimportant. In fact, research has found that the usefulness of knowledge organizations depends on the tasks they need to support. In a study by Eylon and Reif (1984), high school students learned material on a topic in modern physics. Half of the students learned the material according to a historical framework, and the other half learned the same material but according to physics principles. Then the two groups of students were asked to complete various tasks that drew on what they had just learned. These tasks fell into two categories: tasks that required accessing information according to historical periods versus according to physical principles. Not surprisingly, students performed better when their knowledge organizations matched the requirements of the task, and they performed worse when it mismatched.

A similar mismatch between knowledge organization and task demands is likely to be part of the problem Professor Patel describes in the second story at the beginning of this chapter. The students in the anatomy and physiology course appear to have organized their knowledge of anatomy on separate body systems. Whereas this mode of knowledge organization would facilitate performance on tasks that emphasize intra-system relationships, it may not help students answer questions focused on functional relationships that involve the interaction of systems.

Implications of This Research

Because knowledge organizations develop to support the tasks being performed, we should reflect on what activities and experiences students are

---

engaging in to understand what knowledge organizations they are likely to develop. And because knowledge organizations are most effective when they are well matched to the way that knowledge needs to be accessed and used, we should consider the tasks students will be asked to perform in a given course or discipline in order to identify what knowledge organizations would best support those tasks. Then we can foster the ways of organizing knowledge that will promote students' learning and performance.

Experts' Versus Novices' Knowledge Organizations: The Density of Connections

One important way experts' and novices' knowledge organizations differ is in the number or density of connections among the concepts, facts, and skills they know. Figure 3.2 shows a variety of organizational structures that differ in regard to the connections that exist among pieces of knowledge. In each panel, pieces of knowledge are represented by nodes, and relationships between them are represented by links.

If we look at panels A and B, we see knowledge organizations that are fairly typical of novices in that they show few connections among nodes. The sparseness of links among components in panel A, for instance, probably indicates that the

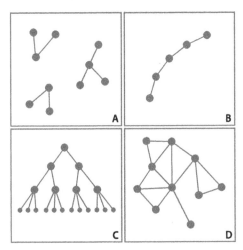

Figure 3.2. Examples of Knowledge Organizations

students have not yet developed the ability to recognize relationships among pieces of knowledge. This kind of organization might be found in a situation in which students absorb the knowledge from each lecture in a course without connecting the information to other lectures or recognizing themes that cut across the course as a whole. Such relatively disconnected knowledge organizations can impede student learning in several ways. First, if students lack a strongly connected network their knowledge will be slower and more difficult to retrieve (Bradshaw & Anderson, 1982; Reder & Anderson, 1980; Smith et al., 1978). Moreover, if students do not make the necessary connections among pieces of information, they may not recognize or seek to rectify contradictions. For example, DiSessa (1982) has repeatedly shown that students whose knowledge of physics is disconnected and lacks coherence can simultaneously hold and use contradictory propositions about the movement of physical objects without noticing the inconsistencies.

Panel B of Figure 3.2 is similar to panel A in that it has relatively sparse connections, but its connections are arranged in the form of a chain of associations. Although this structure affords the sequential access of information (potentially useful for remembering the stanzas of a poem or the steps of a procedure), it can lead to difficulties if one link in the chain is broken, or if some deviation from the specified sequence is required (Catrambone, 1995, 1998). Moreover, the more nodes linked in such a simple chain, the slower and more difficult it is on average to traverse from one piece of knowledge to another. Professor Rothman's students are a case in point: because their knowledge of art history appears to be organized along a time line, they must try to remember each work of art in relation to the one before and after it on the time line, a potentially difficult memory task.

By contrast, panels C and D correspond to knowledge organizations that are more typical of experts. Panel C shows knowledge that is organized hierarchically, indicating an understanding of how various pieces of information fit within a complex structure. An example would be the way an expert distinguishes theoretical schools within her discipline, the scholars whose work falls within each of these schools, and the particular books and articles that exemplify each scholar's work. However, because not all information can be represented as a set of tidy, discrete hierarchies, panel D shows an even more highly connected knowledge structure with additional links that indicate cross-referencing or suggest where strict hierarchies might break down.

These more complex and highly connected knowledge structures enable experts to access and use their knowledge more efficiently and effectively. Indeed, research has shown that experts tend to automatically process information in coherent chunks based on their prior knowledge and then use these chunks to build larger, more interconnected knowledge structures. The power of such highly connected knowledge organizations is illustrated in a classic study by Ericsson et al. (1980). This study (and others that followed it, such as Ericsson & Staszewski, 1989) documented how college students with ordinary memories could develop an ability to recall amazingly long sequences of digits by organizing what they were learning into a multilevel hierarchical structure, much like that in panel C. Because one of these students happened to be a competitive runner, he was able to translate four-digit subsequences into famous running times (e.g., the digits "3432" might be remembered as "34:32, the world record for..."). This strategy, called *chunking*, enabled four digits to be remembered as a single, familiar chunk of knowledge. This initial strategy for organizing the to-be-remembered digits increased his ability to recall from 7 digits to almost 30. But what really boosted his memory performance was organizing these four-digit chunks into even larger groups consisting of three or four chunks, and then organizing these multi-chunk groups hierarchically into higher-level structures, up to the point where he was able to recall up to 100 digits without any external memory aids! In other words, by creating a highly organized knowledge structure for remembering digits, individuals can develop exceptional memory ability and recall a great deal of information.

Although this study focuses on simple recall, it nevertheless suggests that organizing knowledge in a sophisticated, interconnected structure—as experts tend to do—can radically increase one's ability to access that information when one needs it. Professor Rothman (from the first story at the beginning of this chapter) serves as a good illustration. Her own expert knowledge of art history appears to be arranged in an interconnected, hierarchical structure—much like the organization in Figure 3.2, panel C—with links among facts (e.g., dates, artists' names, and the titles of various works) and related knowledge (of artistic movements and historical periods, among other things). This hierarchical organization of knowledge enables her to access the information she needs easily. The only problem is that she expects her students—who lack an analogous organizational structure—to be able to do the same. Instead, they struggle to remember an unwieldy set of isolated facts without an organizational structure to hold them.

Although students may not possess the highly connected knowledge organizations that their instructors possess, they can develop more sophisticated knowledge organizations over time. Indeed, research suggests that when students are provided with a structure for organizing new information, they learn more and better. For example, one classic study (Bower et al., 1969) demonstrated that students who were asked to learn a long list of items (various minerals) performed 60% to 350% better when they were given category information to help them organize the items into a hierarchy (metals versus stones as the main categories and several subcategories under each). Similarly, students show greater learning gains when they are given an *advance organizer*, that is, a set of principles or propositions that provide a cognitive structure to guide the incorporation of new information (Ausubel, 1960, 1978). Indeed, researchers have demonstrated improvements in students' comprehension and recall from advance organizers that rely on familiar structures when they are presented in writing (Ausubel & Fitzgerald, 1962), orally (Alexander et al., 1979), or pictorially (Dean & Enemoh, 1983). These studies indicate that when students are provided with an organizational structure in which to fit new knowledge, they learn more effectively and efficiently than when they are left to deduce this conceptual structure for themselves.

In fact, if we think back to the first story at the beginning of the chapter, we can see applications for these approaches in Professor Rothman's class. Professor Rothman's students needed to learn and retrieve a great deal of factual information, yet probably lacked a hierarchical knowledge organization to help them organize this information for efficient retrieval and use. As a result, they found the memorization task overwhelming. But imagine if Professor Rothman had provided her students with an organizational framework that helped them develop more connections among pieces of knowledge, such as by giving them a template for identifying the characteristics of important artistic schools and movements and categorizing each artist and work in relation to them. With their factual knowledge connected in more—and more meaningful—ways, the students may have found the memorization task less daunting and may have performed better on Professor Rothman's exams, let alone ultimately learned more art history.

Implications of This Research

As experts in our disciplines, we have developed highly connected knowledge organizations that help us retrieve and use information effectively.

> But we cannot reasonably expect students to organize their knowledge in equally sophisticated ways. Instead, it is important that we recognize the difference between expert and novice knowledge structures and provide guidance that highlights to our students how we organize disciplinary knowledge and then draw on our knowledge organizations to perform particular tasks.

Experts' Versus Students' Knowledge Structures: The Nature of the Connections

Novices not only have more sparse knowledge organizations compared to experts, but the basis for their organizational structures also tends to be superficial. This affects their ability to remember and use what they learn effectively (Chi & VanLehn, 1991; Hinsley et al., 1977; Ross, 1987, 1989). Chi and colleagues (1989) demonstrated this in a study in which they asked physics novices and experts to group various problem descriptions into categories. The novices grouped problems according to the superficial "looks" of their diagrams—for example, putting all the problems with pulleys in one group and all the problems with ramps in another group. This way of organizing the different problems, based on surface features, did not reflect the structural relationships among problems, and thus did not facilitate successful problem-solving for the novices. By contrast, the experts in this study organized the problems based on deeper and more meaningful features, such as the physical laws involved in solving each problem. Moreover, when talking through the rationale for their groupings, the experts revealed that sorting each of these problems into a category naturally triggered in their minds the solution template for how "problems like this" are solved. Thus, the experts' organizations were based on a set of deep features that directly related to how they would go about solving the problems.

Experts' ability to classify information in more meaningful—and thus more practically useful—ways than novices is linked to their ability to recognize meaningful patterns. For example, DeGroot (1965) conducted a landmark study in which he showed novice and master chess players a chess board midgame and asked them to generate possible next moves. While both masters and novices considered a roughly equivalent number of possible moves, there were

75

significant differences in the quality of plays they considered: novices tended to choose from among a seemingly random set of options, whereas experts spent their time weighing the pros and cons of a very select set of high-quality moves. From the large amount of research on chess expertise (see also Chase & Simon, 1973a, 1973b; Gobet & Charness, 2006), it is clear that this difference stems from experts' vast experience analyzing chess situations and assessing possible strategies. As a result of this experience, they possess highly developed knowledge organizations that enable them to immediately recognize meaningful board configurations and zero in on a set of high-quality moves.

Indeed, experts' ability to see and instinctively respond to patterns not only helps them solve problems but also enhances their memory. Further research on chess has shown that experts can glance at a chessboard from a particular chess game situation and then take an empty board and replicate the exact positions of 15 or more of the pieces they just saw (Chase & Simon, 1973a, 1973b). This is not a result of superior memory, but rather a reflection of the deep and intricate set of relationships they can see among pieces and that they automatically use during play. This ability among experts to immediately recognize and respond to patterns is not limited to chess but has been demonstrated among experts in many domains (Egan & Schwartz, 1979; Lesgold et al., 1988; Soloway et al., 1988). In one study, for example, skilled electronics technicians and novices were briefly shown symbolic drawings of complex circuit diagrams and then asked to reconstruct the drawings from memory (Egan & Schwartz, 1979). The experts were able to reconstruct a far greater number of elements in the diagrams, even after seeing them for just a few seconds. The researchers attributed this superior recall to two things: the experts' ability to successfully characterize the entire diagram (as "some kind of power supply," for example) and also to identify parts of each drawing that corresponded to recognizable features, such as amplifiers. They were then able to perceive the visual information from the diagrams in terms of these meaningful configurations and use that knowledge organization to help them remember what they had seen.

In addition to organizing their knowledge on meaningful features and patterns, experts have the benefit of flexibly using *multiple* knowledge organizations. A paleontologist's knowledge of dinosaurs, for example, would not be organized on a single organizational hierarchy, but rather would include an interwoven web of classifications and connections based on geological age, habitat, eating habits, relation to modern-day reptiles, strategies for self-protection, and so on. Likewise, a historian could draw on their knowledge in a way that is organized on theories, methodologies, time periods, topic areas, historical figures, or combinations of these. Novices, however, tend not to have as many alternative organizations to tap into. This difference between novice and expert representations is illustrated in the second story at the beginning of this chapter. As an expert in his field, Professor Patel moves flexibly among multiple ways of representing the human body, such as according to body system *and* according to common functions or higher-order principles. Thus, Professor Patel can use his knowledge in multiple ways, tapping into different knowledge organizations according to the current need. His students, however, are more limited.

Obviously, developing the kinds of meaningfully connected knowledge organizations that experts possess takes time and experience. Most of our students are far from attaining that level of expertise. However, even novice students learn and remember more when they can connect information in meaningful ways. In one study that helps to illustrate this point, Bradshaw and Anderson (1982) asked college students to learn various facts about historical figures. They found that students learned the most when they were presented with facts that could be meaningfully related to one another. In other words, it was easier for students to learn and retain multiple facts with a causal dimension (e.g., Isaac Newton became emotionally unstable and insecure as a child, Newton's father died when he was born, and Newton's mother remarried and left him with his grandfather) as compared to a single, isolated fact. However, students showed this advantage only when there was a relationship among the multiple facts that enabled students to make meaningful connections. Thus, the learning advantage did not apply when the multiple facts were unrelated (e.g., Isaac Newton became emotionally unstable and insecure as a child, Newton was appointed warden of the London mint, and Newton attended Trinity College in Cambridge). The value of providing students with meaningfully related information is further highlighted by research showing the opposite phenomenon also holds: adding "extra" words, graphics, or sounds to instructional materials—for example, with the intent of making the instruction more attractive or engaging—actually impedes learning because the extraneous, disconnected information distracts students from what they need to learn (Mayer et al., 2008). To discourage the inclusion of extraneous information, especially in multimedia learning resources where this is rather common, Clark and Mayer (2016) identified the coherence principle, which states that learning is best when extraneous, distracting material is not included (see Clark and Mayer, 2016, for more evidence supporting the

77

coherence principle as well as several other guidelines for designing multimedia learning resources).

Research has also shown that there are instructional approaches that can help students organize their knowledge meaningfully on deep, rather than superficial, features of the domain. For example, studies have shown that when students are given problems that are already solved and are asked to explain the solution to themselves—thereby focusing on the principles that guide the solution—they are better able to solve new problems (Chi et al., 1989). Research also suggests that guiding students through a process of analogical reasoning helps students to see past superficial similarities and instead focus on deeper connections and relationships (Gentner et al., 2003; McDaniel & Donnelly, 1996). Similarly, when students are presented with and analyze contrasting cases, they are better prepared to learn from a lecture or reading assignment (Schwartz & Bransford, 1998). By engaging in such processes, students tend to build more effective knowledge organizations and learn and perform more effectively.

Implications of This Research

One implication of this research is to realize that, as experts in our domain, we may organize our knowledge in a way that is quite different from how our students organize theirs, and that our knowledge organizations play a significant role in our "expert performance." Given that students are likely to come up with knowledge organizations that are superficial and/or do not lend themselves to abstraction or problem-solving, this suggests that, at least initially, we need to provide students with appropriate organizing schemes or teach them how to identify the relevant principles in what they are learning. In addition, it means that we need to monitor how students are processing what they are learning to make sure it gets organized in useful ways.

WHAT STRATEGIES DOES THE RESEARCH SUGGEST?

The following strategies offer ways for instructors to assess their own knowledge organizations relative to students' and help students develop more connected, meaningful, and flexible ways of organizing their knowledge.

Strategies to Reveal and Enhance Knowledge Organizations

Create a Concept Map to Analyze Your Own Knowledge Organization It can be difficult for experts to recognize how they organize their own knowledge, and thus difficult for them to communicate this organization to students. One way to make your own knowledge organization apparent to yourself is to create your own concept map. Concept mapping is a technique that helps people represent their knowledge organizations visually (see Appendix D for more information on what concept maps are and how to create them). Once you have produced your own concept map, the central organizing principles and key features you use should be easier for you to recognize. You can then walk your students through your own concept map as a way of orienting them to the organizational structures in your domain and to illustrate the principles and features on which you want your students to organize their own knowledge.

Analyze Tasks to Identify the Most Appropriate Knowledge Organization Different tasks draw on different kinds of knowledge organizations. For example, a paper that asks students to analyze the theoretical perspectives of different authors may require students to organize their knowledge on theories and the ways they shape research and writing, whereas a paper that requires students to analyze the impact of a historic event demands that they organize their knowledge on economic, political, and social factors. Thus, it can be helpful to analyze the tasks assigned to determine what kind of knowledge organization would best facilitate learning and performance. Then you might consider providing your students with a skeletal outline or template for organizing their knowledge. For example, in the case of the theoretical perspectives paper, you might give students an empty table in which you ask them to identify different theoretical schools in one column, describe the key characteristics of each school in the next column, and list scholars whose work would fall into each school in another column (including, perhaps, a column to list ways in which each scholars' work does not conform to the theoretical norm).

Provide Students with the Organizational Structure of the Course Do not assume that your students, especially those who are new to the content area, will see the logical organization of the material you are presenting. They may not see basic relationships or category structures. Therefore, providing students with a view of the big picture that presents the key concepts or topics in your course and highlights their interrelationships can help students see how the pieces fit together.

This organizational structure can be communicated in your syllabus in various ways: some instructors represent it visually (e.g., through a flow chart or diagram), whereas others communicate it verbally. In addition to presenting and explaining this organization early in a course, periodically remind students of the larger organizational framework and situate particular class days within it (e.g., "If you'll remember, the first unit of this course focused on developing basic negotiation skills. Today we will be starting the second unit, in which we will see how those skills apply to real world work situations.").

Explicitly Share the Organization of Each Lecture, Lab, or Discussion Because students' knowledge organizations guide their retrieval and use of information, it is especially beneficial to help students create a useful organization as they are learning. To this end, providing an outline, agenda, or visual representation of each lecture, lab, or discussion session can give students a framework for organizing the information they are about to learn. Not all outlines or agendas are equally effective for helping students develop meaningful and connected knowledge organizations, so be sure that the organizational structure you provide captures the critical concepts or principles on which you want students to organize the information from the class. (For example, an agenda that includes headings such as "Introduction," "Lecture," "Discussion," and "Recap" is considerably less useful than an agenda entitled "Three rules to guide ethnographic fieldwork, the reasons for these rules, and a discussion of their limitations.")

Use Contrasting and Boundary Cases to Highlight Organizing Features To help students develop more sophisticated and nuanced ways of organizing knowledge, it can be useful to present contrasting cases, or two items that share many features but differ in critical ways. Although cases are often used in teaching, they tend to be most effective when presented not in isolation but rather with some compare-and-contrast analysis. A simple example would be a comparison of sharks and dolphins, which have many similarities but represent different classes of animals. Presenting two such cases together makes the differing features more salient and helps students develop deeper and more finely articulated knowledge structures (e.g., instead of organizing animals superficially by habitat, they begin to organize them according to other features: vertebrate versus invertebrate, warm-blooded versus cold-blooded, live births versus egg-laying, and so forth). Along the same lines, highlighting boundary cases or anomalies (or otherwise commonly misclassified items) can help students identify the salient features of a particular category and develop more nuanced knowledge organizations. For example, the platypus, as an egg-laying mammal, defies some aspects of mammalian classification while possessing other mammalian attributes. Pointing out cases like this focuses students on the critical elements of a particular classification scheme. The use of anomalies also alerts students to the limitations of taxonomies themselves, which can encourage them to develop alternative knowledge organizations.

Explicitly Highlight Deep Features In order to help students develop more meaningful and less superficial knowledge organizations, highlight the deep features of problems, designs, theories, and examples. One way to do this is to provide examples of problems that share deep features but differ superficially or examples of problems that are superficially similar but operate on different structural principles. The use of such comparisons can help students become more adept at identifying underlying features and principles and thus teach them to organize their knowledge more meaningfully.

Make Connections Among Concepts Explicit As you introduce a new concept (or design, theory, example, or problem), explicitly connect it to others students have learned (e.g., "You may remember encountering a similar situation in the case study we read last week"). The connections you draw do not always have to be similarities; they can also be contrasts or discrepancies (e.g., "What makes this artist's work so different from other abstract expressionists?"). In addition to pointing out these connections yourself, it is important to ask questions that require students to make these connections themselves (e.g., "Where have we seen this theoretical orientation before?" "What aspects of this case are similar to or different from the labor management case we discussed yesterday?" "What characteristics of this artist's work are reminiscent of the Bauhaus approach?").

Encourage Students to Work with Multiple Organizing Structures To enable more flexible application of knowledge, students need to develop multiple knowledge organizations that they can draw on as appropriate. One way to help students develop multiple representations is to ask them to categorize a set of items according to more than one organizational schema; for example, you might ask students to classify plants first on the basis of their evolutionary histories and then on the basis of native habitat. This classification task could then be followed by questions that illuminate the implications of organizing knowledge one way or the other. For example, a taxonomy based on evolutionary history might be useful for paleontological analysis, but not for designing a green roof. Giving students practice organizing their knowledge according to alternative schemata or hierarchies helps them see that different organizations serve different purposes and thus builds more robust and flexible knowledge organizations.

Ask Students to Draw a Concept Map to Expose Their Knowledge Organizations Asking students to create concept maps gives you a window not only into how much students know about a particular subject but also how they are organizing and connecting their knowledge. Concept maps are a visual representation of a knowledge domain (see Appendix D for more information on what concept maps are and how to create them). A concept-mapping activity can be used at the beginning of a course—to reveal students' prior knowledge organizations—and then in an ongoing manner to monitor how those organizations change with time and experience. Concept maps, whether graded or ungraded, can help you diagnose problems in students' knowledge organizations, for example, if they have miscategorized pieces of knowledge, inappropriately linked unrelated concepts, failed to connect related concepts, or assigned an item to a superordinate position that belongs in a subordinate position, and so on.

Use a Sorting Task to Expose Students' Knowledge Organizations Another way to expose students' knowledge organizations is to ask them to sort different problems, concepts, or situations into categories. This method reveals how students organize their knowledge without requiring them to identify their sorting criteria explicitly. One example of a sorting task is presenting students with a set of problems that have some superficial and some deep features in common, and asking them to group the problems according to similarities. If students group projects on the basis of superficial similarities, it is an indication that they do not recognize the deep features that would help them develop more meaningful and flexible knowledge organizations.

Monitor Students' Work for Problems in Their Knowledge Organizations One way to detect problems in students' organizations of knowledge is to pay attention to the patterns of mistakes they make in their work for your course. For example, do students frequently mix up two conceptual categories (such as confusing theories and methodologies or force and acceleration problems)? Do they apply a formula, strategy, or solution in a consistently inappropriate way? If so, it is possible that students are making inappropriate connections or categorizations that are impeding their learning and performance.

SUMMARY

In this chapter, we have reviewed research pointing to the fact that it is not just *what* you know but *how you organize* what you know that influences learning and performance. Knowledge organizations that include more interconnections and that are based on deep and meaningful features tend to be effective in supporting learning and performance. Another key aspect of effective knowledge organizations is that they are well matched to the task(s) at hand. For this reason, rich and meaningful knowledge organizations are very helpful. Experts often take advantage of these aspects of their knowledge organizations. However, students—especially ones who are new to a discipline—tend to have knowledge organizations that are sparsely interconnected and that are based on superficial features. These students can benefit from instruction that helps them to see important relationships and build more connections among the pieces of knowledge they are learning, thus leading them to develop more flexible and effective knowledge organizations.

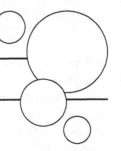

CHAPTER 4

What Factors Motivate Students to Learn?

My Students Are Going to Love This—NOT

This past semester, I finally got to teach a course that relates directly to my primary area of interest and the focus of my research. I was really excited. Over the summer, I put in a lot of time and energy designing the course and preparing materials and learning activities. I used several seminal readings in continental philosophy and assigned a research project based on primary documents from the 19th and 20th centuries. I thought that the students would be excited by the topic and would appreciate reading some of the classic and well-known works. But it did not turn out the way I had hoped, and I was disappointed by their level of engagement and the quality of their work. Except for the two philosophy majors and the one student who "needed an A to get into graduate school," they were not at all interested in the readings and hardly participated in the discussions. In addition, they were not particularly inspired, creative, or motivated when choosing their research topics. Overall, they made little progress across the semester. I guess when it comes right down to it, most students do not care much about philosophy.

Professor Tyrone Hill

A Third of You Will Not Pass This Course

My colleague who usually teaches thermodynamics was on leave for the semester, and I was assigned to take his place. I knew it would not be easy to teach this course: it has a reputation for being really difficult, and engineering students only take it because it is required for the major. On top of that, my colleague had warned me that many students stop coming to lectures early in the semester, and those who come to class often do not come prepared or willing to engage. It seemed clear that I needed a way to motivate students to work hard and keep up with the material. I recalled that when I was a student, any suggestion by the professor that I might not be up to the challenge really got me fired up and eager to prove him wrong. So, on the first day of class, I told my students "This is a very difficult course. You will need to work harder than you have ever worked in a course and still a third of you will not pass." I expected that if my students heard that, they would dig in and work harder to measure up. But to my surprise, they slacked off even more than in previous semesters: they often did not come to class, they made lackluster efforts at the homework, and their test performance was the worst it had been for many semesters. And this was after I gave them fair warning! This class had the worst attitude I have ever seen and the students seemed to be consumed by an overall sense of lethargy and apathy. I am beginning to think that today's students are just plain lazy.

Professor Zoë Obenza

WHAT IS GOING ON IN THESE TWO STORIES?

In both of these stories, students fail to acquire and demonstrate the level of understanding the professors' desires. In both cases, a lack of engagement with the content and material seems to be at the root of the problem. To their credit, Professor Hill and Professor Obenza both think hard about how to motivate their students, yet they make the common—and often flawed—assumption that their students would be motivated in much the same ways that they themselves were as students. When their students are *not* similarly motivated, the instructors conclude that they are apathetic or lazy.

However, a closer examination of these instructors' approaches and their unintended consequences reveals other likely explanations for student disengagement. Because Professor Hill is so passionate about philosophy and finds it so inherently interesting, it does not occur to him that the features of the course that excite him most—the seminal readings and working with primary sources—do not hold the same value for his students. Consequently, they approach the work half-heartedly and never successfully master the material. Professor Obenza, for her part, hopes to re-create the highly competitive classroom environment that had motivated her as a student. However, her warnings about the difficulty of the material and the students' limited chances of passing may fuel preexisting negative perceptions about the course, compromise her students' expectations for success, create anxiety, and undermine their motivation to do the work necessary to succeed.

Although these two stories deal with slightly different issues, the concept of motivation lies at the core of each.

WHAT PRINCIPLE OF LEARNING IS AT WORK HERE?

Motivation refers to the personal investment that an individual has in reaching a desired state or outcome (Maehr & Meyer, 1997). In the context of learning, motivation influences the direction, intensity, persistence, and quality of the learning behaviors in which students engage.

> *Principle:* *Students' motivation generates, directs, and sustains what they do to learn.*

The importance of motivation, in the context of learning, cannot be overstated (Ames, 1990; Hulleman et al., 2016; Loh, 2019; Wigfield & Cambria, 2010). As students enter college and gain greater autonomy over what, when, and how they study and learn, motivation plays a critical role in guiding their behaviors. In addition, because there are many competing goals that vie for their attention, time, and energy, it is crucial to understand what may increase or decrease students' motivations to pursue specific goals related to learning.

As we can see in the first story, if students do not find the content of the course relevant or interesting, they may see little or no value in mastering it and may fail to engage in the behaviors required for deep learning. Similarly, in the second story, if students do not expect to be successful in a course, they may disengage from the behaviors necessary for learning. Imagine how different these two stories might have been if the students in Professor Hill's class saw broadly applicable value in learning to use primary sources and the students in Professor Obenza's class expected their hard work to result in strong performance and good grades!

As these stories demonstrate, there are two important concepts that are central to understanding motivation: (1) the *subjective value* of a goal and (2) the *expectancies*, or expectations for successful attainment of that goal. Although many theories have been offered to explain motivation, most position these two concepts at the core of their framework (Atkinson, 1957, 1964; Wigfield & Eccles, 1992, 2000, 2020). As Figure 4.1 illustrates, expectancies and values interact to influence the level of motivation to engage in goal-directed behavior.

WHAT DOES THE RESEARCH TELL US ABOUT MOTIVATION?

Goals provide the context in which values and expectancies derive meaning and influence motivation. Hence, we begin our exploration of motivation with a brief discussion of goals.

Goals

To say that someone is motivated tells us little unless we say what the person is motivated to do or achieve. Thus, goals serve as the basic organizing feature of motivated behavior (Elliot & Fryer, 2008; Mitchell, 1982; Ryan, 1970). In essence, they act as the compass that guides and directs a broad range of purposeful actions, including those that relate to a person's intellectual and creative pursuits, social and interpersonal relationships, identity, and self-concept, needs for safety and material possessions, and desires to be productive and competent in the world (Ford, 1992). Moreover, several goals are often in operation simultaneously. This is certainly true for college students who may, in any given moment,

Learning and Performance

Goal-directed behavior

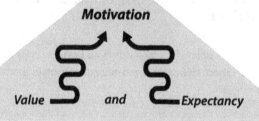

Figure 4.1. Impact of Value and Expectancy on Learning and Performance

seek to acquire knowledge and skills, make new friends, demonstrate to others that they are intelligent, gain a sense of independence, and have fun.

When considering the ways that our students' goals influence their learning behaviors, it is worth noting that students' goals for themselves may differ from our goals for them or from the goals we had for ourselves when we were students. This mismatch was true in the first story at the beginning of this chapter. Professor Hill wanted his students to acquire an understanding of continental philosophy through the use and appreciation of primary sources. This goal clearly did not match his students' goals for themselves. A more general form of mismatch often occurs when we want our students to pursue learning for its own sake, but they are motivated primarily by *performance goals* (Dweck & Leggett, 1988). Performance goals involve protecting a desired self-image and projecting a positive reputation and public persona. When guided by performance goals, students are concerned with normative standards and try to do what is necessary to demonstrate competence in order to appear intelligent, gain status, and acquire recognition and praise. Elliot and colleagues (Elliot, 1999; Elliot & McGregor, 2001) make a further distinction among performance goals. They suggest that goals focused on performance may take two forms: *performance-approach goals* and *performance-avoidant goals*. Students with performance-approach goals focus on meeting normative performance standards to appear competent. Students with performance-avoidance goals, however, focus on meeting normative performance standards to avoid appearing incompetent. Elliot and colleagues suggest that the cognitive framework with which students approach learning is different for those with an approach versus avoidance orientation, and results of research suggest that performance-approach goals are more advantageous to learning than performance-avoidance goals (Cury et al., 2006; Elliot & McGregor, 2001).

When guided by *learning goals*, in contrast to performance goals, students try to gain competence and truly learn what an activity or task can teach them. As you can imagine, if we want our students to gain the deep understanding that comes from exploration and intellectual risk-taking (a learning goal), but they want only to do what is necessary to get a good grade (a performance goal), our students may not engage in the kinds of learning behaviors and achieve the learning outcomes that we desire. Indeed, most research suggests that students who hold learning goals, as compared to those who hold performance goals (particularly performance-avoidance goals), are more likely to use study strategies that result in deeper understanding, to seek help when needed, to persist when faced with difficulty, and to seek out and feel comfortable with challenging tasks. (For more discussion on learning versus performance goals, see Barron & Harackiewicz, 2001; Harackiewicz et al., 2000; McGregor & Elliot, 2002; Miller et al., 1996; Somuncuoglu & Yildirim, 1999.)

Students may also have other goals that conflict with our goals as instructors. *Work-avoidant goals* (Meece & Holt, 1993), for example, involve the desire to finish work as quickly as possible with as little effort as possible. Students guided primarily by work-avoidant goals may show little interest in learning and appear alienated, discouraged, or disengaged. It is important to remember, however, that work-avoidant goals are often context-specific, such that a student who works very hard in one context may avoid work in another. For example, a dedicated engineering student may do as little as possible in Professor Hill's course if he does not see how the knowledge and perspectives from continental philosophy apply to his broader intellectual and professional growth and development.

Even though students' goals may not correspond exactly to our goals for them, these two sets of goals (ours and theirs) do not always conflict. In fact, when our students' goals align with ours, powerful learning situations tend to result. Imagine if the engineering student just mentioned came to see that being able to develop, present, and evaluate a logical argument could help him become a more effective engineer (e.g., by helping him defend an engineering design choice to a client or to communicate engineering limitations to colleagues). With his own goals and his philosophy professor's goals in closer—and therefore more productive—alignment, his motivation to pursue learning goals may be strengthened.

Moreover, if an activity satisfies more than one goal, the motivation to pursue that activity is likely to be higher than if it satisfies only one goal. Relevant to this point is the fact that *affective goals* and *social goals* can play an important role in the classroom (Ford, 1992). For instance, if a student's goals in an industrial design project course include learning and applying fundamental design principles (a learning goal), making friends (a social goal), and engaging in stimulating activity (an affective goal), then allowing the student to work on the course project as part of a group provides her the opportunity to satisfy multiple goals at the same time and potentially increases her motivation. This point is further supported by research demonstrating that students who hold multiple types of goals are more successful than those with just one type of goal (Valle et al., 2003).

It is also possible, of course, that students hold multiple conflicting goals. For example, a student may have the goal of doing well on an upcoming psychology exam for which there is an evening study session scheduled. At the same time, they may also have the goal of bonding with their peers via intramural sports and consequently feel a pull to be at an intramural registration meeting held at the same time as the study session. To complicate matters even more, they may have the goal of remaining healthy and, since they have been experiencing a scratchy throat and other symptoms of a cold, may think it is wise to go straight to bed without attending the study session or intramural registration meeting. Given this range of competing goals, which one do they choose? There are some important variables that can provide insight into which goal the student will be motivated to pursue. Remember that value and expectancies interact to influence motivation. In the next section, we discuss value and, in the following, expectancies.

Value

A goal's importance, often referred to as its *subjective value*, is one of the key features influencing the motivation to pursue it. Indeed, the lack of perceived value among Professor Hill's students almost certainly contributed to their lack of motivation, described in this chapter's first story. The issue here is quite simple. People are motivated to engage in behaviors to attain goals that have a high relative value. Thus, when confronted with multiple goals (such as going to a study session, attending a registration meeting, or fending off a cold by going to bed early), a student will be more motivated to pursue the goal that has the highest value to them.

Value can be derived from a number of different sources. Wigfield and Eccles (1992, 2000) suggest three broad determinants of subjective value for achievement-related activities and goals. The first is *attainment value*, which represents the satisfaction and sense of accomplishment that one gains from mastery and accomplishment of a goal or task. For instance, a student may receive great satisfaction and a sense of accomplishment from solving complex mathematical theorems and consequently work for many hours simply to demonstrate her ability to solve them. Similarly, people can often spend hours playing video games in order to reach higher levels of mastery or be incredibly motivated to complete tasks in order to cross items off a to-do list.

A second source of value is *intrinsic value* (sometimes called *interest value*), which represents the satisfaction that one gains simply from doing the task rather than from a particular outcome of the task. This form of value is operating when students work tirelessly to design and build a beautifully crafted stage set, spend hours writing a computer program, or work hard to understand the complex interplay of variables that regulate blood flow to tumor cells simply because they love it. At its core, this value is intimately tied to the specific content of the goal or activity and is the source of what researchers have traditionally called *intrinsic motivation*.

91

A final source of value, one that Eccles and Wigfield call *utility value* (sometimes called *instrumental value*), represents the degree to which an activity or goal helps one accomplish other important goals, such as gaining what are traditionally referred to as *extrinsic rewards*. Praise, public recognition, money, material goods, an interesting career, a high-status job, or a good salary are all longer-term goals that may provide utility value to shorter-term goals. For example, students who study business only because of the salary and prestige they expect a job in business will bring are motivated to study and attend their classes by the utility value the classes provide toward their desired salary and status.

Most of the students in Professor Hill's continental philosophy course appeared to have been unable to find any of the three sources of value. Like the two philosophy majors, for whom the content of the course held intrinsic value, and the student for whom a good grade in the course was instrumental toward getting into graduate school, a single source of value may motivate behavior. However, in many cases, sources of value operate in combination. Indeed, the distinction between the traditional concepts of intrinsic and extrinsic motivation is rarely as dichotomous as theory posits. For instance, by working hard in a biology course, a student may derive value from multiple sources, including solving challenging problems (attainment value), engaging her fascination with biological processes (intrinsic value), and advancing her chances of getting into a good medical school (utility value). Consequently, it is important not to think of these sources of value as necessarily conflicting but as potentially reinforcing. In fact, a task that initially holds only utility value to a student (something he does primarily to earn a grade or satisfy a requirement) can come to have attainment value as he develops knowledge and competence in the subject area and intrinsic value as he comes to appreciate and like the activity (Hidi & Renninger, 2006).

Self-Determination

When considering value, it's important to recognize that what our students value varies widely (see Chapter 1 on individual differences). Consequently, the task of aligning our courses to the broad and endless range of student values seems daunting. Fortunately, we do know that motivation in general is enhanced when students feel a sense of self-determination (Ryan & Deci, 2000, 2017). Grounded on the assumption that people inherently pursue growth and learning, self-determination theory suggests that students will find value when learning addresses three important needs.

Autonomy refers to the need for choice and control over one's own behaviors. When students have autonomy, they willingly engage in learning activities and do not feel forced, compelled, or controlled. As such, we support our students' need for autonomy when we provide opportunities for choice, input, and control over their learning. In the case of the first story in this chapter, you might imagine how students' perceived value of the philosophy course might have been different if they had been given options about the nature of the activities (e.g., reading contemporary theorists versus classic articles, engaging in positioned role-plays, interviewing experts, writing editorials).

Competence refers to the need to successfully achieve desired outcomes and develop mastery. This means that when students feel as though they are gaining proficiency in our classrooms and they recognize that they are acquiring knowledge and building skills, they are more likely to feel motivated to learn. Indeed, research demonstrates that when people are given unexpected positive feedback, indicating increasing competency, they demonstrate increased levels of motivation (Deci, 1971). This points to the importance of providing frequent formative feedback to students and the role of explicitly helping students recognize the development of their knowledge and skills.

Relatedness refers to the need to feel connected to others and to experience a sense of closeness and belonging. Relationships between a student and instructor and relationships among students help support students' perceptions of relatedness. Students' feelings of relatedness are associated with their believing that an instructor genuinely likes, respects, and values them (Niemiec & Ryan, 2009). Creating opportunities for students to get to know each other and to work collaboratively are important in building relatedness, especially in online learning environments (Zhou et al., 2021).

By increasing the level of perceived autonomy, competence, and relatedness among our students, we can leverage potent aspects of the learning environment that increase the value of learning for all students and help support motivation.

Expectancies

Although one must value a desired outcome to be motivated to pursue it, value alone is insufficient to motivate behavior. People are also motivated to pursue goals and outcomes that they believe they can successfully achieve.

Conversely, if they do not expect to successfully achieve a desired goal or outcome, they will not be motivated to engage in the behaviors necessary to achieve it. Motivational theorists refer to these expectations as *expectancies*. Here we describe two forms of expectancies that help inform our understanding of motivated behavior.

To be motivated to pursue specific goals, students must hold positive *outcome expectancies*. Outcome expectancies reflect the belief that specific actions will bring about a desired outcome and can be based on a variety of factors, including, among other things, previous experience, available resources, and dispositional characteristics (Carver & Scheier, 1998). A student holds positive outcome expectancies when he thinks, "If I do all the assigned readings and participate in class discussions, I will be able to learn the material well enough to solve problems on the exam and achieve a passing grade." In this case, there is a positive outcome expectancy linking the student's behavior and the desired outcome. By contrast, negative outcome expectancies involve a belief that specific actions have no influence on a desired outcome. For example, a student may think, "No matter how hard I work in this course, I won't get a good grade." This dynamic was likely to be at work among some of Professor Obenza's students in the story at the beginning of this chapter. Professor Obenza warned her students that a third of them were likely to fail, even after working harder than they had ever worked before. As a result, many of them may have developed negative outcome expectancies; in other words, they began to doubt that hard work would, in fact, result in a passing grade and so lost their motivation. Ironically, what Professor Obenza thought would "fire up" her students might have profoundly demotivated them. In order for students to be motivated to engage in the behaviors that result in learning, they must believe that there is a connection between those behaviors and the outcomes they desire.

Whereas positive outcome expectancies are necessary for motivated behavior, they are insufficient on their own. *Efficacy expectancies* are also essential. Efficacy expectancies represent the belief that one is *capable* of identifying, organizing, initiating, and executing a course of action that will bring about a desired outcome (Bandura, 1997). So, in order to hold a positive expectancy for success, a student must not only believe that doing the assigned work can earn a passing grade but also she must believe that she is capable of doing the work necessary to earn a passing grade. Thus, it is the belief in personal agency that is the potent feature of this expectancy variable and that drives motivation.

What determines a student's expectation for success? One important influence is prior experience in similar contexts. If a student has experienced success in a particular activity in the past, she is more likely to expect success in a similar activity in the future. If she has experienced failure in the past, she is more likely to expect failure in the future. A more complicated analysis of past success and failure suggests, however, that the *reasons* that students identify for their previous successes and failures may be an even more powerful determinant of expectancies. These reasons, or attributions, involve the causal explanations students use to make sense of the outcomes they experience (Weiner, 1986).

When students successfully achieve a goal and attribute their success to internal causes (e.g., their own talents or abilities) or to controllable causes (e.g., their own efforts or persistence), they are more likely to expect future success. If however, they attribute success to external causes (e.g., easy assignments) or uncontrollable causes (e.g., luck), they are less likely to expect success in the future. For instance, if a student attributes the good grade she received on a design project to her own creativity (ability) or to the many long hours she spent on its planning and execution (effort), she is likely to expect success on future design assignments. This is because she has attributed her success to relatively stable and controllable features about herself. These same features form the basis for her positive expectations for similar situations in the future.

When a student fails to achieve a goal, however, his motivation is likely to be low if he attributes his failure to his identify or a lack of ability (e.g., "I am not good at math" or "I am just not a good writer"), especially if he sees his ability as fixed or not amenable to change. However, even in failure situations, motivation is likely to remain high if a student explains his poor performance in terms of controllable and temporary causes such as inadequate preparation, insufficient effort, or lack of relevant information. Under these circumstances, students can maintain the belief that they are capable of changing their behaviors to achieve a more positive outcome.

Thus, in the context of the classroom, motivation and the effort and persistence that accompany it are highest among students who attribute successful performance to a combination of ability and effort, and poor performance to insufficient effort and inadequate information. These attributions form the basis for the expectation that good performance can be sustained and poor performance can be changed.

Adult Learners

When thinking about values and expectancies, it is important to recognize that not all students fall within the traditional college-age demographic (see Chapter 1 on individual differences). In this context, the field of adult learning, or andragogy, provides useful insights regarding motivation among older students. Most closely associated with Malcolm Knowles (1984), andragogy posits that adult learners differ from non-adult learners and is guided by five principles of application.

First, adult learners are self-directed and need to be involved in the planning and evaluation of their learning. Like the notion of autonomy from self-determination theory, choice, options, and self-direction support motivation in adult learners.

Second, adults have rich life experience and robust prior knowledge on which to build new knowledge (see Chapter 2 on prior knowledge). This prior experience is often an important source of expectancies for future success and provides an increasingly robust resource for learning over time. Third, adult learners are oriented toward learning that is relevant to their current social roles, and fourth, adult learners are concerned with learning that is problem-focused rather than subject-centered. Thus, adult learners are most interested in learning that has immediate practical relevance and application to their careers or personal lives. Fifth, as learners mature, their motivation to learn is primarily internal. This means that while many adult learners may find utility value in seeking education for career advancement, increased salaries, disciplinary requirements, or other professional aspirations, it is important to identify and understand the internal reward systems of the adult learner to design meaningful and engaging courses.

Applying these principles to the design, development, and delivery of learning experiences goes a long way in helping support the motivation of adult learners and is particularly relevant for continuing and professional education programs, graduate degrees, and online programs, which all attract adult learners.

How Perceptions of the Environment Affect the Interaction of Value and Expectancies

Value and expectancies do not operate in a vacuum. Indeed, they interact within the broader environmental context in which they exist (see Chapter 7 on course climate). From a student's point of view, this environment can be perceived along a continuum from supportive to unsupportive (Ford, 1992). Without question, the complex dynamics of the classroom, its tone, the interpersonal forces at play, and the nature and structure of communication patterns all combine to either support or inhibit the students' motivation to learn. If students perceive the environment as supportive (e.g., "The instructor is approachable and several of my classmates seem willing to help me if I run into trouble"), motivation is likely to be enhanced. If students perceive the environment as unsupportive (e.g., "This instructor seems hostile to women in engineering, and I have nowhere to get help"), it can threaten expectations for success and erode motivation.

Thus, our framework for understanding motivation suggests that if a goal is valued *and* expectations for success are positive *and* the environment is perceived to be supportive, motivation will be highest. However, if there is little value associated with a goal *or* expectations for success are negative *or* the environment is perceived to be not supportive, motivation is likely to be lower. So, what does this mean for our classrooms and how students behave?

To begin, it is important to realize that we have three important levers (value, expectancies, and the supportive nature of the environment) with which we can influence motivation. Moreover, if we neglect any one of the three, motivation may suffer substantially. Based on the work of Hansen (1989) and Ford (1992), Figure 4.2 presents the range of behaviors that result from the interaction of value and expectancies in both supportive and unsupportive environments.

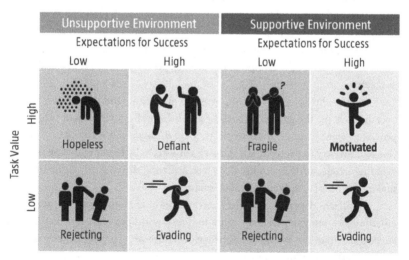

Figure 4.2. Interactive Effects of Environment, Efficacy, and Value on Motivation

When students care little about a goal and have low expectations for success, they see it as both unimportant and undoable. As such, they tend to behave in a *rejecting* manner. Notice that this characterizes students in both supportive and unsupportive environments. These students are prone to disengage from learning situations and may experience apathy, general passivity, alienation, or even a sense of anger, if a supportive environment is perceived as coercive or pressuring.

When students, in both supportive and unsupportive environments, see little value in a goal but have high expectations for success, they may act in an *evading* manner. Since they see the task as doable but unimportant, students often have difficulty paying attention and are frequently preoccupied by social distractions or daydreaming. Often, to avoid overt disapproval and pressure from the instructor or the stigma associated with a poor grade, they may do the minimum amount of work that is needed to just get by.

Those students who see value in a goal but have low expectations for success see the goal as important but undoable. They can manifest two forms of behavior, depending on the nature of the environment. Those who perceive little or no support from the environment tend to be *hopeless*. As such, they appear to have no expectation of success and demonstrate very low levels of motivation, often behaving in a helpless manner. Notice that the students described in the second story at the beginning of this chapter probably represent the hopeless students just described. The students in Professor Obenza's class believe the thermodynamics course is important; however, they don't expect success, and she hasn't made any explicit mention of support or strategies for success. As a consequence, they are likely feeling a sense of hopelessness, which she interprets as laziness.

Those who do perceive a supportive environment tend to be *fragile*. That is, because they see the goal as important and believe the environment offers support, they want to succeed. However, they are dubious about the chance of success and may try to protect their sense of self-esteem by feigning understanding, avoiding situations that require overt performance, denying any difficulty, and making excuses to explain poor performance.

Similarly, depending on their perceptions of the supportive nature of the environment, students who see value in a task and have high expectations for success also manifest two forms of behavior. Those who perceive little or no support from the environment may be *defiant*. That is, because the task is important and they are confident of their own abilities, they may take an "I will show you" or "I will prove you wrong" attitude in response to the perceived lack of support from the environment. It seems reasonable to suspect that this is how Professor Obenza responded to challenging environments when she was a student and how she incorrectly anticipated her students would respond to her announcement that only some students would pass the course. By contrast, those students who see value in a task, have positive expectations, and who perceive the environment to be supportive demonstrate the most *motivated* behavior. In essence, all three levers that influence motivation are aligned in a positive direction. Consequently, these students seek to learn, integrate, and apply new knowledge and view learning situations as opportunities to extend their understanding.

Implications of This Research

Several important points should be evident thus far. First, value, expectancy, and environment interact to produce an array of distinctive student behaviors. Thus, no single variable is universally deterministic with regard to motivating students. That said, changes in any one dimension can change students' levels of motivation and thus alter their behaviors. For instance, providing support and encouragement to students who tend toward defiance can edge them toward greater motivation. Similarly, by helping "fragile" students build positive beliefs about their chances of success, we may support them to become more highly motivated. Indeed, each of the dimensions in Figure 4.2 represents features of the learning environment over which we, as instructors, can have substantial influence. Finally, if we neglect any single dimension, motivation may suffer substantially. As a case in point, if we fail to address students' perceived lack of value for a given task or goal, at best they are likely to demonstrate an evading pattern of motivation (see the bottom row of Figure 4.2). Similarly, if students perceive the environment in which they learn as unsupportive, even those who find value in the goal and hold positive efficacy expectancies may fall short of highly motivated behavior. Indeed, when the environment is perceived as unsupportive, the best we can hope for is a defiant pattern of motivation (see the top row of Figure 4.2).

WHAT STRATEGIES DOES THE RESEARCH SUGGEST?

In this section we present a number of strategies that may help you increase the value that students place on the goals and activities that you have identified and created for them, as well as strategies to help you strengthen students' expectancies and create an environment that supports motivation.

Strategies to Establish Value

Connect the Material to Students' Interests Students are typically more motivated to engage with material that interests them or has relevance for important aspects of their lives, especially for adult learners. For example, courses on the history of rock 'n' roll, philosophy and the *Matrix* films, the statistics of sexual orientation, how technology can combat global poverty, how to build virtual reality worlds, and management principles for a remote work force may strongly connect with students' interests. All of these courses can be rigorous and yet demonstrate high demand because they tap into issues that are important to students. Recognize, however, that what interests one student or one group of students may not interest others. Being too narrow or contextualized can alienate minoritized students.

Provide Authentic, Real-World Tasks Assign problems and tasks that enable students to see the relevance and value of otherwise abstract concepts and theories vividly and concretely. For example, an economics professor might use a case study of economic instability to illustrate market forces. Analyzing a real-world event provides students with a context for understanding economic theories and their applicability to current situations. Similarly, in an information systems course, the instructor might assign a service-learning project in which students must build a database for an actual client in the community. This kind of authentic task enables students to work within real constraints, interact with real clients, and explore the profession. It might also create possibilities for future internships or jobs.

Show Relevance to Students' Current Academic Lives Students sometimes do not appreciate a current learning experience because they do not see its value relative to their course of study. For instance, psychology students may see little value in taking a math course because they do not realize that the knowledge they acquire will serve them well when they take a required statistics or research methods course. If you make explicit connections between the content of your course and other courses to come, students can better understand the utility value of each course as a building block for future courses.

Demonstrate the Relevance of Higher-Level Skills to Students' Future Professional Lives Students often focus on specific course content without recognizing how the skills and abilities they develop across courses (e.g., quantitative reasoning, public speaking, persuasive writing, teamwork skills) will benefit them in their professional lives. For example, students often complain about being graded on the quality of their writing in lab reports, failing to recognize the importance of

100

written communication skills in a wide range of professions. We can help motivate students by explaining how various skills will serve them more broadly in their professional lives.

Identify and Reward What You Value It is important to explicitly identify for students what you value in their work. This can be done in the syllabus, through feedback, and through modeling. Having identified what you value, be sure to reward it through assessments that are aligned with course objectives. For instance, if you value the quality of group interactions in a project course, you should identify and describe the aspects of such interactions that are important (e.g., clear communication, effective resolution of disagreements, consideration of multiple perspectives) and include an evaluation of the group as part of the final grade. Similarly, if you want students to take intellectual or creative risks, identify these features as important and assess students' work based on the extent to which they pushed the limits, whether or not they were ultimately successful.

Show Your Own Passion and Enthusiasm for the Discipline Your own enthusiasm and passion can be powerful and contagious. Even if students are not initially attracted to or interested in your course, don't be afraid to let your excitement for your discipline show. Your enthusiasm might raise students' curiosity and motivate them to find out what excites you about the subject, leading them to engage more deeply than they had initially planned or discover the value they had overlooked.

Strategies That Help Students Build Positive Expectancies

Ensure Alignment of Objectives, Assessments, and Instructional Strategies When these three components of a course are aligned—when students know the goals, are given opportunities to practice and get feedback, and are able to show their level of understanding—learning is supported. Students also have a more coherent picture of what will be expected of them and thus are more motivated because they feel more confident and in control of their learning, as well as their grade.

Identify an Appropriate Level of Challenge Setting challenging but attainable goals is critical for optimally motivating students. However, identifying the appropriate level at which to frame your expectations may be difficult. To do so, you need to know who your students are—in terms of their prior knowledge and experience, as well as their future plans and goals (see Chapter 1 on individual differences). A pre-assessment may be useful in evaluating both prior knowledge and future goals. Examining the syllabi of courses that immediately precede your course in the curricular sequence (when relevant) may also provide insight into your students' prior academic experiences. Syllabi from instructors who have taught the course in the past may also offer clues about the appropriate level at which to frame your expectations. Finally, talk to colleagues about their process for identifying appropriate expectations or ask to observe their classes.

Create Assignments That Provide the Appropriate Level of Challenge On the one hand, if your course or an assignment is pitched at a level that students do not expect will enable them to be successful with reasonable effort, they will not be motivated to engage with the assignment. On the other hand, if the course or the assignment is too easy, students will not think that it has value or is worth their time to engage with it, deeming it busy work. Consequently, we need to set standards that are challenging but attainable with student effort. Determining these standards is not always easy given that student cohorts differ, so administering diagnostic or early assessments can help you determine the right level for each cohort.

Provide Early Success Opportunities Expectations for future performance are influenced by past experiences. Hence, early success can build a sense of efficacy. This strategy is incredibly important in courses that are known as "gateway" or "high-risk" courses or for students who come into your course with anxiety for whatever reason. For example, you might incorporate early, shorter assignments that account for a small percentage of the final grade but provide a sense of competence and confidence before you assign a larger project.

Articulate Your Expectations Articulate your course goals clearly to students so that they know what the desired outcomes are. Then make it clear to students what you expect them to do to reach those goals. This will help make the connection between a course of action and a desired outcome more concrete and tangible, thus creating a more positive outcome expectancy. Help students set realistic expectations by identifying areas in which they might encounter difficulty and support their sense of agency by communicating your confidence and expectation that they will overcome those challenges and succeed. At the same time, let students know what support they can expect from you in pursuit of those goals (e.g., office hours or review sessions).

Provide Rubrics Rubrics and checklists are ways of explicitly representing performance expectations and thus can direct students' behaviors toward your intended goals. For example, a rubric for a research paper can identify the components of the task (e.g., hypothesis, evidence, conclusion, writing) and the expectations for performance for each component at several levels of sophistication (e.g., developing, competent, exemplary). See Appendix E on rubrics and Appendix F on learner checklists for examples.

Provide Targeted Feedback Because feedback provides information about achievement and progress toward a goal (i.e., achievement value), it can have a powerful motivating effect. Feedback is most effective when it is timely and constructive. Timely feedback is close enough in proximity to the performance to have impact and to enable incorporation of the feedback into the next iteration. Constructive feedback identifies strengths, weaknesses, and suggestions for future action that can support expectations for future success (see Chapter 6 on practice and feedback).

Be Fair Be sure that the standards and criteria used to assess students' work are administered fairly. This is particularly relevant when multiple graders are involved (e.g., teaching assistants). If students perceive that their work is being assessed differently from their peers or differently from one time to the next, their expectations for success may be compromised.

Educate Students About the Ways We Explain Success and Failure To give students a better sense of control over the outcomes that they experience and in turn influence their expectations for success, educate them about the attributions that people make for success and failure. For example, we frequently attribute success to things about us (i.e., internalize) and attribute failures to things about the external world (i.e., externalize). Help them shape their attribution for success to include appropriate study strategies, good time management, and hard work. Similarly, help them avoid attributing failure to factors such as "not being good with numbers," "not being good with details," or "not being very smart." Rather, help them focus on controllable features, such as the way they studied (e.g., how much, when, the nature of their study habits).

Describe Effective Study Strategies Students may not be able to identify ways in which they should appropriately change their study behaviors following failure. In this case, it is important to discuss effective study strategies to give them alternatives to the behaviors that resulted in poor performance. In doing so, we may help adjust their expectations about being able to successfully obtain their goals.

103

Strategies That Address Value and Expectancies

Provide Flexibility and Control When possible, provide autonomy by allowing students to choose among options and make choices that are consistent with their goals and the activities that they value. One way to give students greater flexibility is to allow them choices in portions of the course content, topics for papers, and questions for class discussion. Flexibility lends a sense of control, which can contribute to a student's expectation of success.

Give Students an Opportunity to Reflect It is important to give students an opportunity to reflect on assignments. Facilitating their reflection with specific questions can help structure the process to support motivation. For example, asking students "What did you learn from this assignment?" or "What was the most valuable feature of this project?" helps them identify the value of their work. Asking students "What did you do to prepare for this assignment/exam? What skills do you need to work on? How would you prepare differently or approach the assignment differently if you were doing it in the future?" can help them to identify specific strategies that leverage their strengths and overcome their weaknesses, thus bolstering their expectations for future success.

Provide Frequent Feedback to Help Students Recognize Their Development of Competence Students often don't recognize the knowledge, skills, and abilities they are developing. Explicitly point out when students successfully acquire new knowledge and talent. At the end of the course, to demonstrate how much students have learned, contrast their current knowledge and abilities relative to the beginning of the course. The sense of developing competency can bring value to a task or area of study and can lay the foundation for expectations for future success.

Provide Opportunities for Relatedness Relatedness comes from opportunities for members of a learning community (instructors and students) to build connections. Offer students the opportunity to get to know each other with ice breakers, introduction/biography threads in discussion forums, or pair/group activities that enable students to get to know each other. Similarly, demonstrate your interest in your students' learning and your allyship in their success in your class.

SUMMARY

In this chapter, we have discussed some of the variables that underlie student motivation. We have used the concept of goals as an organizing feature and have argued that students frequently have multiple and diverse goals, many of which may not align with ours. We described a model in which the subjective value that students place on goals and their expectancies of success play a critical role in influencing their motivation. We highlighted how autonomy, competence, and relatedness, key elements from self-determination theory, support motivation and how andragogy informs our practices to motivate adult learners.

We have described how subjective value, expectations for success, and beliefs about the supportive nature of the environment interact to affect the specific ways in which students behave. Our hope is that by understanding how some of these variables influence motivation and by arming yourself with some practical strategies, you can increase the motivation of your students and improve the quality of learning in your courses.

CHAPTER 5

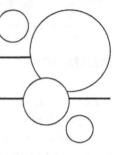

How Do Students Develop Mastery?

A Sum of Their Parts

I love teaching our department's first-year design studio. It energizes me to see students get excited about graphic design for the first time. In recent years, I've made it a point to integrate the kinds of technology tools that are increasingly used in the industry, tools that offer sophisticated editing capabilities, filters, color management . . . that sort of thing. I want students to become comfortable with these tools as early as possible, and I think they appreciate being treated like design professionals. And, heck, this generation takes to technology like fish to water! So that part is great. But what I've noticed over the last few years is that students' design work is, to put it bluntly, mediocre, and lacking the creativity I've seen from student work in the past. Moreover, they seem to be struggling with the conceptual content of the course. When I ask them to apply basic design principles in critiques, I often get blank looks. Or else they misapply the terminology. These concepts aren't hard, mind you, but my students from five years ago did fine. I hear a lot about how this generation of students is distracted and lacks focus, so maybe that explains it. I could use some advice on how to help students to learn this material more effectively. If they don't learn key design principles, they'll struggle in downstream courses. And Lord knows they'll never become successful designers . . .

Professor Jamel Davis

Shouldn't They Know This by Now?

I just came from observing a group of medical students in clinic and am feeling more discouraged than I've felt in months. I know for a fact that these students have studied and practiced how to take a patient's medical history because I've led the workshops focused on those skills. They've gotten didactic training on what goes into a patient history, they've learned communication strategies, they've role-played taking histories from classmates, they've even been video-recorded taking histories from simulated patients and received peer and instructor feedback on their videos. I really thought they knew this stuff! But watching them with patients today in the clinic made me wonder if they've learned anything at all. They struggled with clinical management and differential diagnoses, and their carefully honed communication skills flew straight out the window. I observed one resident, someone I know to be a particularly empathetic and effective communicator, botch her history-taking badly, not only presenting as brusque and impersonal to the patient but failing to ask critical questions about the patient's family medical history and medications. And this wasn't a particularly challenging patient or an especially hectic time in the clinic. Frankly, I was embarrassed, not only for my students but for myself. How is it possible that I worked so hard yet prepared them so poorly?

Dr. Pamela Kozol

WHAT IS GOING ON IN THESE TWO STORIES?

The instructors in these two stories believe that their students have the skills and knowledge to perform well in key areas, yet students' performance has been disappointing, and neither instructor knows why. The instructors are confused, wondering (in Professor Davis's case) what is wrong with their students or (in Dr. Kozol's case) where they went wrong as teachers. What might be happening in each case that can help us understand why the students have failed to meet their instructor's expectations?

In fact, the tasks these instructors have assigned may require more from students than the instructors realize, and their students may be less prepared than their instructors assume. In the first story, for example, Professor Davis expects his students to learn a set of unfamiliar design concepts and apply them

107

to the creation of innovative designs while also mastering a slew of new technology tools. He assumes, as many instructors do, that the younger generation of students is at home with all digital technologies and can easily learn the tools of the trade (an assumption that is often unfounded, particularly for technologies that lack the user-friendly interfaces of standard phone apps). By adding these design tools to his course, Professor Davis has unwittingly added significant additional challenges without dedicating time for students to learn the tools, never mind use them effectively to accomplish creative goals. Moreover, each tool comes with small but significant cognitive burdens, such as creating accounts and managing log-in information, that add to the cognitive demands of the task and draw intellectual resources away from the conceptual learning that is ostensibly Professor Davis's primary focus.

Dr. Kozol's medical students, by contrast, appear to have the necessary component skills. They have had ample opportunity to practice taking patient histories in realistically simulated contexts and demonstrate their competence. Yet when they are asked to do so in a real clinical context, their communication skills fall apart, and they make multiple errors in data collection. There are several possible explanations for this. First, Dr. Kozol's students have practiced taking patient histories in contexts where they could focus intently on building rapport with patients, communicating clearly, and collecting the appropriate information. When placed in a genuine clinical setting, they faced a whole new set of challenges, including integrating history-taking with other tasks, such as formulating diagnoses and making treatment recommendations. All of this was happening, moreover, in an environment with far more sensory inputs (e.g., chatty patients, the presence of family members, hallway noise.) The students in this scenario do not necessarily lack the component skills but rather the ability to use them in combination. A second possibility is that the students, finding themselves in a new context, do not fully recognize the applicability of skills they learned in a different and more simplified context. If so, the problem was not that students lacked component skills or that they were unable to integrate them successfully, but that they failed to transfer their knowledge successfully to a new context and apply it appropriately.

WHAT PRINCIPLE OF LEARNING IS AT WORK HERE?

As this chapter's stories suggest, tasks that seem simple and straightforward to instructors often involve a complex combination of skills. Think back to when you learned to drive. You had to keep in mind a sequence of steps (e.g., adjust the mirrors, apply the brakes, turn the key in the ignition, put the car in reverse, check the rear view mirror, release the brake, press the accelerator), a set of facts (e.g., traffic rules and laws, the meaning of street signs, the functions of the car's controls and gauges), and a set of skills (e.g., accelerating smoothly, parallel parking, performing a three-point turn). You also had to learn how to integrate all of these component skills and knowledge in order to execute them together, such as checking your mirror and moving into another lane. Finally, you had to recognize the appropriate context for particular knowledge and skills, such as adapting speed and braking behavior when driving on icy versus clear roads.

To an experienced driver, driving is effortless and automatic, requiring little conscious awareness to do well. But for the novice driver it is complex and effortful, involving the conscious and gradual development of many distinct skills and abilities. A similar process exists in the development of mastery in academic contexts, as described in the following principle.

> **Principle:** To develop mastery, students must acquire component skills, practice integrating them, and know when to apply what they have learned.

Mastery refers to the attainment of a high degree of competence within a particular area. That area can be narrowly or broadly defined, ranging from discrete skills (e.g., using a Bunsen burner) or content knowledge (e.g., knowing the names of all U.S. presidents) to extensive knowledge and skills within a complex disciplinary domain (e.g., French theater, thermodynamics, or game theory). For students to achieve mastery within a domain, whether narrowly or broadly conceived, they need to develop a set of key component skills, practice them to the point where they can be combined fluently and used with a fair degree of automaticity, and know when and where to apply them appropriately (see Figure 5.1).

WHAT DOES THE RESEARCH TELL US ABOUT MASTERY?

Common sense suggests that having achieved mastery within a domain should position an instructor well to help novices develop mastery. But this is not necessarily the case. In the following sections we examine why expertise can potentially be a problem for teachers; we then explore research relevant to each element of mastery and discuss implications for teaching.

109

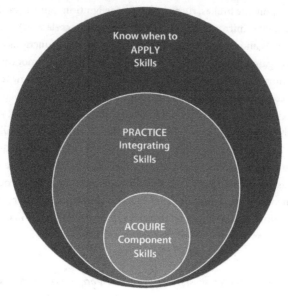

Figure 5.1. Elements of Mastery

Expert Blind Spot

Ironically, expertise can be a liability as well as an advantage when it comes to teaching. To understand why, consider the model of mastery offered by Sprague and Stuart (2000) and illustrated in Figure 5.2. It describes a four-stage trajectory from novice to expert focused on two dimensions: competence and consciousness.

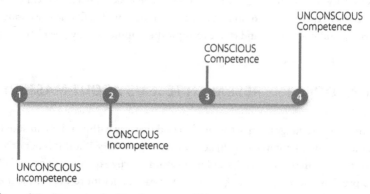

Figure 5.2. Stages in the Development of Mastery

As illustrated in the diagram, novice students are in a state of unconscious incompetence in that they have not yet developed skill in a particular domain, nor do they have sufficient knowledge to recognize what they need to learn. Put simply, they do not know what they do not know. As they gain knowledge and experience, they advance to a state of conscious incompetence, where they are increasingly aware of what they do not know and, consequently, of what they need to learn. As their mastery develops, students advance to a state of conscious competence wherein they have considerable competence in their domain, yet they still must think and act deliberately and consciously. Finally, as students reach the highest level of mastery, they move into a state of unconscious competence in which they exercise the skills and knowledge in their domain so automatically and instinctively that they are no longer consciously aware of what they know or do. As this model suggests, while competence develops in a more-or-less linear way, conscious awareness first waxes and then wanes, so that novices (in stage one) and experts (in stage four) both operate with relatively little conscious awareness of their knowledge and skills, though for very different reasons.

It is easy to see why novices lack conscious awareness of what they do not know, but less obvious why experts lack conscious awareness of what they do know. Research on expert-novice differences helps to illuminate the issue. Experts, by definition, possess vastly more knowledge than novices, but they also organize, access, and apply their knowledge very differently (see Chapter 2 on prior knowledge; Ericsson & Lehmann, 1996; Ericsson & Smith, 1991). For instance, experts organize knowledge into large, conceptual "chunks" that enable them to access and apply their knowledge efficiently and with little effort (Chase & Ericsson, 1982; Chase & Simon, 1973a; Koedinger & Anderson, 1990). Moreover, because experts immediately recognize meaningful patterns and configurations based on their previous experiences, they are able to employ shortcuts and skip steps that novices cannot (Anderson, 1992; Blessing & Anderson, 1996; Chase & Simon, 1973b; DeGroot, 1965; Koedinger & Anderson, 1990). Also, because experts have extensive practice in a narrowly defined area (e.g., planning a problem-solving strategy or critiquing a theoretical perspective), they can perform with ease and automaticity tasks that are much more effortful for novices (Beilock et al., 2002; Lansdown, 2002; Smith & Chamberlin, 1992). Finally, experts link specific information to deeper principles and schemas and are consequently better able than novices to transfer their knowledge across contexts in which those principles apply (see Chapter 2 on prior knowledge; Boster & Johnson, 1989; Chi et al., 1981; Larkin et al., 1980).

111

These attributes of expertise are an obvious advantage when instructors are working within their disciplinary domains, but they can be an obstacle to effective teaching. For example, the way instructors chunk knowledge can make it difficult for them to break a skill down so that it is clear to students. Moreover, the fact that instructors take shortcuts and skip steps with no conscious awareness of doing so means they will sometimes make leaps that students cannot follow. In addition, the efficiency with which instructors perform complex tasks can lead them to underestimate the time it will take students to learn and perform these tasks. Finally, the fact that instructors can quickly recognize the relevance of skills across diverse contexts can cause them to overestimate students' ability to do the same.

When expert instructors are blind to the learning needs of novice students, it is known as *expert blind spot* (Hinds, 1999; Nathan & Koedinger, 2000; Nathan & Petrosino, 2003; Nickerson, 1999). To get a sense of the effect of expert blind spot on students, consider how master chefs might instruct novice cooks to "sauté the vegetables until they are done," "cook until the sauce is a good consistency," or "add spices to taste." Whereas such instructions are clear to chefs, they do not illuminate matters to novice students, who do not know what "done" entails, what a "good consistency" is, or what spices would create a desired taste. Here we see the unconscious competence of the expert meeting the unconscious incompetence of the novice. The likely result is that students miss vital information, make unnecessary mistakes, and function inefficiently. They may also become confused and discouraged. Although they might muddle through on their own, it is unlikely that they will learn with optimal efficiency or thoroughness.

Both Professor Davis and Dr. Kozol in the stories at the beginning of the chapter demonstrate expert blind spot. Professor Davis has developed such ease and fluency with tools used in the design industry that he has forgotten the time it took to learn them, thus underestimating the learning curve for students. Likewise, Dr. Kozol has become so accustomed to functioning in a clinical context that she forgets how overwhelming it can be to relative novices to integrate multiple skills in a complex, real-world setting.

This is by no means unusual. As experts in our fields, we are all susceptible to expert blind spot. However, we can reduce the problems it poses for student learning by becoming more consciously aware of three discrete elements of mastery that students must develop: (1) the acquisition of key component skills, (2) practice in integrating them effectively, and (3) knowledge of when to apply what they have learned.

Acquiring Component Skills

As the driving and cooking examples just given suggest, tasks that seem simple to experts can hide a complex combination of component skills. For example, the ability to analyze a case study requires component skills such as the capacity to identify the central question or dilemma of the case, articulate the perspectives of key actors, enumerate constraints, delineate possible courses of action, and recommend and justify a solution. Similarly, problem-solving might involve component skills including (but not limited to) representing the problem, determining an appropriate solution strategy, doing the calculations necessary to execute that strategy, and evaluating the result. These component skills are particularly difficult to identify when they, involve purely cognitive processes (e.g., recognizing, planning, and formulating) that are not directly visible.

If students lack critical component skills—or if their command of those skills is weak—their performance on the overall task suffers (Resnick, 1976). This is demonstrated in studies wherein researchers decompose complex tasks, identify weak or missing component skills, and track the effect of those gaps on student performance. Lovett's (2001) research with introductory statistics students, for instance, identified two key skills involved in statistical data analysis: the ability to recognize the relevant variables and the ability to categorize them according to types. Lovett found that when students lacked these component skills, they were less able to choose appropriate forms of analysis, and their performance on the overall problem-solving task was compromised (Lovett, 2001). We see a similar phenomenon in the first story at the beginning of the chapter: Professor Davis has overlooked key component skills—the mastery of design tools—and the lack of these skills is eroding overall student performance.

In order to teach complex skills systematically—without missing pieces—instructors must be able to "unpack" or decompose complex tasks. This can be challenging because of expert blind spot, but it offers tangible payoffs for student learning. Indeed, research indicates that when instructors identify and reinforce students' component skills (especially weaker ones) through targeted practice, performance on the overall task often improves significantly. For example, Koedinger and Anderson (1990) found that, relative to experts, novice geometry students lacked the ability to plan problem-solving strategies. After assigning students exercises to specifically reinforce this skill within the context of the larger task, the researchers found that students became much more adept problem-solvers (Koedinger & Anderson, 1993). Lovett (2001) found that if beginning students were given a mere 45 minutes of practice identifying statistical problem types, and were given feedback on this particular skill, they were able to select appropriate analyses as adeptly as students who had had a semester-long course. In other words, even a small amount of focused practice on key component skills had a profound effect on overall performance. This same effect is demonstrated in research on cognitive tutors (computer-based tutoring programs), which are designed to detect the component skills that students lack and direct them to exercises that strengthen their abilities in those areas (Anderson et al., 1989, 1995; Ritter et al., 2007; Singley, 1995).

While we know that students need to practice component skills in order to improve their performance on the complex tasks involving those skills, the question of whether students should practice component skills in isolation or in the context of the whole task is more complicated. The advantage of practicing a component skill in isolation is that it enables students to focus their attention solely on the skill that needs work. Think, for example, of the benefits to a basketball player of drills that emphasize dribbling or shooting. Drilling these component skills in isolation gives players more repeated practice with each skill than they could ever get in the context of a game or scrimmage and enables them to devote their energy and concentration exclusively to the skill in question. The advantage to practicing the whole task, however, is that students see how the parts fit into the whole in a context that is authentically complex. Think, for example, how much more difficult it is to shoot under defensive pressure in a game situation than when taking practice shots during a drill!

Whether or not students benefit more from practicing component skills in isolation or in the context of the overall task depends to a large extent on the nature of the task. Although the research results are mixed, it seems generally true that whole-task practice is preferable if the overall task is fairly simple or if components cannot be realistically extracted from the whole (Naylor & Briggs, 1963; Teague et al., 1994; Wightman & Lintern, 1985). However, if the task is highly complex and can be easily divided into component parts, students often learn more effectively if the components are practiced initially in isolation, and then progressively combined (Salden et al., 2006; White & Frederickson, 1990; Wightman & Lintern, 1985). The extent to which isolated practice facilitates learning also depends in part on the skill level of the student. Studies have shown that explicit instruction and isolated practice of component skills, while helpful for novice learners (Clarke et al., 2005), might be counterproductive for advanced learners if they have already integrated these components into a coherent whole

(Kalyuga et al., 2003). Finally, the extent to which isolated practice is beneficial depends on the learning objectives of the class. For example, if Professor Davis truly wants his design students to learn to use professional design tools, he might want to create structured opportunities for students to practice these tools before asking them to use them for assignments. Since this would take time away from some of Professor Davis's other course goals, he would do well to weigh his priorities and consider scaling back the new technologies.

Implications of This Research

In order to build new skills systematically and to diagnose weak or missing skills, instructors must be able to break complex tasks down into their component parts. Analyzing complex tasks into their parts helps instructors pinpoint skills that students need to develop through targeted practice. However, in designing practice opportunities to reinforce component skills, instructors should consider whether their learning goals are best accomplished through isolated practice, whole-task practice, or some combination of the two.

Integrating Skills

Acquiring component skills does not by itself prepare students to perform complex tasks. This is because mastering complex tasks requires not only practice of the component skills that comprise them but also the opportunity to practice them in combination. Integrating component skills can be difficult and demanding, as is evidenced in the second story at the beginning of this chapter in which Dr. Kozol's medical students struggle to combine skills they have learned separately. The performance deficits that Dr. Kozol's students exhibit when attempting to combine skills are not unusual. Many studies have shown that people's performance tends to degrade when they are asked to do more than one task at a time, a phenomenon known as *dual task effects* (Navon & Gopher, 1979; Neider et al., 2011; Pashler, 1994; Wickens, 1991). This degradation occurs because performing multiple tasks simultaneously tends to require attention to and processing of a great deal of information, and yet people have a limit to how much they can attend to and process at once. This brings us to the research on cognitive load.

Cognitive psychologists have called our attention to the limits of working memory (Baddeley & Hitch, 1974; Cowan, 2008). Working memory is the part of the brain's cognitive apparatus charged with processing and using information before that information is encoded in long-term memory. While long-term memory is capacious (think of it like a library or archive), working memory is limited (think of it as a physical desktop). The total information-processing demands imposed by a given task or set of tasks is known as *cognitive load*. When cognitive load is excessive, we are left with insufficient cognitive resources to complete tasks effectively: the desktop gets crowded and items on it begin to slide off.

Cognitive load increases—and performance often declines—when learners combine skills. For example, Strayer and Johnston (2001) found that when they asked adults to perform a simulated driving task, various measures of performance (e.g., the number of traffic signals obeyed and reaction time for braking at red lights) declined when a cell phone conversation task was added to the driving task. Furthermore, as the complexity of the cell phone task increased, driving performance worsened. In other words, although the participants in this study likely had sufficient cognitive resources to perform well on the driving task in isolation, the more resources that were demanded by the secondary (cell phone) task, the fewer resources there were left for driving—leading to worse driving performance. The same phenomenon often occurs when learners perform a single complex task that is new to them. Think back to Professor Davis's design studio where the combined burden of using new technologies, applying design principles, and producing a creative design appears to have overwhelmed students' working memory, leading to designs that lacked originality and poor command of conceptual material.

Not surprisingly, experts do not have the same experience as novices when performing complex tasks that involve combining skills. Because experts have extensive practice within a circumscribed domain, the key component skills in their domain tend to be highly practiced and automated. Each of these highly practiced skills then demands relatively few cognitive resources, effectively lowering the total cognitive load that experts experience. Thus, experts can perform complex tasks with relative ease (Beilock et al., 2002; Lansdown, 2002; Smith & Chamberlin, 1992). This is not because they have more cognitive resources than novices; rather, because of the high level of fluency they have achieved in performing key skills, they can do more with what they have. Novices, however, have not achieved the same degree of fluency and automaticity in each of the component skills. Thus, they struggle to combine skills that experts combine easily and efficiently.

Because instructors, as experts, do not experience the same cognitive load as novices, they may have performance expectations for students that are unrealistically high. This can lead to the kinds of errant conclusions Professor Davis draws about students' work ethic and focus or to Dr. Kozol's worries that she has failed to properly teach her medical students how to take a patient history. Fortunately, as students gain mastery over time, the knowledge and procedures required for complex tasks become automatized and thus require fewer cognitive resources. Thus, with practice, students gain greater fluency in executing and combining component skills.

How then can we help students manage cognitive load as they learn to perform complex tasks? To begin with, we can distinguish among three types of cognitive load: intrinsic, extraneous, and germane. *Intrinsic cognitive load* refers to the cognitive burden imposed by the task itself (let's say, reading and critiquing an article). *Extraneous cognitive load* refers to the cognitive cost exacted by things unrelated to learning (e.g., confusing document formatting or unclear task instructions). Extraneous cognitive load only detracts from learning. *Germane cognitive load* goes beyond the immediate task to encourage deeper learning (e.g., asking learners to draw connections or think of new applications). Cognitive load theory has proven essential in the realm of online learning (Griskevica & Iltners, 2021; Skulmowski & Xu, 2021). In online courses, where students interact extensively with digital course materials and course communication is largely via text, poor visual design and confusing instructions can impose significant extraneous cognitive load that interferes with learning (Mayer, 2001; Mayer & Moreno, 1998). So, too, can the inclusion of multiple tools and platforms, as Professor Davis's experience (albeit in an in-person setting) demonstrates. The key to managing cognitive load effectively lies in identifying which of the demanding aspects of a task are related to the skills students need to learn and which may be disruptive to (or distracting from) those learning goals. While as instructors, we do not have control over *all* forms of cognitive load that affect student learning (think of financial stressors and family obligations, for instance; see Chapter 1 on individual differences), we *can* look for ways to decrease extraneous load wherever possible. At the same time, we can seek to reasonably increase germane load to foster deeper learning (Kalyuga, 2011; Paas et al., 2003, 2004; Sweller, 2010; Van Merriënboer & Ayres, 2005).

One way to reduce cognitive load in the interests of learning is to allow students to focus on one skill at a time, enabling them to get the opportunity to develop fluency in component skills before they are required to integrate multiple skills. For example, Clarke et al. (2005) found that math students who knew little about spreadsheets learned less and performed less well when they were taught new mathematical concepts in the context of spreadsheets. This is because they had to learn both the spreadsheet skills and the math concepts concurrently, and they became overwhelmed. However, when these students first learned spreadsheet skills and later used those skills to learn the math concepts, learning and performance improved. Professor Davis's story has direct parallels. If students in his design studio were able to practice using the required technology tools *before* trying to produce graphic designs with them, those designs may well have been better.

Another way to manage cognitive load is to support some aspects of a complex task while students perform the entire task (Cooper & Sweller, 1987; Paas & van Merrienboer, 1994; Sweller & Cooper, 1985). For example, Sweller and Cooper (1985) demonstrated this with students learning to solve problems in a variety of quantitative fields from statistics to physics. They found that when students were given typical word problems, it was possible for them to solve the problems without actually learning much. This is because the problems themselves were sufficiently demanding that students had no cognitive resources available to learn from their own problem-solving. But when students were given "worked examples" (such as presolved problems) interspersed with problems to solve, studying the worked examples freed up cognitive resources that enabled students to see the key features of the problem and to analyze the steps and reasons behind problem-solving moves. The researchers found this improved students' performance on subsequent problem-solving. This result, called the *worked example effect*, is one example of a process called *scaffolding*, whereby instructors temporarily relieve some of the cognitive load so that students can focus on specific dimensions of learning.

Implications of This Research

Performing complex tasks can be cognitively demanding for students, particularly when they have not yet developed fluency or automaticity in all the component skills. Thus, instructors should have reasonable expectations about the time and practice students will need, not only to develop fluency in component skills but also to learn to integrate those skills successfully. It can be helpful under some circumstances for instructors to strategically lighten aspects of the task that introduce extraneous cognitive load so that students can focus their cognitive resources on the aspects of a task most germane to the learning objectives. Several specific ways to do this are discussed in the "Strategies" section.

Application

As we have seen, mastery requires component skills and the ability to integrate them successfully. However, it also requires that students know when and where to use what they have learned. When students acquire skills but do not learn the conditions of their appropriate application, they may fail to apply skills that are relevant to a task or problem, or, alternatively, apply the wrong skill for the current context.

The application of skills (or knowledge, strategies, approaches, or habits) learned in one context to a novel context is referred to as *transfer*. If the learning context and transfer context are similar, researchers call it *near transfer*. If the learning context and transfer context are dissimilar, it is called *far transfer*. For example, far transfer comes into play when a student is given a task in his public policy course that requires him to apply a formula he learned two semesters previously in Statistics 101. Not only has the knowledge domain changed from statistics to public policy but the physical and temporal contexts (a new class, two semesters later) have as well. If the transfer task were in a different functional context altogether, say outside academia, additional transfer distance would be introduced (for a discussion of different dimensions of transfer, see Barnett & Ceci, 2002).

Far transfer is, arguably, the central goal of education: we want our students to be able to apply what they learn far beyond the classroom. Yet most research has found that (1) transfer occurs neither often nor automatically and (2) the more dissimilar the learning and transfer contexts, the less likely successful transfer will occur. In other words, much as we would like them to, students often do not successfully apply relevant skills or knowledge in novel contexts (Cognition and Technology Group at Vanderbilt, 1994; Holyoak & Koh, 1987; McKeough et al., 1995; Reed et al., 1974; Singley, 1995; Singley & Anderson, 1989; Thorndike & Woodworth, 1901). In this section, we examine this phenomenon by exploring issues that can affect transfer negatively and positively.

There are a number of reasons students may fail to transfer relevant knowledge and skills. First, they may associate that knowledge too closely with the context in which they originally learned it and thus not think to apply it—or know how to apply it—outside that context. This is called *over-specificity* or *context dependence* (Mason Spencer & Weisberg, 1986; Perfetto et al., 1983). To illustrate: students in a statistics course might perform well on their chapter quizzes that

119

require application of statistical concepts and techniques from that same chapter, yet perform poorly on a final exam involving questions of precisely the same type and difficulty, but from multiple different chapters. If students relied on superficial cues to figure out which concept or technique to apply on chapter quizzes (e.g., if it is Chapter 12, it must be a *t*-test), then in the absences of these cues, they may be unable to identify the salient features of each problem and select an appropriate statistical test. Their knowledge, in other words, was overly context dependent and thus not flexible. Context dependence may also account for why students in Professor Kozol's class struggled to apply history-taking skills they had learned in prior workshops; in the new, clinical context, they no longer had the contextual cues that had guided them in previous experiences.

Second, students may fail to transfer relevant skills, knowledge, or practices if they do not have a robust understanding of underlying principles and deep structure—in other words, if they understand what to do but not why. If, for example, Dr. Kozol's medical students had memorized the steps of taking a patient history without understanding deeply enough *why* this information was important to collect, it could inhibit their ability to transfer their learning to new contexts.

Fortunately, much of the same research that documents transfer failure also suggests instructional approaches that can bolster transfer. For example, studies have shown that students are better able to transfer learning to new contexts when they can combine concrete experiences from particular contexts with abstract knowledge that cuts across those contexts (Schwartz et al., 1999). A classic study by Schoklow and Judd (in Judd, 1908) illustrates this point. The researchers asked two groups of students to throw darts at a target 12 inches under water. Predictably, the performance of both groups improved with practice. Then one group was taught the abstract principle of refraction, while the other was not. When asked to hit a target four inches under water, the group that knew the abstract principle adjusted their strategies and significantly outperformed the other group. Knowing the abstract principle helped students transfer their experiential knowledge beyond the context in which it was learned and to adjust their strategies for new conditions. Similarly, when students are given opportunities to apply what they learn across multiple contexts, it fosters less context-dependent and more "flexible" knowledge (Gick & Holyoak, 1983).

Structured comparisons—in which students are asked to compare and contrast different problems, cases, or scenarios—have also been shown to facilitate transfer. For example, Loewenstein et al. (2003) asked two groups of management students to analyze negotiation training cases. One group analyzed each case individually; the other group was asked to compare cases. The researchers found that the group that compared cases demonstrated dramatically more learning than the group that considered them individually. Why? Because when students were asked to compare cases, they had to recognize and identify the deep features of each case that would make it analogous or non-analogous to other cases. Having identified those deep features, students could link the cases to abstract negotiation principles, which then allowed them to learn more deeply and apply what they learned more effectively. Other methods that have been found to facilitate transfer include analogical reasoning (Catrambone & Holyoak, 1989; Gentner et al., 2001; Holyoak & Koh, 1987; Klahr & Carver, 1988), using visual representations to help students see significant features and patterns (Biederman & Shiffrar, 1987), and asking students to articulate causal relationships (Brown & Kane, 1988).

Finally, research indicates that minor prompts on the part of the instructor can aid transfer. In Gick and Holyoak's (1980) study, college students were presented with a passage describing a military conundrum in which an army is trying to capture a fortress and must ultimately divide into small groups, approach the fortress from different roads, and converge simultaneously to attack. After memorizing this information, students were presented with a medical problem that required a similar solution (the use of multiple laser beams coming from different angles and converging on a tumor). Despite having just encountered the military solution, the large majority of students did not apply what they had learned to the medical problem. Even though the physical, social, and temporal contexts were the same, the knowledge domains (military strategy versus medicine) and functional contexts (storming a fortress versus treating a tumor) were sufficiently different that students did not recognize their analogous structures or think to apply knowledge from one problem to the other. However, when students were asked to think back to the military problem when solving the medical one, they were far more likely to solve it (Gick & Holyoak, 1980). Similar results have been shown in other studies as well (Bassok, 1990; Klahr & Carver, 1988; Perfetto et al., 1983). A little prompting, in other words, can go a long way in helping students apply what they know.

Implications of This Research

Transfer does not happen easily or automatically. Thus, it is particularly important that we "teach for transfer"—that is, that we employ instructional strategies that reinforce a robust understanding of deep structures and underlying principles, provide sufficiently diverse contexts in which to apply these principles, and help students make appropriate connections between the knowledge and skills they possess and new contexts in which those skills apply. We consider some specific strategies under the heading "Strategies to Facilitate Transfer" later in this chapter.

WHAT STRATEGIES DOES THE RESEARCH SUGGEST?

The following strategies include those faculty members can use to (1) decompose complex tasks so as to build students' skills more systematically and to diagnose areas of weakness, (2) help students combine and integrate skills to develop greater automaticity and fluency, and (3) help students learn when to apply what they have learned.

Strategies to Expose and Reinforce Component Skills

Anticipate and Challenge Your Own Expert Blind Spot Because of their expertise, instructors may have lost conscious awareness of the many components—individual skills, facts, and concepts—required to complete complex tasks. Consequently, when teaching students, instructors may inadvertently omit skills, steps, and information that students need to learn and perform effectively. The first step toward overcoming this expert blind spot is simply to be aware of it. Are you underestimating the challenge for relative novices? Have you provided sufficient opportunities for students to acquire the key component skills, as well as to practice combining them and learn to apply them in a range of contexts?

Decompose Complex Skills When teaching complex skills (e.g., grant writing, survey design), it is wise to spend time identifying the skills that comprise them. Ask yourself: "What would students have to know—or know how to do—in order to achieve what I am asking of them?" For example, grant writing requires the ability to conduct a literature review and develop a budget: complex skills in their own right. Decompose the task until you have identified the key component skills at a grain size that makes sense for your students' level. Many instructors stop decomposing the task too soon and thus fail to identify critical skill gaps that can impede both learning and performance.

Enlist a Graduate Student to Help You Identify Expert Blind Spot As experts in our disciplinary domains, we operate in a state of "unconscious competence" that can make it difficult to see the component skills and knowledge that students must acquire to perform complex tasks. While graduate students are in the process of developing mastery themselves, they are often closer than experienced faculty members to the "conscious competence" stage of mastery (see Sprague and Stuart's model as illustrated in Figure 5.2) and are more aware of the steps along the way, as well as the challenges of specific tasks. Thus, if you have a teaching assistant, it can be helpful to ask them to watch for and point out areas of expert blind spot, to help you decompose complex tasks, and to identify areas where students might struggle.

Seek Out Other Perspectives It can be helpful to ask someone outside your discipline to review specific teaching materials (e.g., syllabus, assignments) to look for expert blind spot. A person (such as a teaching consultant or colleague outside your discipline) who is intelligent and insightful but does not share your disciplinary expertise can help you identify areas in which you may have omitted or skipped over important component knowledge or skills. Another option is to compare notes with colleagues in your field to see how *they* decompose complex tasks, such as research papers, oral presentations, or design projects. Although your colleagues have their own expert blind spots to overcome, they may have identified skills that you have not. Thus it can be helpful to talk with them and ask to examine their syllabi, assignments, and performance rubrics for ideas (see Appendix E on rubrics).

Explore Available Educational Materials Most fields have journals focused on teaching in the discipline, and these can be valuable resources. There may be published work in your field that presents completed task analyses that can help you think about the component skills in a course or learning situation, or simply to recognize where students might struggle. For instance, it might have helped Dr. Kozol to read articles about taking patient histories, both to identify component skills she might have missed and to anticipate challenges her students might encounter when applying these skills in real-world contexts.

Make Sure Students Know Where to Focus Their Attention If students are spending their cognitive resources on extraneous features of the task, it diverts those resources from the germane aspects of the task. Thus, one way to help students manage cognitive load is to clearly communicate your goals and priorities for assignments and tell students where—and where not—to direct their energy. For example, let's say you assign students in your architecture class a task meant to help them explore a wide range of creative design solutions. You might tell them to generate as many different design solutions as possible but *not* to spend time getting the details right or making their designs aesthetically pleasing. Rubrics that spell out your performance criteria for assignments can help students focus their cognitive resources where they best serve your learning objectives (see Appendix E on rubrics and Appendix F on learner checklists).

Diagnose Weak or Missing Component Skills To assess your students' competence vis-à-vis component skills and knowledge, consider giving a diagnostic exam or assignment early in the semester (see Appendix C on student self-assessments). If a small number of students lack key skills, you can alert them to this fact and direct them to resources (academic support on campus, tutoring, additional readings) to help them develop these skills on their own. If a large number of students lack key prerequisite skills, you might opt to devote some class time to addressing them or hold an informal review session outside class. You can also assess your students' understanding of subject matter in your own course by analyzing the patterns of mistakes students make on exams, papers, oral presentations, and so on. The information you gain from these kinds of ongoing analyses can help you design instruction to reinforce critical skills or improve the next iteration of the course.

Provide Isolated Practice to Address Weak or Missing Skills Once you have identified important missing skills, create opportunities for students to practice these skills in relative isolation. For example, if students are writing conclusions to their papers that simply restate the topic paragraph or descend into banalities—and you perceive this as an obstacle to achieving one of your learning objectives—you might (1) ask students to read the conclusions of several articles and discuss what makes them compelling or not compelling, (2) have them write a conclusion for an article that is missing one, and (3) critique their conclusions together. For in-person courses, these can be in-class activities; for online learning, they could be synchronous or asynchronous group activities. Similarly, in a class focused on quantitative problem-solving, you might ask students to plan a problem-solving strategy without actually executing the plan. This focuses students' energies on one aspect of the task—planning—and builds that particular skill before allowing them to jump into calculations.

Strategies to Build Fluency and Facilitate Integration

Provide Practice Opportunities Specifically Designed to Increase Fluency If diagnostic assessments, such as those just described, reveal that students can perform key component skills but do so slowly and effortfully, you might want to assign exercises specifically designed to increase students' speed and efficiency. In a language class, for example, this might involve asking students to drill verb conjugations until they come easily. In a quantitative class, it might involve assigning supplementary problem-solving exercises to build automaticity in a basic mathematical skill—vector arithmetic, for example. When providing practice intended to increase automaticity, explain your rationale to your students. For example: "It is important not only that you can do these calculations but also that you can do them quickly and easily, so that when you are solving a complex problem you do not get bogged down in the basic mathematical calculations. These exercises are to increase your efficiency." You should also be explicit about the level of fluency you expect students to achieve, as illustrated in these examples: "You should practice these to the point that you can solve an entire page of problems in less than 15 minutes without the use of a calculator" or "You should be able to scan a 20-page journal article and extract its main argument in less than five minutes."

Temporarily Constrain the Scope of the Task It can be helpful to minimize cognitive load temporarily while students develop greater fluency with component skills or learn to integrate them. One way to do this is by initially reducing the size or complexity of the task. For example, a piano teacher might ask students to practice only the right hand part of a piece, and then only the left hand part, before combining them. If the student still struggles to integrate the two parts successfully, the teacher might ask her to practice only a few measures, until she develops greater fluency at coordinating both hands. Similarly, a typography instructor might give an assignment early in the semester in which students must create a design using only font and font size but no other design elements. Once students have practiced these particular components, the instructor can then add additional elements, such as color or animations, adding to the level of complexity as students gain fluency in the component skills.

125

Explicitly Include Task Integration in Your Performance Criteria As we have seen, integrating skills is a skill in itself. Thus, it is reasonable to include the effective integration of component parts in your performance rubrics for complex tasks. For example, on the rubric for a group project and presentation, you could include the seamless integration of every member's contribution to the project, or a consistent voice, as a feature of high-quality performance (see Appendix E on rubrics). Likewise, on an analytical paper, you could identify the coherence or "flow" of the argument as an important dimension of performance (see Appendix F on learner checklists).

Reduce Extraneous Cognitive Load Look for ways to reduce extraneous cognitive load to free up cognitive resources for learning. Make sure directions are clear and concise, use document headers effectively to organize information, and reduce text on slides so students are not reading when they should be listening. Pay particular attention to visual design in online courses, where students rely heavily on digital interfaces and text to navigate the course. Read about and apply multimedia design principles (Clark & Mayer, 2016) and seek help from an instructional designer when possible. Again, it is not feasible to reduce all the factors imposing cognitive burdens on students (think of taking online courses from a small apartment while managing the online schooling of small children!) but you can help by reducing cognitive load in areas you can control.

Limit Use of New Technologies Tech tools can be tremendously useful but learning them imposes additional cognitive load that must be factored into the design of a course. If using a tool is an essential part of your course, make time for students to learn it on its own before using it to perform complex tasks. For example, in a qualitative research course, you might give students practice using data analysis software with a simplified data set *before* asking them to use it for an extensive or high-stakes assignment. If tools are not fundamental to your learning goals but rather a means to an end (e.g., asynchronous engagement), limit how many you use. For instance, rather than using three different tools for asynchronous discussion as requirements of course interaction, limit yourself to one or two and use the same ones often enough that students develop fluency with them.

Strategies to Facilitate Transfer

Discuss Conditions of Applicability Do not assume that because students have learned a skill they will automatically know where or when to apply it. It is important to explain the contexts in which skills are—or are not—applicable and to do so clearly and explicitly. For example, when might one collect qualitative versus quantitative data, use a *T*-test, or transcribe lines of dialogue phonetically? There will not always be a single "best" solution or approach, in which case it is helpful to ask students to discuss the pros and cons of different approaches (e.g., "What do you gain and lose by using a questionnaire instead of a face-to-face interview?" or "What objectives are and are not served by staging a play in a minimalist style?"). Explicitly discussing the conditions and contexts of applicability can help students transfer what they know more successfully.

Give Students Opportunities to Apply Skills or Knowledge in Diverse Contexts When students practice applying skills across a range of contexts it can help them overcome context-dependence and prepare them better to transfer that skill to new situations. When possible, give students opportunities to apply skills and knowledge in multiple contexts. For example, if you are teaching students a set of marketing principles, you might assign multiple case studies to give students the opportunity to apply those principles in the context of very different industries. In a product design course, you might ask students to use the same set of ideation techniques to brainstorm solutions across a variety of design problems.

Ask Students to Generalize to Larger Principles To increase the flexibility of knowledge, and thus the likelihood of transfer, encourage students to generalize from specific contexts to abstract principles. You can do this by asking questions such as "What is the physical principle that describes what is happening here?" or "Which of the theories we have discussed is exemplified in this video case study?" Asking students to step back from the details of specific problems or cases and focus on higher-order principles can help them recognize the applicability of these principles in new contexts and facilitate transfer.

Use Comparisons to Help Students Identify Deep Features Students may fail to transfer knowledge or skills appropriately if they cannot recognize the meaningful features of the problem. Providing your students with structured comparisons—of problems, cases, scenarios, or tasks—helps them learn to differentiate the deep features of the problem from the surface characteristics. For example, in a physics class you might present two problems in which the surface features are similar (they both involve pulleys) but the physics principles at work are different (momentum versus energy). Or you could present two problems in which the surface features are different (one involves a pulley and one involves an inclined plane) but the physics principle is the same. Structured comparisons such as

127

these encourage students to identify and focus on underlying, structural similarities and differences and caution them not to be fooled by superficial features. This can then help them recognize the deep features of novel problems and thus facilitate successful transfer.

Specify Context and Ask Students to Identify Relevant Skills or Knowledge Help students make connections between problems they might confront and the skills and knowledge they possess by giving them a context—a problem, case, or scenario—and asking them to generate knowledge and skills (e.g., rules, procedures, techniques, approaches, theories, or styles) that are appropriate to that context. For example, "Here is a statistical problem; which of the tests you know could be used to solve it?" or "Here is an anthropological question you might want to investigate; what data-gathering methods could you use to answer it?" Then vary the context by asking what-if questions, such as "What if this involved dependent variables? Could we still use this test?" or "What if the subjects of your research were children? Could you still employ that methodology?" It is not always necessary for students to do the actual application (apply the statistical test, conduct the ethnographic research) but rather to think about the features of the problem in relation to specific applications.

Specify Skills or Knowledge and Ask Students to Identify Contexts in Which They Apply To further help students make connections between the skills and knowledge they possess and appropriate applications, turn the strategy just described around. In other words, specify a particular skill (e.g., a technique, formula, or procedure) or piece of knowledge (e.g., a theory or rule) and ask students to generate contexts in which that skill or knowledge would apply. For example, "Give me three statistical problems that a *T*-test could help you solve" or "Here is a data-gathering method used in ethnographic research; what questions could it be used to investigate?" Again, it is not necessary for students to do the actual application, but rather to think about the applicability of specific skills and knowledge to particular problems.

Provide Prompts to Relevant Knowledge Sometimes students possess skills or knowledge that are relevant to a new problem or situation but do not think to apply what they know. Small prompts to relevant knowledge and skills (such as "Where have we seen this style of brushwork before?" or "Would this concept be relevant to anything else we have studied?" or "Think back to the bridge example we discussed last week") can help students make connections that facilitate transfer. Over time, prompts from the instructor may become unnecessary as students learn to look for these connections on their own.

SUMMARY

In this chapter we have argued that to develop mastery, students must acquire a set of component skills, practice combining and integrating these components to develop greater fluency and automaticity, and then understand the conditions and contexts in which they can apply what they have learned. Students need to have these three elements of mastery taught and reinforced through practice. However, because instructors have often lost conscious awareness of these aspects of expert practice, they may inadvertently neglect them in their instruction. Consequently, it is of particular importance that instructors deliberately regain awareness of these elements of mastery so they can teach their students more effectively.

CHAPTER 6

What Kinds of Practice and Feedback Enhance Learning?

When Practice Does Not Make Perfect . . .

I teach a public policy course, and I believe strong communication skills are essential to moving up the ranks in the public sector. As a result, I require my students to write frequently. The three papers I assign focus on the different types of writing my students will potentially do: a policy briefing, a persuasive memo to their boss, and an editorial for a newspaper. I had expected the students' writing on these assignments to be at least decent because all of our students are required to take two writing courses in their first year. Then, when I saw the serious problems in their first paper submissions, I thought I could help them improve by giving feedback on the multiple aspects that needed improvement. So I have been spending an enormous amount of time grading and writing detailed margin comments throughout their papers, but it does not seem to be doing any good: the second and third assignments are just as bad as the first. As much as I think these assignments are useful because they prepare students for their future professional lives, I am ready to nix them because the students' writing is so poor and my efforts are bringing about little or no improvement.

Professor Norman Cox

130

They Just Do Not Listen!

Last semester, when I taught medical anthropology, the students' research presentations were all glitz and very little substance. So this time, because this final project is worth 50% of the final grade, I tried to forewarn my students: "Do not be seduced by technology; focus on substantive anthropological arguments as you create engaging presentations." And yet, it happened again. Last Tuesday, student after student got up in front of the class with what *they* believed to be strong presentations—fancy fonts in their PowerPoint slides, lots of pictures swishing on and off the screen, embedded video clips, and so on. It was clear they had spent hours perfecting the visuals. Unfortunately, although their presentations were visually appealing, the content was very weak. It had seemed like a good idea to give them free rein on these projects so they could have flexibility and "be creative," but that did not work out well at all! Some of the students had not done thorough research, and those who did tended merely to describe their findings rather than craft an argument. In other cases, students' arguments were not supported by sufficient evidence, and most of the images they included were not even connected to the research findings. I thought I was clear in telling them what I wanted and did not want. What is it going to take to make them listen?

Professor Tanya Strait

WHAT IS GOING ON IN THESE TWO STORIES?

In both stories, the professors and their students seem to be putting in time and effort without reaping much benefit. For example, Professor Cox makes lengthy and detailed comments on his students' writing but fails to see any improvement across assignments. Professor Strait's students spend an inordinate amount of time on aspects of the presentation that actually matter least to her, despite the guidance she gave. And both professors are understandably frustrated that students' learning and performance is not up to expectations. A theme running through both stories is that time is being misspent—just the kind of mistake that neither students nor instructors can afford to make.

In the first story, Professor Cox's students may be entering his course with fairly basic writing skills. Even though his students may be developing some new writing skills through the practice they get during the first writing assignment, these skills are not built on through the later assignments. Recall that Professor Cox's assignments involve different genres (policy briefing, memo, and editorial). Each assignment likely involves somewhat different writing skills to address the distinct goals, audiences, and writing styles specific to each (see Chapter 5 on mastery). Moreover, even though Professor Cox gives plenty of comments on his students' papers, the students probably have little opportunity—or incentive—to apply the feedback in subsequent practice because each assignment is so different from the previous.

In the second story, Professor Strait tells her students that their arguments should have substance and their presentations should be engaging. However, her students seem not to understand what constitutes a substantive anthropological argument or what characteristics she identifies with engaging presentations. Although it is true that Professor Strait's students have spent the bulk of the semester reading and analyzing anthropological arguments, they have had relatively little opportunity to conduct library research and construct arguments of their own. So this partly explains the disconnect. Similarly, although these students have accumulated a good deal of prior experience with presentations, they have not done so previously in her course, so they mistakenly equate putting glitz in their presentations with what Professor Strait wants. Thus, the students probably have only minimal skill at argument construction and yet ample skills related to preparing PowerPoint slides (e.g., adding animations, pictures, and sound). Thus, it appears that these students are falling back on the more comfortable task of working on visuals at the expense of articulating an effective argument in their presentations. Professor Strait reasonably assumes that her warnings should be sufficient to guide students, but students often need significantly more guidance and structure than we would expect in order to direct their efforts productively. With only one chance to get it right with regard to this large-scale project, these students end up losing a key learning opportunity.

WHAT PRINCIPLE OF LEARNING IS AT WORK HERE?

We all know that practice and feedback are essential for learning. Unfortunately, the biggest constraint in providing students with sufficient practice and feedback is the time they take—both on the part of students and faculty members.

Although we cannot control the length of a semester or class period, we can be more *efficient* in designing practice opportunities and giving feedback. Thus, this chapter focuses on ways to "work smarter" by exploring what kinds of practice and feedback are most productive.

It is important to acknowledge that all practice is not equal. In particular, there are more and less effective ways students can practice. Consider two music students who spend the same amount of time practicing a piece after having made several errors in a difficult passage. If one of the students practices for an hour, spending the majority of that time working on the difficult passage and then playing that passage in the context of the whole piece, this student will be likely to show sizable performance gains. However, if the other student spends the same hour but uses that time playing through the whole piece until they make an error and then returning to the start, much of their time will be spent repeating the early parts of the piece, even after they are already mastered. This is reminiscent of Professor Strait's students, who seem to spend much of their time on what they already know—how to make fancy PowerPoint slides—only to miss their main chance at practicing less developed skills. In other words, *how* students spend their time on a learning activity (either in or out of class) determines the benefits they gain.

This problem of unproductive practice is even worse when students fail to receive sufficient feedback along the way. Think about the first music student who spent considerable time on the problematic passage. Even though this student's approach has greater potential to strengthen the areas in need of improvement, this student still could have spent their time poorly. If they received no feedback while practicing the problematic passage, they might have entrenched bad habits or introduced new errors without realizing it. This music example thus also highlights the critical role that feedback plays in keeping learners' practice moving toward improvement. In other words, students need both productive practice *and* feedback.

> **Principle:** *Goal-directed practice coupled with targeted feedback are critical to learning.*

At one level, this principle states the obvious: practice and feedback are both important and helpful to learning. To be clear about terminology, we define

133

practice as any activity in which students engage their knowledge or skills (e.g., creating an argument, solving a problem, or writing a paper). We define *feedback* as information given to students about their performance that guides future behavior. However, the full potential of practice and feedback is not realized unless the two are aligned with each other and ultimately with the particular learning goals they are intended to promote. For example, Professor Cox provides an enormous amount of feedback, but it does little good because it is not coordinated with subsequent practice opportunities in which students could apply the feedback and refine their skills. By contrast, when repeated practice and feedback are focused on the same aspects of students' performance, students have the chance to practice and refine a consistent body of knowledge and skill. Figure 6.1 depicts this interaction as a cycle: practice produces observed performance that, in turn, allows for targeted feedback, and then the feedback guides further practice. In other words, practice and feedback opportunities are given in tandem so they can build on each other. Also note: this repeating cycle is directly

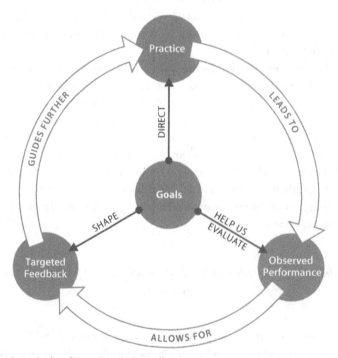

Figure 6.1. Cycle of Practice and Feedback

linked to the student's learning goals—the central hub that ideally influences each aspect of the cycle. For example, goals direct the nature of focused practice, provide the basis for evaluating observed performance, and shape the targeted feedback that guides students' future efforts.

Although practice and feedback ideally go hand in hand—as this chapter's principle and Figure 6.1 indicate—each has a sizeable body of literature. So we will discuss the research on each in separate sections, highlighting the importance of their coordination, and then summarize the research on *active learning*, a pedagogical approach that incorporates practice and feedback into class time.

WHAT DOES THE RESEARCH TELL US ABOUT PRACTICE?

Research has shown that learning and performance are best fostered when students engage in practice that (1) focuses on a specific goal or criterion for performance, (2) targets an appropriate level of challenge relative to students' current performance, and (3) is of sufficient quantity and frequency to meet the performance criteria. The following sections focus on these three characteristics of practice.

Focusing Practice on a Specific Goal or Criterion

Research shows that the amount of time someone spends in *deliberate practice*—rather than time spent in more generic kinds of practice—is what predicts continued learning and development of expertise in a given field (Ericsson et al., 2003). One of the key features of deliberate practice is that it involves working toward specific goals. As an illustration of the power of goal-focused practice, note that world-class musicians spend much of their time engaging in rather demanding practice activities, continually monitoring their performance toward a particular goal, and then, once it is achieved, pushing themselves to strive for a new goal (Ericsson & Charness, 1994; Ericsson & Lehmann, 1996). By contrast, we all know of people who have studied a musical instrument—even spending considerable time practicing it—but who do not achieve a very high level of performance. Ericsson's explanation of these contrasting outcomes is that those who spend their considerable practice time working deliberately toward specific

135

goals tend to go on to be expert musicians, whereas those who do not engage in such deliberate practice do not.

Intuitively, it makes sense that having specific goals for practice would be helpful to learning. Goals provide students with a focus for their learning, which leads to more time and energy going to that area of focus. Consistent with this, Rothkopf and Billington (1979) found that students who had specific goals when they were learning from a text paid more attention to passages that were relevant to their goals and hence learned the passages better. Another advantage of having a goal to direct one's learning is that one can monitor (and hence adjust) one's progress toward that goal along the way (see Chapter 8 on self-directed learning).

A key challenge in providing goal-directed practice is that instructors often think they are conveying specific goals to students when, in fact, they are not. This is natural because, as experts, we often see things very differently from our students (see Chapter 5 on mastery), and so we tend not to recognize when our stated goals are unclear to students or when students are likely to misinterpret our criteria. A case in point is Professor Strait, who thought she was being clear by advising her students to focus on "substantive anthropological arguments" and "engaging presentations"—two ideas that carried specific meaning in her field of expertise. However, her students did not share that expertise, so they did not share her sense of the specific goals for their work. Without a clear idea of what Professor Strait wanted, the students filled in the blanks based on their prior experience (see Chapter 2 on prior knowledge). Unfortunately, in this case, students' interpretations of the goals led them to spend their time in a way that gave more practice to skills they already had developed (such as creating glitzy PowerPoint presentations) and less practice to skills they needed to develop (such as creating anthropological arguments). When instructors do not clearly articulate their goals, it is difficult for students to know what (or how) to practice. For example, giving students the goal of "understanding a key concept" tells rather little about the nature or level of understanding that students should be trying to attain. By contrast, the goals of "recognizing when a key concept is applicable" or "explaining the key concept to a particular audience" or "applying the key concept to solve problems" are more concrete and directive. Note that these more specifically stated goals share several key features. First, they all are stated in terms of something students *do*, which automatically leads to more concrete specifications that students can more easily and accurately interpret. Second, all of these goals are stated in such a way that students' performance can be monitored and measured (by instructors as well as students themselves), which enables the provision of feedback to help students refine their performance or learning. For more information on articulating effective learning goals (also called *learning outcomes* or *objectives*), see Appendix G.

The notion of articulating goals in a measurable way still leaves open the question (to students and instructors) of *how much* of that measurable quality is enough for the goal to be achieved. Research has shown that clearly specified performance criteria can help direct students' practice and ultimately their learning. For example, Goodrich Andrade (2001) found that creating a rubric (a clear description of the characteristics associated with different levels of performance; see Appendix E on rubrics) and sharing it with students when an assignment is distributed leads to better outcomes—both in terms of the quality of work produced and students' knowledge of the qualities associated with good work.

An important caveat here, however, is that the goals one specifies must be in accord with what one really wants students to learn. For example, Nelson (1990) studied a case in which students were given detailed *and quantitative* specifications for what to include in a research paper, such as the requirement for at least three pieces of evidence supporting the central argument. In writing their papers, students took this and other similar prescriptions to heart—that is, including the required pieces of evidence in their papers. An important missing piece, however, was that the assignment specifications did not reference any higher-level goals, such as having a well-organized paper or making a coherent argument. Thus, the students often included three *unrelated* pieces of evidence in their papers (meeting the requirement but missing the point), and hence they tended to fall short on unstated criteria that were equally (if not more) important. A key implication of this work is that explicitly communicating goals for students' performance can indeed guide their work, but one must be sure that the stated goals accurately represent what students really need to do and learn.

Studying for exams and completing assigned readings are two common situations in which students' natural tendencies do not include goal-directed practice and where instructors' guidance is often insufficient. A typical scenario is that, when students are told to study for an exam, they reread their notes or the textbook without practicing what they really need. Or when students are given a text to read before class, they passively scan it without really processing or learning the material. A robust body of research has identified an alternative approach, called *retrieval practice*, as much more productive. Retrieval practice involves giving students low-stakes tests—not for the purpose of assessment but rather to

137

give students a concrete goal to guide their practice. The benefits of retrieval practice on learning are notable. For example, Roediger and Karpicke (2006b) had students read a text passage and then either (1) continue studying the passage (by rereading it) three more times or (2) take three open-ended tests where they were asked to recall information from the passage. Even though both groups of students spent the same amount of time in this initial phase, when tested on the passage a week later, those who had taken the tests performed significantly better than those who had "studied," even though the students rereading the text were exposed to 100% of the material multiple times whereas the students being tested were only exposed to the information they could recall.

Similar experiments have been implemented in real courses (Lyle & Crawford, 2011; McDaniel et al., 2011), across a range of materials (e.g., foreign language, statistics, world history, science), and with different test formats (e.g., multiple choice, short answer, essay). Across these different contexts, the results are remarkably consistent—namely, that engaging in retrieval practice by taking retrieval-practice tests is more effective for long-term retention than simply studying (see Roediger & Karpicke, 2006a, for a review). The benefit students get from this retrieval practice approach is often called "test-enhanced learning" or the "testing effect" to highlight the fact that the mere act of testing oneself, which involves actively retrieving information from memory, improves the likelihood that the information will be recalled at a later time. In the context of the current chapter, a key insight from this research is that tests not only measure learning but also they create deliberate practice opportunities that promote learning.

In the context of online learning environments, researchers have similarly studied the learning benefit of different types of instructional elements—namely, those requiring students to do a specific task versus those simply presenting information to students without a specific goal or criterion in mind. By analyzing students' learning gains in relation to the choices they made and time they spent completing different instructional elements in an online course—for example, reading text, watching instructional videos, or doing practice activities—Koedinger and others were able to tease out the learning benefits students derived from each type of instructional element. Results showed that doing practice activities led to six times the learning benefit of reading text or watching videos (Koedinger et al., 2015). Just like the "testing effect," this "doer effect" highlights that students learn more—and their time is better spent—when they are producing answers to specific questions or solutions to concrete problems, as compared to when they are consuming study materials like instructional text and videos. In other words, when students complete structured practice tasks, they are actually retrieving information and applying skills and, in so doing, are more likely to be engaging in productive practice.

Identifying the Appropriate Level of Challenge for Practice

Focusing on particular learning tasks and performance criteria is not enough. To ensure that students' practice has a significant effect on learning, the practice they do should be at an appropriate level of challenge and, as necessary, accompanied by the appropriate amount and type of support. An appropriate level of challenge is that which is neither too hard (the student struggles, makes many errors, and possibly gives up) nor too easy (the student completes the goal with little to no effort and is not pushed to improve). This relates to the notion of deliberate practice mentioned previously. As it turns out, deliberate practice more specifically is defined as working toward a *reasonable yet challenging goal* (Ericsson et al., 2003).

Identifying the appropriate level of challenge seems possible, albeit potentially time-consuming, to accomplish in one-on-one teaching and learning situations. Indeed, research has shown that the success of one-on-one tutoring is in large part driven by this capacity to tailor instruction to an individual student's needs (Anderson et al., 1995; Bloom, 1984; Merrill et al., 1992). Instructors who, given practical constraints, cannot provide different levels of challenge for individual students will be glad to know that research has also shown benefits from adjusting the difficulty of a practice task at the group level. In one study, Clarke et al. (2005) designed an instructional unit to teach students mathematical concepts and procedures through the use of a spreadsheet application. Instruction was either sequential (focused on learning spreadsheet skills first and then using those skills to learn the mathematics) or concurrent (learning and using these skills simultaneously). They found that, for students with little prior knowledge of spreadsheets, the concurrent learning condition was too demanding; these students showed better mathematics learning and performance in the sequential condition where the tasks were presented in isolation, making the challenge level more reasonable. Correspondingly, the opposite pattern held for more knowledgeable students. These results reinforce the idea that when novices are given too great a challenge, learning is hampered. This was probably part of the problem faced by Professor Strait's students, who were asked to take on challenges they had not practiced before (doing research in medical anthropology, constructing an argument of their own, and creating an engaging presentation).

Given a particular instructional activity, then, how can one effectively adjust its challenge level downward, particularly to address the needs of students who might not be quite ready to take on the activity in its full form? Research has shown that adding structure and support—also called *instructional scaffolding*—to a practice activity promotes learning when it helps students practice the target skills that would otherwise be too challenging. This relates to Vygotsky's zone of proximal development, which defines the optimal level of challenge for a student's learning in terms of a task that the student cannot perform successfully on his or her own but could perform successfully with some help from another person or group. A research study by Palinscar and Brown (1984) shows the success of this approach in helping students who were learning to read texts actively rather than passively. In particular, the researchers developed a protocol for pairs of students to follow in which students switched back and forth between the role of teacher and student, with the "teacher" asking the "student" a set of questions designed to exercise four strategic subskills of active reading—questioning, clarifying, summarizing, and predicting. These researchers found that when active reading skills were explicitly supported in this way, students' overall comprehension and retention improved markedly.

Research also indicates that instructional support does not need to come directly from another person to be helpful. For instance, Bereiter and Scardamalia developed a set of written prompts to help writing students target their efforts on two oft-neglected stages of the writing process: planning and revision. Because students did not naturally engage in these two stages on their own, following the prompts shifted their attention and effort toward (1) generating, refining, and elaborating their ideas and (2) evaluating their own writing, diagnosing problems, and deciding on revisions. As a result, students' writing process and product showed significant improvements, including a ten-fold increase in the frequency of idea-level revisions (Bereiter & Scardamalia, 1987). This set of research results suggests that if Professor Strait had employed various kinds of instructional scaffolds to support her students in completing their final project presentations, they probably would have spent their practice time more effectively, learned more from it, and lived up to her expectations on the final project presentation.

While instructional scaffolding is a powerful strategy for making overly challenging tasks more approachable for students, a different approach is needed when practice is too "easy." This can naturally happen when students are devising or selecting their own practice—that is, inadvertently choosing a level of difficulty that does not stretch them enough to learn and grow. It can also happen when instructors conceive of their role as creating practice activities that are smooth and easy for students—so students avoid making errors. But again, research on deliberate practice indicates that we should target practice on reasonable yet challenging goals in order to enhance learning. So how do we find an approach that will hit the mark in creating "desirable difficulties" (Bjork & Bjork, 2020)—that is, just enough challenge to promote learning but not too much so as to undermine it?

Research has identified a few approaches that target this sweet spot and tend to work across groups of students. One mentioned previously, called *retrieval practice*, involves giving students low-stakes tests such that students need to retrieve knowledge and engage skills they might otherwise avoid if left to their own (more passive) study strategies. The other two approaches to practice that tend to create desirable difficulties are (1) spaced practice and (2) interleaved practice.

Spaced practice involves adjusting the relative timing of multiple practice opportunities so that they are spread out in time (rather than massed together). For example, Rawson and Kintsch (2005) asked students to read a long text passage either once, twice massed, or twice spaced—that is, spread apart by a week. Then, students from each group were further divided and given a test on the passage either immediately after their last study session or two days after their last study session. Although massed practice led to the best performance for students taking the immediate test, it was the spaced practice that led to better performance on the delayed test. Given that real-world learning situations call for retention beyond an immediate test, these results demonstrate the value of spacing one's practice opportunities. In terms of creating "desirable difficulties" for learning, students who studied the passage for the second time after a week's delay likely had to work a bit harder to process it (because it was not something they had just read moments ago). Engaging that extra mental work was desirable for their learning in that it created stronger memories than simply reading the passage twice in immediate succession.

Interleaved practice is another way to create desirable difficulties from a given set of practice activities. Instead of manipulating how practice is distributed across time (as in spaced practice), interleaved practice involves adjusting how the practice activities are sequenced. Suppose you have a set of practice

141

problems where half of the problems draw on one body of knowledge and skill (call these type A problems) and the other half draw on a different body of knowledge and skill (type B problems). Interleaved practice involves assigning the practice problems in an alternating ABABAB sequence, whereas blocked practice would involve assigning all the A problems before all the B problems (i.e., AAABBB). Interleaved practice creates desirable difficulties because students cannot merely apply a similar solution multiple times in row; instead they must switch up their solution approach on each problem. (Note that with three problem types, interleaved practice could be any sequence without repeated problem types, e.g., ABCBCA. . . .)

Just as the desirable difficulty of spacing practice leads to better learning than massed practice, many research studies demonstrate that interleaved practice dominates blocked practice, even when the amount of time spent and/or the number of problems is kept the same (Kornell & Bjork, 2008; Rohrer & Taylor, 2007). Interestingly, however, when students in these studies are asked which type of practice is more effective, they often report, in error, that blocked practice seemed more effective. Researchers surmise that the relative ease of blocked practice misleads students to believe that they have learned more. So besides highlighting that some level of difficulty can be good for learning, this research also highlights the value of preparing students to see challenge (and even making mistakes) as a productive part of effective learning (see research on student beliefs about learning in Chapter 8 on self-directed learning).

Another advantage of finding an appropriate challenge level for student practice is that it can help students remain motivated to sustain their efforts (see Chapter 4 on motivation). For example, if a challenge is too small or too great, learners may become disengaged or apathetic. By contrast, if students feel that the challenge is reasonable, they will be more likely to persevere and work hard for the goal. Finally, engaging in a task that is at the right level of challenge for a person's knowledge and skills is one of the key predictors of *flow*—the state of consciousness in which a person is totally engaged in and experiencing deep enjoyment of a particular task (Csikszentmihalyi, 1991).

Accumulating Practice

In addition to identifying the two features that make practice most productive—goal-directed and appropriately challenging—research in this area also reiterates the importance of *time on task*. In other words, even if students have engaged in high-quality practice, they still need a sufficient *quantity* of practice for the benefits to accumulate (Healy et al., 1993; Martin et al., 2007). The idea that the benefits of practice accumulate only gradually may seem obvious, but the practical constraints of time and resources often lead faculty members to move from concept to concept or skill to skill rather quickly, giving students no more than a single opportunity to practice each. For example, Professor Cox is giving his students exposure to multiple genres, but this comes at the expense of giving students only a single opportunity to practice their skills in each of the genres he has assigned. If his goal is to simply expose students to the three different genres, without expecting them to gain proficiency in any of them, then the design of his activities is appropriate. But if his goal is for students to be able to write in each of the three genres at a professional level by the end of the course, then they would need more time on each.

Generally speaking, both professors and students underestimate the need for practice. Students often assume that if they can perform a task on one occasion in one context, their knowledge is secure, when in fact it is much more difficult than that (see Chapter 5 on mastery). It takes much more than one trial to learn something new, especially if the goal is for that new knowledge to be retained across time and transferred to new contexts.

Students at different phases of the learning process are especially likely to underestimate the value of practice. Even though practice (especially deliberate practice) gradually shows improvements, the amount of improvement often depends on where the student is in their learning process. As Figure 6.2 indicates, the early and late phases of learning tend to show relatively little effect of practice relative to the middle phase. These flatter portions at both ends of the curve tend to occur for two reasons.

The first reason is that the measures students often use to monitor their learning, such as accuracy, tend to be less sensitive at the extremes. So even though learning may be occurring, students do not see evidence of the change and hence feel like they are at a plateau. For example, consider a student who has just started learning to play the violin. Even though this student may be improving in several ways (better recall of the finger positions for different notes, increased accuracy in placement of the bow), the sound produced may be so poor that improvements are hard to detect. Or imagine a student learning to program in a new computer language. Early on, the student may be making so many errors in programming syntax that it is hard to discern that they are formulating increasingly better algorithms. A similar lack of sensitivity to

143

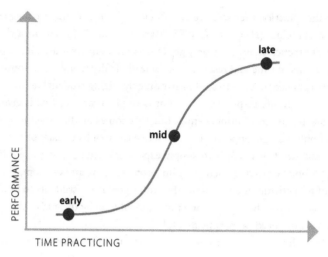

Figure 6.2. Unequal Effects of Practice on Performance

changing performance tends to occur on the upper end of learning because in this later phase students have managed to refine their performance to such a degree that they do not perceive changes, or the changes may occur in aspects of performance to which they are not attending. For example, advanced students may not recognize that they have actually improved in their ability to complete tasks more quickly and with less effort than they could before, or they may not realize that they are now able to reflect on their own processes *while* they complete complex tasks. Thus, because of this phenomenon at the early and late phases of learning, it is all the more important for instructors to highlight for students how their performance is changing or to provide more refined goals and criteria so that students can discern that they are improving.

The second reason that the learning curve in Figure 6.2 tends to be flatter at both ends is that the tasks we naturally assign for practice tend to pose too great a challenge for beginning students and too little challenge for accomplished students. As discussed, when students engage in practice that is either too challenging or not challenging enough, their learning is hampered. This reason offers additional support for the notion of setting an appropriate level of challenge for students.

In contrast to the early and late phases of learning, the middle part of the curve in Figure 6.2 is steep, which indicates students are able to see large improvements in performance with additional practice. This is because students in this phase have a foundation of knowledge and skills on which to build and because they are more likely to be able to detect improvements in their performance. This may also explain why students sometimes appear to take off in their development of knowledge and skill only after they have achieved a certain amount of learning.

Implications of This Research

Overall, the implications of the body of research on practice are that to achieve the most effective learning, students need *sufficient* practice that is *focused* on a specific goal or set of goals and is at an *appropriate level of challenge*. Given the constraints of time and resources that we must face, however, it is often difficult or impossible to increase students' practice time (either in or out of the class). Instead, the results in this chapter highlight the benefits of using a given amount of practice time more efficiently by focusing students' efforts on what they need to learn (rather than what they already know or may be more comfortable doing) and maintaining their practice at an appropriate and productive level of challenge.

WHAT DOES THE RESEARCH TELL US ABOUT FEEDBACK?

Goal-directed practice alone is insufficient to foster student learning. Goal-directed practice must be coordinated with targeted feedback in order to promote the greatest learning gains. The purpose of feedback is to help learners achieve a desired level of performance. Just as a map provides key information about a traveler's current position to help them find an efficient route to a destination, effective feedback provides information about a learner's current state of knowledge and performance that can guide them in working toward the learning goal. In other words, effective feedback can tell students *what* they are or are not understanding, *where* their performance is going well or poorly, and *how* they should direct their subsequent efforts.

Taking this map analogy a step further, imagine trying to find your way through a maze without any guiding information as to where you are relative to the entrance or exit; you could wander in circles without even realizing it, waste time, and become confused—even if you ultimately do find your way out of the maze. This situation is akin to the position that students are in without effective feedback. It is not surprising, then, that effective feedback can greatly facilitate students' learning. For example, consider two students who have the same misconception that leads them to solve several problems incorrectly. Suppose, however, that these two students receive feedback on their work at different times and with different content. One student solves all of these problems in a single, large homework assignment and, after submitting the assignment, gets it back a week later with the letter grade C. He notices from the points marked off that he failed to get full credit for even a single problem, so he infers that he is totally lost on this topic. Suppose the other student is in a course where the instructor includes a bit of problem-solving practice in each class session and then highlights some natural mistakes and how to remediate them after students have a chance to try a couple on their own. This student rather quickly gets some input from the instructor, indicating that in two of the practice problems he was making the same error. Once this is identified, the student is able to correct his understanding and then go on to solve that week's homework problems with this in mind.

Note that based on the different timing and content of the feedback, these two students may take very different paths from this point onward in the course. The first student, not realizing that it was only a single misconception that led to his level of performance, may believe he is unable to learn the current topic and hence skip any opportunities for further practice (e.g., not bothering to study for the upcoming exam). The second student, armed with information about where he went wrong, can work on additional problems to strengthen his new understanding of this tricky issue. In other words, feedback at the right time and of the right nature can promote student learning not only in the present but also in the future.

Consistent with this example, research points to two features of feedback that make student learning more effective and efficient: content and timing. First, feedback should communicate to students where they are relative to the stated goals and what they need to do to improve. Second, feedback should provide this information when students can make the most use of it, based on the learning goals and structure of activities you have set for them. Like so many aspects of teaching and learning, there is no single approach to feedback that will work across the variety of situations students and instructors encounter. Rather, the content and timing of feedback need to be considered in terms of the learning goals we have for our students, students' incoming level of knowledge and proficiency, and the practical constraints of the course. Research on what tends to make the content and timing of feedback most effective is discussed in the following two sections.

Communicating Progress and Directing Subsequent Effort

Feedback is most effective when it explicitly communicates to students about some specific aspects of their performance relative to specific target criteria and when it provides information that helps students progress toward meeting those criteria. This kind of feedback, which informs students' subsequent learning, is often called *formative* feedback. By contrast, *summative* feedback is that which gives a final judgment or evaluation of proficiency, such as grades or scores.

Extending our earlier analogy between using a map to navigate and receiving feedback to learn, consider the additional benefits of an electronic navigation system like Google Maps. This system has the capability of tracking the traveler's current position *relative to the destination*. It can communicate how far the traveler is from the destination and provide step-by-step directions to help the traveler reach it. Similarly, feedback can do much more than simply telling students that they are right or wrong; effective feedback involves giving students a clear picture of how their current knowledge or performance differs from the goal and providing information on adjustments that can help students adjust to reach the goal.

Research has long shown that feedback is more effective when it identifies particular aspects of students' performance they need to improve rather than providing a generic evaluation of performance, such as a grade or abstract praise or discouragement (Black & William, 1998; Cardelle & Corno, 1981). As illustrated by the example of the student who received a C with no comments on his homework, giving only a letter grade or numerical score tends not to be effective feedback. Although grades and scores provide some information on the *degree to which* students' performance has met the criteria, they do not explain *which aspects* did or did not meet the criteria and *how*. Moreover, feedback that is specific to the processes students are engaging in (e.g., helping students to properly approach a problem or to detect their own errors; see Chapter 8 on self-directed learning) has been associated with deeper learning (Balzer et al., 1989). In one study, students were learning to solve geometry problems on the computer, with feedback automatically provided whenever the computer detected an error in students' solutions. One group of students received generic messages indicating that they had

147

made an error, and another group received specific information about their errors and how to remediate them. The group with the more targeted feedback significantly outperformed the generic feedback group on a posttest assessing problem-solving skills (McKendree, 1990).

At the other extreme, simply giving students lots of feedback about their performance is also not necessarily an example of effective feedback. This is because too much feedback tends to overwhelm students and fails to communicate which aspects of their performance deviate *most* from the goal and therefore how they should focus their future efforts. For example, research has shown that too many comments in the form of margin notes on student writing are often counterproductive because students are either overwhelmed by the number of items to consider or because they focus their revision on a subset of the comments—that is, ones that involve detailed, easy-to-fix elements rather than more important conceptual or structure changes (Lamburg, 1980; Shuman, 1979).

Remember Professor Cox's lament of spending so much time making comments on his students' papers but seeing no improvement in later assignments? Providing too much information in his comments may have been part of the problem. In his case, giving fewer comments that addressed one or two top-priority issues would have provided his students with more targeted feedback. However, it is important to note that even if Professor Cox had given this kind of targeted feedback, it might not have been fully effective unless his students also had an opportunity to use the feedback in a rewrite or related assignment. The key idea here is that *targeted* feedback gives students prioritized information about how their performance does or does not meet the intended goal so they can understand how to improve their future performance.

Indeed, the full benefits of feedback can be realized only when the feedback adequately directs students' subsequent practice *and* when students have the opportunity to incorporate that feedback into further practice. Recall that in Professor Cox's course, students had only one opportunity to practice writing in each of the three genres he assigned. Although he may have conceived of this as repeated practice at the general skill of writing, these three assignments probably required rather different subsets of skills (see Chapter 5 on mastery). So, even if Professor Cox had provided targeted feedback on the first assignment, students might not have benefited much from it unless they had an opportunity to carry it into the next assignment.

How could Professor Cox use feedback in a way that ties in with students' opportunities for further practice? One option is that he could have included more repetition of assignments within the same genre and then asked students to incorporate his feedback into subsequent assignments. Alternatively, he could have asked students to submit a rough draft of each assignment, made targeted comments on those drafts, and then explicitly articulated that the final draft's goal was to address his comments. This scenario highlights the interaction between feedback and practice. Indeed, one can conceive of the practice that follows targeted feedback as a particularly tailored form of goal-directed practice.

Timing Feedback Appropriately

Whereas the research just discussed involves the content of feedback, it is also important to consider the appropriate timing of feedback. This involves both *how soon* feedback is given (typically, earlier is better) as well as *how often* (typically, more frequently is better). The ideal timing of feedback, however, cannot be determined by any general rule. Rather, it is best decided in terms of what would best support the goals you have set for students' learning. For example, going back to our Google Maps analogy, it is clear that a key feature of this system is that it gives feedback *when the driver needs it* to support the goal of reaching a particular destination as quickly as possible.

Generally, more frequent feedback leads to more efficient learning because it helps students stay on track and address their errors before they become entrenched. Ample research supports this conclusion (see Hattie & Timperley, 2007, for a review). However, given practical constraints, this is often difficult. Fortunately, research shows that even minimal feedback on student writing can lead to better second drafts because the feedback gives students a better sense of what their readers do and do not understand (Traxler & Gernsbacher, 1992). This result highlights that giving even a modest amount of feedback, especially when it is given early, can be helpful. This result also suggests that if Professor Strait had established milestones early in her students' project work, it could have enabled her to offer feedback earlier on in the process, before her students went off track.

This research does not mean, however, that greater frequency of feedback is always better. Again, *timeliness* of the feedback is a significant factor. For example, consider a study in which college students were learning to write mathematical functions in a spreadsheet application (Mathan & Koedinger, 2005). The particular goal for student learning in this situation was not only that they be able to write these functions accurately but also that they be able to recognize and fix

149

their own errors. Students who received feedback immediately after they made a mistake scored lower on final assessments compared to students who received delayed feedback. Although surprising at first, this result makes sense when one realizes that the immediate feedback group was missing the opportunity to practice recognizing and repairing their own errors. By contrast, the students receiving delayed feedback had a chance to fix their own errors so they had more practice at the corresponding skills. That is, when the delayed feedback group made errors, feedback was given only when they (1) showed sufficient signs of not having recognized their error or (2) made multiple failed attempts at fixing their error. In this way, one could argue that even though it was not immediate, their feedback was given in a more timely manner relative to the learning goals at hand.

Implications of This Research

There are three key implications of this research on what makes feedback more effective. The feedback must (1) focus students on the key knowledge and skills you want them to learn, (2) be provided at a time and frequency when students will be most likely to use it, and (3) be linked to additional practice opportunities for students. As we saw in some of this chapter's sections, each of these aspects of feedback must align with the goals you have set for students' learning. It is best to find a type and frequency of feedback that enables students to reap the benefits of feedback while staying actively engaged in monitoring their own learning—in other words, feedback that does not undermine students' progress in becoming independent, self-regulated learners. Giving too little detail in feedback can leave students unclear on what they need to do to improve, whereas giving too much detail can overwhelm them or mislead them as to what aspects are higher priority. Similarly, giving feedback too infrequently can leave students floundering without enough information to direct their learning, whereas giving feedback too frequently can potentially irritate students or lead them to depend on the feedback rather than on themselves.

In addition to balancing the amount and timing of feedback to make it most effective, it is often necessary to pay attention to the practical aspects of giving feedback. For example, the instructor's time in composing or tailoring feedback and the students' time in processing and responding to feedback is a key consideration in guiding how and when to give feedback. Note that feedback can be usefully targeted without being individualized or coming from the instructor, therefore increasing efficiency (see "Strategies That Address the Need for Targeted Feedback" at the end of this chapter).

WHAT DOES THE RESEARCH TELL US ABOUT ACTIVE LEARNING?

In recent years, *active learning*—that is, "the process of learning through activities and/or discussion in class, as opposed to passively listening to an expert" (Freeman et al., 2014, pp. 8413-8414)—has become a commonly referenced approach to teaching and learning. It is arguably not a single strategy or intervention but rather a label used to represent a variety of strategies that involve students making overt actions and (ideally) generating new outputs, such as solving a sample problem or contributing to in-class groupwork (Chi & Wylie, 2014). Examples of active learning strategies include the following:

Think-pair-share—Students think individually about their response to an instructor-posed prompt, they pair up with a neighbor, and then the partners share their responses and discuss. Optionally, instructors may invite students to share their responses with the whole class at different points in this sequence.

Polling/concept tests—Students respond individually to a conceptual question (often posed in multiple-choice format) in a way that the instructor can easily process their responses. This strategy may involve the use of technology (e.g., clickers or targeted apps students can access on their smartphone to enter their responses) and is often used in combination with think-pair-share.

In-class collaborative group work—Students work in small groups to tackle a specific, assigned task.

Because active learning involves each student doing something relevant to the course learning goals (i.e., practicing) in a situation where the instructor and/or peers can comment on what the student did (i.e., receiving feedback), we dedicate this last research section on practice and feedback to discussing the literature on active learning and its implications.

The body of research on active learning—encompassing both how to enact active learning in one's teaching and the impact of active learning on student outcomes—is big and broad. Although much of this research is conducted in the context of STEM courses, active learning is applicable across disciplines. Many active learning studies have focused on its efficacy, leveraging a study design in which one active learning strategy (or possibly more than one) is compared

151

against traditional lecture as the "control." For example, Armbruster et al. (2009) measured student performance on the final exam across three years of the same introductory biology course (all taught by the same instructor), where the first year was taught via traditional lecture and the second and third years, after a course redesign, were taught using an active learning approach. By contrast, Deslauriers et al. (2011) compared two different sections of the same course (taught during the same semester) in which a single week was taught by different methods and instructors—one section via lecture and the other via active learning—and then assessed via the same quiz questions. Even though these two research studies were designed very differently, the active learning approach was similar—for example, small-group problem-solving, conceptual clicker questions, and instructor feedback on students' responses during class time—as were the results. In both studies, students experiencing active learning showed higher performance, on average, than those experiencing lecture.

Given that many such studies comparing active learning to lecturing have been conducted, Freeman and others (2014) conducted a meta-analysis to quantitatively combine the results and estimate the overall impact of active learning in the context of STEM courses. Results showed that, averaging across 225 studies, active learning led to better outcomes than lecture, both in terms of examination scores (6% better, on average, for active learning) and failure rates (1.5 times worse for traditional lecture). In addition to overall effects, this meta-analysis investigated the size of active learning's benefits for different categories of studies. For example, the researchers found that, regardless of the STEM discipline (e.g., biology, math, chemistry, engineering, physics, etc.), active learning showed a consistent advantage over lecture, across both exam scores and failure rates. And active learning was more effective than lecture across all class sizes, but with the largest effects arising in small classes, that is, classes with fewer than 50 students.

Building on this important work, Theobald and others (2020) conducted a follow-up meta-analysis, using a similar approach but studying active learning's potential to reduce inequities in student outcomes in STEM courses. In other words, this meta-analysis was addressing the question: How does active learning versus traditional lecturing affect underrepresented minority and low-income students across a wide array of STEM disciplines, courses, instructors, and intervention types? Averaging over 15 studies (9,238 total students) that compared the effect of active learning versus lecture on exam scores, and 26 studies (44,606 total students) comparing the effect of these two approaches on failure rates, the researchers found compelling and encouraging results: relative to lecture, active learning on average "reduced achievement gaps in examination scores by 33% and narrowed gaps in passing rates by 45%" (Theobald et al., 2020, p. 6476). Looking further into differential effects across different categories of studies, results indicated that active learning's benefits were focused on classes that implemented high-intensity active learning (i.e., the bulk of class time spent in active learning). This suggests that instructors seeking to reduce inequities in student outcomes via active learning should target implementing active learning for a high proportion of class time.

Another review of the active learning literature that takes a more qualitative approach identifies four different levels of active learning and shows that they convey different levels of learning benefits (Chi & Wylie, 2014). The top level, producing the greatest learning benefit, is called *interactive* and involves students collaboratively generating output (e.g., jointly solving problems or discussing a case study). Interactive is followed by *constructive*, which involves students generating output independently (e.g., answering a question or solving a problem solo) and is, in turn, followed by *active*, which involves students doing something but not actually generating output (i.e., hands on but not necessarily minds on). Finally, *passive* is the bottom level and is associated with the smallest learning benefit. This framework, called interactive constructive active passive (ICAP), helps clarify the features that make active learning strategies more effective. Indeed, Chi and Wylie cite several examples showing that a given instructional strategy, when implemented at different ICAP levels, leads to predicted differences in learning impact. As such, ICAP can be used as a tool (and mnemonic device) to guide instructors in implementing active learning strategies in more effective ways.

Implications of This Research

Amidst the overwhelming evidence that active learning approaches dominate lectures in terms of student outcomes, there are several specific implications of this research worth reiterating. First, active learning appears to benefit learning across a variety of situations (e.g., different active learning strategies, class sizes, and disciplines), so it is worthwhile trying some active learning strategies in your own teaching. Second, it appears that the more class time spent in active learning the better, so instructors should target implementing active learning for a good proportion of their class

---

time if they can. Third, when implementing active learning strategies, aim for those in which students are not just active with their bodies but are also constructing novel responses and/or ideally interacting with other students as they do so. And finally, instructors should feel encouraged to incorporate active learning approaches into their teaching regardless of modality, because research has demonstrated its benefit in both in-person and online learning contexts.

WHAT STRATEGIES DOES THE RESEARCH SUGGEST?

Here we present strategies that can help you provide students with (1) goal-directed practice and (2) targeted feedback. In both cases, the focus is on how to do so in the most efficient and feasible ways.

Strategies That Address the Need for Goal-Directed Practice

Conduct a Prior Knowledge Assessment to Target an Appropriate Challenge Level Students come into our classes with a broad range of preexisting knowledge, skills, and competencies. Giving a prior knowledge assessment (such as a survey, pretest, or early ungraded assignment) can help you gauge students' strengths and weaknesses in order to better target their practice at the right level (based on where they are, not where you wish they were). A performance assessment (e.g., actual problems to solve or terms to define) will provide the best indication of what students actually know or can do, while a survey asking them about the level of their knowledge (e.g., can they define or apply, do they know when to use) will give you a sense of what students *believe* they know or can do. (See additional related strategies in Chapter 2 on prior knowledge and Appendix C for more information on incorporating student self-assessments.)

Be More Explicit About Your Goals in Your Course Materials Without specific goals for the course as a whole or for individual assignments, students often rely on their assumptions to decide how they should spend their time. This makes it all the more important to articulate your goals clearly (in your course syllabus and with each specific assignment), so students know what your expectations are and can use them to guide their practice. Students are more likely to use the goals to guide their practice when the goals are stated in terms of what students should be able to *do* at the end of an assignment or the course. (See Appendix G for more information on articulating learning objectives.)

Use a Rubric to Specify and Communicate Performance Criteria When students do not know what the performance criteria are, it is difficult for them to practice appropriately and to monitor their progress and understanding. A common approach to communicating performance criteria is through a *rubric*—a scoring tool that explicitly represents the performance expectations for various aspects of a given assignment. (See Appendix E for more information on rubrics.)

Build in Multiple Opportunities for Practice, Including Low-Stakes Tests Because learning accumulates gradually with practice, multiple assignments of shorter length or smaller scope tend to result in more learning than a single assignment of great length or large scope. With the former, students get more opportunity to practice skills and can refine their approach from assignment to assignment based on feedback they receive. For example, instructors who typically give a mid-term and a final exam might incorporate weekly quizzes for more frequent, focused practice. Even without counting the quiz scores toward the final grade (and without incurring an increased grading burden), the research from this chapter suggests that such quizzes could be quite beneficial for student learning. Indeed, some instructors have found success from breaking their big exams into multiple, shorter mini-tests, administered across several weeks, and then eliminating the in-class exam. This strategy can also be applied to free one's thinking beyond the traditional term paper and consider multiple, shorter writing assignments instead (e.g., a letter, program notes, or a short policy memo). Bear in mind, however, that a single opportunity to practice a given kind of assignment is likely to be insufficient for students to develop the relevant set of skills, let alone to be able to incorporate your feedback on subsequent, related assignments.

Ensure Multiple Practice Opportunities Are Spread Out in Time While a key first step in promoting better practice is to include *multiple* practice opportunities for the various skills, concepts, or assignment types you want your students to master, the second step is to make sure that these multiple opportunities are spread out over time. In courses where the learning is cumulative, repeated practice of key concepts and skills *across* the semester is natural. In other contexts, think about how you might deliberately return to something from earlier in the course and give students an extra dose of practice. For example, consider taking a problem from one homework and assigning a version of that problem later—say, at a few weeks' delay. Or, for smaller-scale written or project work that students complete early in the semester, make sure there are additional opportunities for similar practice later in the semester as well. Otherwise, positive learning gains that are achieved all in one burst may not be well retained.

Intersperse Lectures with Active Learning Even though your teaching role models may have been excellent lecturers, the evidence in favor of active learning over lecturing is overwhelming. Active learning—in which students are doing more during class than passively listening and taking notes—leads to significantly better learning outcomes and can even reduce some of the inequities we see in learning outcomes. Remember, there are many different options for active learning strategies, so you can select the one(s) that fit your course format and size, discipline, and time available. Some instructors find it useful to aim for interspersing a few active learning activities into each class period (e.g., at least one every 20 minutes or so). Feel encouraged to experiment with different active learning strategies until you hone in on the ones that work best for your students and your teaching context. (See Appendix H for a table of active learning strategies.)

Build Scaffolding into Assignments Adjust scaffolding to a task so that it continues to target an appropriate level of challenge for students. Scaffolding refers to the process by which instructors give students instructional supports early in their learning and then gradually remove these supports as students develop greater mastery and sophistication. One way to apply scaffolding to a more complex assignment is to ask students to first practice working on discrete phases of the task and, later, ask students to practice integrating them.

Set Expectations About Practice Students can underestimate the amount of time an assignment requires. As a result, it is vital to provide students with guidelines for the amount, type, and level of practice required to master the knowledge or skills at the level you expect. There are at least two ways to help you estimate the time students will need. Some faculty members collect data by asking students, over a number of semesters, how long an assignment took to complete. They can then report to their current students the average and range of time spent by past students. Other faculty members adhere to a general rule of thumb that it takes students approximately three to four times as long as it would take them to complete an assignment. This ratio may vary from situation to situation, however, so it is worthwhile to try multiple strategies for this estimation and to adjust based on one's experience, as necessary.

Give Examples or Models of Target Performance In addition to clear assignment descriptions, rubrics, and other explanations of your expectations, it can also be helpful to *show* students examples of what the target performance looks like (such as a model design, an effective paper, or a robust solution to a problem). Sharing samples of past student work can help students see how your performance criteria can be put into practice in an actual assignment. For example, some instructors illustrate how a sample or model of student work meets the assignment criteria by demonstrating how it would be evaluated, that is, by annotating its strong and weak features or even by applying the assignment rubric to the sample and showing how each rubric criterion maps onto particular features.

Show Students What You Do Not Want In addition to sharing exemplary models of target performance (i.e., highlighting what you want students to do), it can be helpful to contrast those with examples of what you do *not* want, by illustrating common misinterpretations students have shown in the past or by explaining why some pieces of work do not meet your assignment goals. For example, in the case of writing or giving presentations, it is often helpful to share samples that are annotated to highlight weak features. Such samples can also be used to give students practice at distinguishing between high- and low-quality work. To get students more actively involved and check their understanding, you can ask students to grade a sample assignment by following a rubric. (See Appendix E on rubrics.)

Refine Your Goals and Performance Criteria as the Course Progresses As students move through a course practicing various skills, you may need to add new challenges, refine your goals to meet students' continually changing proficiency, or both. For example, once students have acquired competency with a skill, you may want them to be able to apply that skill more quickly, with less effort, or in more diverse contexts. You need to continually articulate the increasingly sophisticated goals you want students to work toward.

Strategies That Address the Need for Targeted Feedback

Look for Patterns of Errors in Student Work Within a class, students can often share common errors or misconceptions that are revealed only when you make a concerted effort to look for patterns. For example, you might identify an exam question that many students missed or a homework assignment that was particularly difficult for many students. You may also notice that during your office hours multiple students are asking the same type of question or are making the same kind of mistake. If you are grading student work, you have access to this information and can seek out the patterns of errors. If you have TAs grading, ask them to summarize any major patterns of errors or misconceptions and report these to you. Once you have identified common patterns across students, you can provide feedback to the class as a whole using the following strategies.

Prioritize Your Feedback The question of exactly what information feedback should include is dependent on many aspects of the course context: your learning objectives (for the course and the particular assignment), level of students, what they most need to improve, and the time you have available. So the key to being efficient while still providing effective feedback is to think carefully about what information will be most useful to students at a particular point in time and to prioritize that information in your feedback. In many cases, it is not necessary or even best to give feedback on all aspects of students' performance but rather focus your feedback on key aspects of the assignment. One way to do this is to offer feedback on a single dimension at a time (e.g., one aspect of presenting an argument, one piece of the design process, or one step in problem-solving). This strategy avoids overwhelming students with too much feedback and enables them to engage in targeted practice—that is, with a specific goal in mind.

Balance Strengths and Weaknesses in Your Feedback Students are often unaware of the progress they are making, so communicating to them the areas where they are doing well or have improved is just as important as communicating to them the areas where they lack understanding or need further improvement. The positive feedback indicates which aspects of their knowledge and performance should be maintained and built on, whereas the negative feedback indicates what aspects should be adjusted (and, ideally, how). Moreover, beginning with targeted feedback that is positive can increase students' sense of efficacy and hence enhance their motivation. How you balance positive versus negative feedback for a given class or for a particular student should depend on your priorities and their needs.

Design Frequent Opportunities to Give Feedback The prerequisite to giving frequent feedback is to provide multiple opportunities for students to practice using their knowledge and skills. More tasks of shorter length or smaller scope provide the frequency of feedback that enables students to refine their understanding. This also makes a more manageable workload for you and your students. As indicated in other strategies in this section, not all feedback needs to be focused on individual students or come from the instructor. These strategies reduce the load on instructors in giving frequent feedback.

Provide Feedback at the Group Level Not all feedback has to be individual to be valuable. Although you might want to write notes on individual assignments (which takes more time and hence decreases how quickly you can get feedback to students), you might at times identify the most common errors that students committed, provide the group with this list, and discuss those errors. In a similar vein, you can show the group two examples of high-quality performance and discuss the features that make this work A level.

Provide Real-Time Feedback at the Group Level In a classroom situation, especially large lectures, instructors often assume that it is impossible to give effective feedback. However, by posing questions to the class in a format that enables easy collection of their responses, instructors can overcome this challenge. You can collect students' responses quickly in a paper-based way (with color-coded index cards) or with interactive technology (often called personal response systems, or clickers). In either case, the instructor poses a question and students respond (either by raising the index card corresponding to their answer or by submitting their answer choices via clicker). The instructor can then easily glean the proportion of correct/incorrect answers (either by scanning the room for the different colors of index cards or viewing the computer screen that tallies the clicker responses). Based on this information, the instructor can decide how to give appropriate feedback to the class as a whole. For example, the instructor may simply indicate that there was a high proportion of incorrect answers and ask students to discuss the question in small groups before polling them again. Alternatively, the instructor might recognize a common misconception in students' responses and provide further explanation or examples, depending on the nature of the misconception.

Incorporate Peer Feedback Not all feedback has to come from you to be valuable. With explicit guidelines, criteria, or a rubric, students can provide constructive feedback on each other's work. This can also help students become better at identifying the qualities of good work and diagnosing their own problems. In addition to the advantages to students, peer feedback enables you to increase the frequency of feedback without increasing your load. Keep in mind, however, that for peer feedback to be effective, you need to clearly explain what it is, the rationale behind it, how students should engage in it, and—as this chapter attests—give students adequate practice at doing it (with feedback!) for it to reach its potential. (See Appendix I on peer review.)

Leverage Technology Tools to Provide Automated Feedback Sometimes the barrier to providing feedback is that it is too time-consuming. To make it more feasible, in addition to leveraging peers and providing feedback at the group level, technology tools can sometimes be helpful. Whether your course is online, in-person, or some combination of both, consider assigning students to complete some of their practice via an appropriate technology tool that provides automated feedback. Most learning management systems have quizzing functions that can provide targeted feedback on specific question types (e.g., multiple choice, fill in the blank). Other tools are available that provide practice and automated feedback on more complex problems (especially look for this if you are in a STEM field, where a greater prevalence of automated practice and feedback tools appear to be available). Even peer feedback can become more efficient for the instructor by leveraging the relevant technology tools. Bear in mind: if you would like to use technology in your course, ensure that all of your students have appropriate access to it and the relevant preparation or training (which you might need to provide) so they can use it effectively. Do not assume that all students have access to the devices, apps, and internet connectivity that your tool choice might require, and do not assume that all students are equally tech savvy.

Require Students to Specify How They Used Feedback in Subsequent Work Feedback is most valuable when students have the opportunity to reflect on it so they can effectively incorporate it into future practice, performance, or both. Because students often do not see the connection between or among assignments, projects, exams, and so on, asking students to explicitly note how a piece of feedback affected their practice or performance helps them see and experience the complete learning cycle. For example, some instructors who assign multiple drafts of papers require students to submit with each subsequent draft their commented-on prior draft with a paragraph describing how they incorporated the feedback. An analogous approach could be applied to a project assignment that included multiple milestones.

SUMMARY

In this chapter, we have tried to move beyond simple maxims such as "practice makes perfect" or "the more feedback, the better" in order to hone in on the critical features that make practice and feedback most effective. Key features of effective practice include (1) focusing on a specific goal or criterion for performance, (2) targeting an appropriate level of challenge relative to students' current performance, and (3) being of sufficient quantity and frequency so students' skills and knowledge have time to develop. Key features of effective feedback are that it (1) communicates to students where they are relative to the stated goals and what they need to do to improve and (2) provides this information to students when they can make the most use of it. Then practice and feedback can work together such that students are continuing to work toward a focused goal and incorporating feedback received in a way that promotes further development toward the goal. To increase the practice and feedback students can experience *during class*, active learning is a pedagogical approach that can be implemented at small or large scale, with many benefits for student learning. Then, whether they are incorporated in class or outside of class, practice and feedback opportunities that are designed with these beneficial features in mind can help make the learning-teaching process not only more effective but also more efficient.

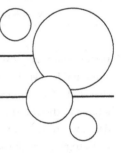

CHAPTER 7

Why Does Course Climate Matter for Student Learning?

How Did That Get by Me?

I *thought* my online sociology of the family course was going well. The metrics from our learning management system showed robust engagement, and I had not heard any complaints from students. So I was caught off guard when Sharice, my TA, called me to say she had concerns. "The feeling of the class has changed," she said. "At the beginning of the semester, there was a good vibe but now something has . . . gone sour." She speculated that the change stemmed from an argument about arranged marriage on a course discussion thread about divorce a few weeks previously. Apparently, a student—Rafi—had written that the divorce rates in Bangladesh, where his parents were born, were low because they have arranged marriages. He suggested—maybe joking?—that Americans should give arranged marriage a try. According to Sharice, several of Rafi's classmates thought he was criticizing American culture, and they started throwing out derogatory comments about Muslim societies: who would agree to marry a stranger and what do you expect in cultures where women have no rights—that kind of thing. Eventually a classmate pointed out that the discussion was getting off topic and redirected conversation back to the prompt. "The argument seemed to end," said Sharice, "but I feel like the class lost its mojo right about then. It hasn't been the same since." To her credit, Sharice had reached out to Rafi to see how he was doing. "He's okay," she said, "but he told me he wishes the course represented a wider range of views on marriage and the family and was more open to considering customs and practices in other parts of the world. He said he didn't expect ethnocentrism in a sociology course."

I hung up the phone with an awful feeling in the pit of my stomach. I know I should pay more attention to discussion boards, but *how*, with so many classes to teach, grant deadlines looming, and more committee work than is remotely reasonable? I feel terrible that this whole discussion board kerfuffle got by me. Rafi's comment about the course also really stung. I appreciate and value cultural differences and thought I'd created a course that is a safe space for dialogue, but maybe it isn't. Geez, how did I mess this up? And how can I get my course back on track?

Professor Susannah Jenkowski

No Good Deed Goes Unpunished

There's been a lot of discussion in my department about how to get more female students into electrical engineering. This is something I believe is very important, so I've gone out of my way to support and encourage the women in my classes. I know engineering can be an intimidating environment for women, so I always try to provide extra help and guidance to female students when they're working on problem sets in small groups. I've also avoided calling on women in class, because I don't want to put them on the spot. So you can imagine my frustration when a student reported to me a few weeks ago that one of my teaching assistants had made a blatantly derogatory comment during recitation about women in engineering. I've had a lot of problems with this TA, who has very strong opinions and a tendency to belittle people he doesn't agree with, but I was particularly unhappy about this latest news. I chastised the TA, of course, and gave him a stern warning about future misconduct, but unfortunately the damage was already done: one female student in that recitation (who seemed particularly promising) has dropped the course, and I can tell from facial expressions and body language that others are unhappy, too. I braced myself for complaints on the early course evaluations I collected last week, and some students did complain about the sexist TA, but what really baffled me was that they complained about me, too! One student wrote that I "patronized" female students while another wrote that the class was "unfair to us guys" since I "demanded more from the men in the course." I have no idea what to make of this and am beginning to think there's simply no way to keep everyone happy.

Professor Felix Guttman

WHAT IS GOING ON IN THESE TWO STORIES?

In both of these cases, something has gone wrong in the social and emotional fabric of a course that appears to have affected students' ability to engage productively with course material and with one another. Moreover, in both cases, the actions of the instructor (or lack thereof) contributed to or exacerbated the situation, creating a course climate that impeded rather than facilitated learning.

In the first scenario, Professor Jenkowski, busy with other work, has neglected her course discussion boards, missing a significant argument among students and failing to address the ensuing tensions in a constructive and timely manner. As a result, students who were once engaged and happy have withdrawn. The classroom discussion space has ceased to be a safe one for honest exchange, and the once-productive learning environment has soured. It is difficult to know whether trust can be restored. In addition, Professor Jenkowski appears to have an issue with her course content, which seems to have taken Western cultural conventions as the default or norm, thus leaving at least one student feeling like an outsider.

In the second scenario, we see a well-meaning instructor—Professor Guttman—doing his best to reach out to female students, whom he worries (with good reason) may be marginalized in a male-dominated field. He is justifiably upset by the blatantly sexist behavior of his TA and chastises him, but he may not have addressed it with the students it affected. Moreover, he seems unaware of how students perceive his own behavior. In fact, his attempts to support female students by providing extra help and reduced pressure has backfired. To the women in the class, it signals a lack of faith in their competence and abilities, while the men perceive it as just plain unfair to them. As a result, students seem dissatisfied and disaffected, to the point where one promising student has dropped the course altogether.

In both stories, we see instructors who care about their students and consider their classrooms inclusive and welcoming. Yet in both cases, their actions—or their failure to act—have generated a course climate that is not conducive to learning—at least not for everyone.

WHAT PRINCIPLE OF LEARNING IS AT WORK HERE?

As educators, we are primarily concerned with building intellectual and creative skills in our students. But students are not merely cognitive beings. Indeed, the social and emotional dimensions of learning are arguably far more influential than purely cognitive ones (Cavanagh, 2016). Social and emotional factors can either direct attention and energy toward learning (if students are motivated and curious) or away from learning (if students are fearful or lack motivation.) Because social and emotional factors are so significant, the classroom climates instructors create are of critical importance, shaping learning, engagement, achievement, and persistence in significant ways (Cavanagh, 2016; Immordino-Yang, 2016). While a broad and growing literature speaks to the negative influence a toxic or alienating classroom climate can have on learning, this same research provides insight into how instructors can build classroom environments that are both intellectually challenging and welcoming of all students, thus enhancing learning in powerful ways.

> **Principle:** *The classroom environment we create can profoundly affect students' learning, positively or negatively.*

WHAT DOES THE RESEARCH TELL US ABOUT COURSE CLIMATE?

Course climate refers to the intellectual, social, emotional, and physical environments in which students learn. Climate is determined by a constellation of interacting factors operating both within and outside the physical or virtual classroom, including course content, the degree to which students feel they belong in the course and discipline, the tone instructors maintain across a range of contexts, and the extent to which instructors help to create a sense of presence or connection within the course. Note that courses do not exist in a vacuum but rather in social and political contexts distinguished by systemic inequities and power hierarchies. These realities must be grappled with, not ignored. It is incumbent on instructors to take this broader context into account as they consider how to foster a learning environment that welcomes, embraces, and empowers all students but most urgently students from groups that have been historically marginalized.

The same course climate, of course, can be experienced very differently by different students. For example, in both Professor Guttman's and Professor Jenkowski's courses, male and female students had negative reactions to the

165

same course, but for different reasons. By the same token, the same course climate may feel welcoming and validating to some students (usually, though not always, students from majority cultures) but unwelcoming and invalidating to other students (usually, though not always, students from minoritized cultures). As discussed in Chapter 1, students and faculty members both enter the learning environment shaped by their backgrounds and cultures, not to mention the biases, accumulated slights, and historical traumas of the larger world. Thus, no course climate is neutral, much as we might like it to be. The goal, then, should be to work to shape the environment so that all learners feel seen, heard, and supported, as well as challenged intellectually.

A common but simplistic way of thinking about climate is in binary terms: climate is either good (inclusive, productive) or bad (chilly, marginalizing). However, research suggests that it may be more accurate to think of climate as a continuum (see Figure 7.1). A framework identified in one study by DeSurra and Church (1994) is worth exploring in some detail. Although it is somewhat dated, more recent research arrives at similar conclusions (Wall & Evans, 1999). DeSurra and Church explored the experiences of LGBTQIA college students, asking those students to categorize the climate of their courses as either *marginalizing* or *centralizing*, depending on student perceptions of whether an LGBTQIA perspective would be included and welcomed in the course or excluded and discouraged. In order to further categorize these perceptions, the students indicated whether the messages were *explicit* (evidenced by planned and stated attempts to include or to

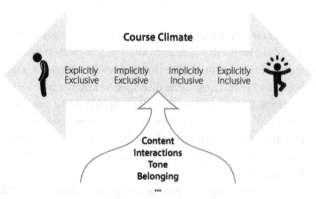

Figure 7.1. Factors That Influence Course Climate and Thus Learning and Performance

marginalize) or *implicit* (e.g., inferred from the consistent absence of an LGBTQIA perspective). This classification produced a continuum that we believe is useful for thinking about classroom climate in a broader sense than in relation to LGBTQIA issues only.

At the most inclusive level of the continuum, we find *explicitly centralizing* climates. In courses with explicitly centralizing climates, marginalized perspectives are not only validated when students spontaneously bring them up but also they are intentionally and overtly integrated in the content. The climate here is characterized by obvious and planned attempts to include a variety of perspectives. Often, syllabi in these courses contain provisions (such as discussion ground rules and course policies) to foster sensitivity to the perspectives that students bring to the classroom. If Professor Jenkowski included discussion of non-Western marriage practices (or, for that matter, nontraditional marriage arrangements in the west) as part of her course, it would help to create a more explicitly centralizing course climate.

Moving toward the less inclusive end of the continuum, we find *implicitly centralizing* climates. These climates are characterized by unplanned responses that validate alternative perspectives and experiences. Imagine, for instance, if Professor Jenkowski had been monitoring her discussion board when Rafi commented and had stepped in to say, "Rafi, you may be joking but you've drawn our attention to an important point: the expectations put on marriage and the social structures that support married couples differ markedly from culture to culture and that, of course, affects divorce rates. Let's talk about that more." She might have been able to validate Rafi's perspective, explain the usefulness of thinking about marriage and divorce from a cross-cultural perspective, and avert the defensiveness with which her other students responded. If students made culturally insensitive or insulting comments, she could have immediately addressed them. Instead, though, the unmoderated discussion created an explicitly marginalizing environment that was not conducive to risk-taking and disclosure and likely discouraged participation in subsequent discussions.

Moving along the continuum, we find *implicitly marginalizing* climates. These are climates that exclude certain groups of people, but in subtle and indirect ways. These off-putting messages might even come from well-meaning instructors. For instance, Professor Guttman unintentionally created an implicitly marginalizing climate for women, even though he was trying to be welcoming and encouraging. The lack of non-Western perspectives in the sociology of the family course demonstrates how content can contribute to implicitly marginalizing environments.

167

Finally, we find *explicitly marginalizing* climates. These are climates that are overtly hostile, discriminatory, or unwelcoming to certain students. In the first story, the students' explicitly anti-Muslim posts in the discussion board clearly contribute to this kind of environment. Similarly, in the second story, the TA's openly sexist comments and demeaning attitudes create an explicitly marginalizing climate. Sadly, DeSurra and Church's study found that most students located their courses on the marginalizing side of the spectrum.

It is important to note that course climate does not have to be blatantly exclusive or hostile in order to have a marginalizing effect on students. Indeed, while each instance of subtle marginalization may be manageable on its own, the sum total of accumulated "micro-inequities" can have a profoundly negative impact on learning (Hall & Sandler, 1982). DeSurra and Church's study shows marginalization based on sexual orientation, but much of the earliest work on classroom climate, collectively known as the "chilly climate studies," documents marginalization on the basis of gender (Hall & Sandler, 1982, 1984; Sandler & Hall, 1986). And, of course, similar observations have been made about course climate in relation to race and ethnicity (e.g., Hurtado et al., 1999; Soria, 2018; Watson et al., 2002).

The effects of a marginalizing climate are significant, moreover. Ackerman-Barger et al. (2020) found that racial microaggressions seriously affected the academic performance of medical and nursing students from underrepresented groups. Pascarella and others (1997) studied women in two-year colleges and concluded that perceptions of a negative climate were associated with lower scores on composite measures of cognitive development that included reading comprehension, mathematics, and critical thinking. Their study also found that perceptions of a marginalizing climate had a negative relationship with self-reported academic preparation for a career. In a follow-up longitudinal study, Whitt et al. (1999) studied women students at 23 two- and four-year institutions in 16 states and followed them through their junior year. They found that perception of a chilly climate was negatively associated with self-reported gains in writing and thinking skills, understanding science, academic preparation for a career, and understanding arts and humanities.

Many factors contribute to climate. Climate, moreover, is not set in a "once and done" fashion at a single moment in time; rather, it needs to be established, reinforced, and reestablished at multiple points: when a course is planned and content chosen, on the first day of class when expectations are set, and via interactions throughout the semester. The instructor, while influential, also does not have full control over the course climate. Finally, individual courses do not exist in a vacuum but are affected by events and trends in the larger social, political, and economic environment. Suffice it to say, course climate is a complex issue. For the purposes of this chapter, we focus on four areas where we believe instructors can make the biggest difference: belonging, tone, content, and presence/immediacy. While closely related, we discuss them separately, highlighting the mediating mechanisms by which they affect student outcomes.

Belonging

Like all human beings, students have limited cognitive resources. When they perceive threat in the learning environment, it is common for those cognitive resources—which would otherwise be directed toward learning—to be diverted toward vigilance and self-protection (Cohen & Sherman, 2014; Cohen et al., 2012; Inzlicht & Schmader, 2011; Steele, 2010; Walton & Cohen, 2007). Perceptions of threat can arise in a number of different contexts. Students may experience overt hostility from a belittling teacher, a bullying classmate, or a wide variety of microaggressions (to be discussed in the following section). But threat can take subtler forms as well.

One form of perceived threat arises when individual students do not feel they belong, whether in a particular classroom, a specific discipline, or even in higher education. Fitting into one's environment influences our ability to succeed in it, as theories of student retention and success have noted (Bentrim & Henning, 2022; Braxton, 2012; Tinto, 2012). Some experts, in fact, have used the abbreviation GPS to denote three elements necessary for successfully navigating college. The G is for growth mindset (see Chapter 8 on self-directed learning), the P is for purpose, and the S is for a sense of belonging (Hulleman & Happel, 2018). First-generation college students, students of color, and women are particularly vulnerable to a feeling of not belonging, as they may see few people like them in certain academic and professional environments (Good et al., 2012; Smith et al., 2014; Walton & Cohen, 2007). When students feel that they do not belong, they can become hypervigilant, attending with far greater sensitivity to cues that they do not belong than to cues that they do. This hypervigilance exacts a high cognitive toll, draining cognitive resources that would otherwise be put toward learning, performance, and relationship-building (see cognitive load in Chapter 5 on mastery).

Luckily, small interventions can have outsized positive effects on the performance decrements caused by a low sense of belonging. A number of interventions focus on demonstrating that feelings of not belonging are common. For example, Walton and Cohen (2011) asked students to reflect on the results of a survey that showed that many college students feel that they don't belong in college at first but develop a stronger sense of belonging over time. Students were then asked to write an essay and prepare a presentation for incoming students about how their own feelings of not belonging changed. (Students in the control condition did the same tasks but focused on other topics.) The researchers found that Black students in the experimental condition earned higher GPAs *over their entire college careers* than students in the control group, reducing the racial achievement gap by 52%. These students were also more likely to be in the top 25% of their class and to report higher levels of happiness and well-being.

Binning et al. (2020) took this one step farther by showing that belonging interventions can be inculcated at an environmental level, using a set of group-focused interventions designed to change collective understandings about the nature of belonging, competence, and adversity. The results were similarly dramatic, improving the performance of students from underrepresented groups significantly. The researchers speculate that when students who are vulnerable to imposter syndrome realize how common those feelings are among their peers, they reassign attributions, linking the feeling of not-belonging to being new, rather than linking it to their social identify (e.g., Black, Hispanic, a woman, first-generation college student.)

Other "belonging interventions" focus on the attributions students make when they encounter challenges or failure. In one study by Wilson and Linville (1985), two groups of first-year college students were shown videos of seniors describing their college experience. In the experimental group, the videos showed seniors talking about how their grades in college were low at first but improved over time. In the control group, videos showed seniors talking about social and academic interests. Students in the experimental condition performed better on a GRE exam one week later, earned higher college grades overall, and were 80% less likely to drop out. A study by Good et al. (2003) showed that a similar intervention eliminated the gender difference in math performance on a standardized test. When students attribute their struggles to fixed qualities in themselves ("I got a C on the midterm; I'm not smart enough to make it in this program."), it contributes to low resilience and can exacerbate imposter syndrome. But when they see that other students also struggle, overcome those struggles, and go on to succeed, it helps them adjust their attributions, moving from "I'm not good enough" to "It's hard. Struggle is normal. If they can do it, so can I."

Closely related to the sense that one does not belong is stereotype threat (Beasley & Fischer, 2012; Inzlicht & Schmader, 2012; Steele & Aronson, 1995). In simple terms, stereotype threat refers to the anxiety that arises in members of a stereotyped group (e.g., the elderly) when they are faced with a challenging task (e.g., a test of memory) and feel internal pressure to perform well so as not to confirm the stereotype. This pressure—that is, a sense of threat imposed by the stereotype—can sap cognitive resources and have a negative impact on affected individuals' performance on tasks, regardless of their ability, level of preparation, self-confidence, or their own belief in the stereotype. In their seminal study, Steele and Aronson (1995) focused on one stereotype of African Americans—that they perform poorly on standardized tests. They gave two groups of African American students a standardized test, asking one group to indicate their race prior to taking the test. The researchers found that simply by calling attention to race, a negative stereotype was activated in the minds of the African American participants. The activation of the stereotype in turn significantly depressed the performance of those African American students relative to other African American students for whom the stereotype was not activated. Similar studies have used common stereotypes about certain groups (e.g., women are bad at math, older people are forgetful) and have demonstrated parallel findings. The effects of stereotype threat has been demonstrated in Black students (Beasley & Fischer, 2012), Hispanic students (Gonzales et al., 2002), Asian American students (Shih et al., 1999), women (Inzlicht & Ben-Zeev, 2000), older people (Levy, 1996), and students of lower socioeconomic status (Croizet & Claire, 1998).

The activation of a stereotype does not need to be intentional, and in fact seemingly innocuous comments can trigger stereotype threat, for instance assumptions instructors make about students' religion, upbringing, or socioeconomic status (e.g., assuming that all Hispanics are Catholics or that criminal justice reform is a priority for all Black people). Tokenism can be a trigger as well—instructors relying on students from minoritized groups to represent the "minority point of view" rather than speaking for themselves. Professor Guttman in scenario 2 is certainly conscious of the predicament of women in engineering, but the way he deals with it—refusing to call on women and insisting on giving them extra help—might trigger stereotype threat because it communicates problematic assumptions (i.e., that women will be unprepared when he calls on them or that women need the extra help because of an ability deficiency). Regardless of whether the stereotype is activated blatantly or subtly, the effects on performance are similar.

How can stereotypes influence performance in students who do not even believe the stereotype? Steele and Aronson investigated two competing hypotheses. The first one attributed poor performance to lowered self-esteem and efficacy triggered by the stereotype. Measures of students' self-esteem failed to support this hypothesis. The second hypothesis, which their data confirmed, was that stereotypes have their impact by generating emotions that disrupt cognitive processes. In fact, students reported focusing on their anger at the stereotype or the instructor instead of on the test, not being able to think clearly, checking every answer multiple times only to run out of time for later questions, and so on (Steele & Aronson, 1995). In addition, as a coping mechanism to protect their self-concept against the self-fulfilling prophecy of their low performance, students might disidentify from their chosen discipline, deciding that the discipline was not good for them in the first place (Major et al., 1998). Thus, stereotype threat operates through two related mediating mechanisms, one cognitive and one motivational. Stereotype threat is an intriguing and complex phenomenon, and there are many nuances highlighted by this line of research that cannot be adequately addressed here. However, one key takeaway is that the way we frame the material and the task matters—and it has implications for learning and performance. Fortunately, research shows that, just as easily as stereotype threat can be activated, it can also be removed (see strategies at the end of this chapter).

A number of interventions can mitigate stereotype threat. One type bolsters students' core values through affirmations. A recent meta-analysis demonstrates the power of these simple interventions (Wu et al., 2021). For example, Miyake et al. (2010) conducted a study in which college students in a physics class wrote about values for 15 to 20 minutes. The experimental group wrote about values that were important to them personally, while the control group wrote about values that might be important to someone else. The researchers found that this intervention alone eliminated a significant gender gap in grades and scores on a nationally normed physics test. Similar interventions substantially reduced a race-based performance gap in other subjects (e.g., Cohen et al., 2009). Researchers postulate that focusing on core values bolsters a sense of identity and helps to inoculate students against threats. Another way to reduce stereotype threat is to convey high standards while communicating your confidence in all your students' abilities (Cohen & Steele, 2002). A number of other interventions also reduce stereotype threat, including the belonging interventions discussed previously.

Tone

Course climate is also determined by the way the instructor communicates with students, the level of hospitableness that students perceive, and the more general range of inclusion and comfort that students experience. For instance, Ishiyama and Hartlaub (2002) studied how the tone an instructor uses affects climate by manipulating course syllabi. They created two versions of the same syllabus, with policies identical in substance but one worded in a punitive tone, the other in an encouraging one. They discovered that the tone used influenced students' judgments about instructor approachability. In their study, students are less likely to seek help from the instructor who worded those policies in punitive language than from the instructor who worded the same policies in rewarding language. Rubin (1985) dubs those instructors "scolders"—those who word policies in boldface block letters and promise harsh punishments rather than offering a pedagogical rationale for the policy. Similar findings have demonstrated that students reading a syllabus with a friendly versus unfriendly tone were more likely to perceive the instructor as more approachable, warm, caring, and motivating (Denton & Valoso, 2017; Harnish & Bridges, 2011). Even though these studies of tone were focused on syllabi, it is reasonable to assume that its impact is more pervasive. Other facets of tone include the kind of language used in the classroom (encouraging or demotivating), especially in the way feedback is offered (constructive and focused on the task or demeaning and focused on the person). In fact, in their study of why undergraduates leave the sciences, Seymour and Hewitt (1997) found that sarcasm, denigration, and ridicule by faculty members were some of the reasons reported by students as drivers in their decisions to no longer pursue the study of the sciences. The belittling tone of the TA in the second story at the beginning of the chapter makes him unapproachable to many students. An instructor's negative or unwelcoming tone has also been shown to increase classroom incivilities (Klebig et al., 2016; Miller et al., 2014).

A discussion of tone would not be complete without mention of microaggressions. Microaggressions are "subtle expressions of hostility and discrimination, intended or unintended, toward people with marginalized or underrepresented social identities" (Byers et al., 2020, p. 484). Racial microaggressions might include statements like "I don't see color" that deny the reality of race and gaslight those who experience racism. They might also involve backhanded compliments directed to people of color, such as an insultingly surprised "You're so articulate!" An example of an ethnic microaggression might be asking

173

a non-White person born and raised in the United States "Where are you from? No, where are you *really* from?" in a way that conveys that they will never fully belong here. In academic settings, microaggressions can come from instructors or classmates. Individual microaggressions may not be devastating; however, they have a cumulative effect, building over time in ways that erode academic self-esteem (Forrest-Bank & Cuellar, 2018), inhibit performance (Solorzano et al., 2000), and even negatively affect health (Ong et al., 2013). Thus we see that tone affects learning and performance through a number of motivational and socioemotional mechanisms (see Chapter 4 on motivation).

Content

The climate variables explored thus far are all process variables—explicit and subtle speech and behaviors of faculty members and students. But what about the content of our courses? Is there something inherent to *what* we teach—not *how*—that can influence climate? Marchesani and Adams (1992) describe a continuum of inclusion for course content from the exclusive curriculum, where only a dominant perspective is represented, to the exceptional outsider stage, in which a token marginalized perspective is included only to comply with a requirement (e.g., one Native American poet in an American poetry course), to ever more inclusive stages, culminating with the transformed curriculum, where multiple perspectives are placed at the center. Course content is broader than that. It includes the examples and metaphors instructors use in class and the case studies and project topics we let our students choose. Just as important as those used are those omitted, because they all send messages about the field and who belongs in it.

What if Professor Jenkowski had framed the discussion about divorce to include other cultural practices and norms, even if simply to situate American practices and the assumptions in which they are embedded? Perhaps then Rafi would have felt more welcome to introduce Bangladeshi perspectives on marriage. Perhaps more to the point, his classmates may not have been so dismissive of cultural practices they did not understand. Similarly, what if instead of offering extra help to his female students—which came across as patronizing and may have triggered stereotype threat—Professor Guttman had worked differently to make his course inclusive? What if he sought out examples highlighting the contributions of women in the field or used articles by prominent female engineers? What if he incorporated a unit on socially responsible engineering or led a discussion of the barriers women and other minoritized groups faced in engineering careers? What if he highlighted how diversity on engineering teams brought more innovative approaches to problem-solving?

For students who are just developing their sense of identity, purpose, and competence, the subtle messages conveyed by the content included or omitted can be powerful. When students do not see the communities they come from and the issues they care about reflected in course content, they may conclude "this isn't for me" and shift toward other majors or disciplines. On the flip side, when students feel themselves reflected in course content, it can create a powerful draw. Astin (1993) identified a factor, which he called *faculty diversity emphasis*, comprising elements such as inclusion of readings on gender and racial issues in the curriculum. He found that this factor positively affects student GPA by conveying that these issues are up for discussion and not to be avoided. In fact, Seymour and Hewitt (1997) found that many of the women and minoritized students who left the sciences transferred to fields where race and gender are legitimate lenses of analysis instead of "a dirty little secret over in the engineering school." In conclusion, content can affect learning through cognitive, motivational, and socioemotional mechanisms because it conveys what topics, perspectives, and people are welcome in the field.

Presence and Immediacy

One issue that has gained increasing attention, particularly in the context of online learning, is "social presence," which refers to the feeling of being present with a real person or people in a virtual space (Oh et al., 2018). It has proven essential to successful online learning, and there are strong correlations between presence and student satisfaction and perceived learning in online courses (Richardson & Swan, 2003). In digital spaces, which can feel lonely and alienating to students (Lehman & Conceição, 2010), social presence must be created and sustained deliberately, both through the thoughtful integration of technology tools that facilitate meaningful human interaction and through instructor behaviors that foster a sense of community and connection (Lehman & Conceição, 2010). Garrison et al. (1999) expanded the idea of social presence in their community of inquiry framework, identifying three kinds of presence needed to create successful online courses: (1) *social presence*: a sense of trust and connection between students and instructor and among students; (2) *teaching presence*: a well-designed and coherent learning experience, ably and authentically

175

led by the instructor; and (3) *cognitive presence*: students' intellectual engagement with the material (Garrison et al., 1999). In the first story in this chapter, Professor Jenkowski has abdicated teaching presence in her online course, neglecting to engage with her course discussion boards and thus failing to notice or respond to an argument that could have been an important learning opportunity. Her absence not only allowed negative feelings to fester but also it eroded the sense of connection and engagement so essential for the success of online courses.

Teaching presence is closely related to *instructor (or teacher) immediacy*, a measure of social and psychological connection between instructors and students. Instructor immediacy behaviors are defined as verbal or nonverbal behaviors that reduce the psychological distance between teachers and students (Christophel & Gorham, 1995). Nonverbal immediacy behaviors include eye contact, smiling, and nodding. Verbal behaviors include using humor, engaging informally with students before and after class, asking students to share their opinions, and so on. High levels of instructor immediacy behaviors have been associated with increased student motivation (Baker, 2010; Ballester, 2013), more participation (Mandernach et al., 2006; Roberts & Friedman, 2013), higher satisfaction with the course (Arbaugh, 2001), better perceived learning outcomes (Joksimović et al., 2015; Roberts & Friedman, 2013; Violanti et al., 2018; Witt et al., 2004), higher achievement expectations (Creasey, 2009), and the perception that instructors showing such behaviors are more credible, trustworthy, and caring (Santilli et al., 2011; Schrodt & Witt, 2006; Trad et al., 2014). Interestingly, instructor immediacy can even neutralize situations that might otherwise lower motivation and morale. In one study, for instance, high immediacy preserved student perceptions of instructor credibility even when course workloads were higher than students expected (Malott, 2014). As with social presence, immediacy behaviors have proven especially important online, where instructors must overcome physical as well as psychological distance (D'Agustino, 2016; Schutt et al., 2009). However, both concepts are equally important in in-person learning, where building a strong sense of community and connection, and reducing the distance between instructor and learner, are essential for creating a productive course climate.

While instructor presence must be created and maintained most deliberately in online courses, it matters in in-person courses as well. In his study of more than 200,000 students and 25,000 faculty members at 200 institutions, Astin (1999) identified several factors contributing to the college experience. The factor that relates to course climate the most is what he termed *faculty student interaction,* and includes items such as student perceptions of whether faculty members are interested in students' academic problems, care about the concerns of minoritized groups, are approachable outside of class, and treat students as persons and not as numbers. He found that this factor positively affects retention, the percentage of students who go on to graduate school, and self-reported critical thinking, analysis, and problem-solving skills. Seymour and Hewitt (1997) found that one of the reasons students switch out of majors in the sciences is faculty unavailability, and that, conversely, one of the variables that changed the minds of students who were thinking about switching was the intervention by a faculty member during a critical point in the student's academic or personal life. Similarly, Pascarella and Terenzini (1977) discovered that the absence of faculty contacts or the perception that those are largely formalistic exchanges is one of the determinants of student withdrawal from college. Of course, students also contribute to the classroom climate with their own behaviors, like the students who responded to Rafi in the first story. However, the way the instructor responds to those behaviors is the final determinant of climate. If Professor Jenkowski had been able to manage the discussion regarding arranged marriage more strategically, the discussion might have ended in a very different way.

Implications of This Research

What are the implications of the findings on climate for teaching and learning? First, effective teaching requires that we give the same consideration to social and emotional dynamics in the classroom as we do to intellectual processes as the former affects the latter profoundly. Second, because course climate works in both blatant and subtle ways, many well-intentioned or seemingly inconsequential decisions can have unintended negative effects with regard to climate. Finally, as instructors, we have a great deal of control over the climate we shape, and can leverage climate in the service of learning.

WHAT STRATEGIES DOES THE RESEARCH SUGGEST?

Here are a number of strategies for creating a productive course climate. Many of these address multiple issues (belonging, tone, presence) simultaneously.

These strategies sometimes require instructors to stretch outside their comfort zone, but making a concerted effort to foster an explicitly inclusive course climate matters and is worth the effort.

Strategies to Foster a Strong Sense of Belonging

Examine Your Assumptions About Students Our assumptions about students' backgrounds, experiences, and viewpoints influence the way we interact with them, which in turn affects their learning. Instructors may inadvertently exclude students simply by assuming a shared political perspective, family composition, or common set of experiences. Consider, for instance, an economics instructor who asks students to reflect on spending patterns during their last vacation. Then imagine a student whose family has never taken a vacation, and the sense of alienation, even shame, this casual request might create. Or think about a sociology professor whose analysis of family structures only references heterosexual families. How would that feel to an LGBTQ student or a student raised by gay parents? It takes practice to recognize the assumptions embedded in lecture material, assignments, questions, and so on, but deliberately working to recognize and challenge these assumptions can help to foster a strong sense of belonging among students, making the course climate considerably warmer and more productive.

Educate Yourself About Identities Other Than Your Own Societies change rapidly, and norms and language are quickly outdated. In order to teach effectively and foster a course climate that models lifelong learning, open-mindedness, and growth, instructors should continually seek out opportunities to educate themselves about identities other than their own, as well as changing social mores and linguistic conventions. It would be hypocritical indeed to expect students to learn, grow, and challenge themselves if we do not do the same.

Strive to Be Explicitly (and Not Just Implicitly) Inclusive It is better to be implicitly inclusive than either implicitly or explicitly marginalizing. However, it is better still to be *explicitly* inclusive. In other words, the goal should not be to create a classroom environment in which every student is treated the same but rather to foster an environment in which differences are embraced, issues of inequity and injustice are acknowledged and grappled with overtly, and attention is given to intersecting identities. Acknowledging the realities (e.g., poverty, racism, classism, homophobia, transphobia) so many students live with paves the way for deeper, more impactful discussions and more informed and effective problem-solving.

Beware of Conveying Unintentional Messages About Ability Instructors sometimes inadvertently convey messages about students' abilities which can actually undermine students' confidence and reduce academic performance. Think of a physics professor who, in an attempt to build his students' confidence, continually talks about how brilliant one must be to succeed in physics. Such messaging encourages students to see success as a product of immutable conditions, such as native intelligence, instead of effort and persistence: you've either got it or you don't. When students who take in these messages encounter difficulties or setbacks, they are more likely to attribute these challenges to equally immutable qualities in themselves, such as gender, race, ethnicity, or age. This, in turn, diminishes students' sense of agency and self-efficacy, particularly students from groups already underrepresented in the field. To avoid this, instructors should focus on messaging that learning takes practice and diligence, and convey their confidence in the abilities of all students in the course to meet these challenges.

Do Not Ask Individuals to Speak for an Entire Group Students from minoritized groups often report feeling invisible in class or, conversely, feeling like tokens. Self-consciousness is heightened when students from an underrepresented group are treated as spokespeople for the entire group ("Ricardo, you're the child of immigrants. Give us your take on this."). Because such tokenism can exacerbate feelings of not belonging or trigger stereotype threat, instructors should take pains not to put students in that position. At the same time, it is important that students from all backgrounds feel safe *volunteering* their experiences and perspectives, so work to create the kind of course environment where doing so feels safe. Other strategies here can help to create an environment that fosters psychological safety.

Use Strategies That Specifically Enhance Belonging When students feel as though they belong in a course, in a field of study, and at the institution in which they have enrolled, they are more likely to persist and succeed. There are a number of things the research on belonging, mindset, and stereotype threat suggest that can help you, as the instructor, create a climate where students feel a strong sense of belonging. One is to convey high standards, along with your conviction that all the students in your course can meet them and your commitment to provide support. Also, if appropriate, give students opportunities to discuss or write about the values that brought them into a course or field of study. Focusing on these core values helps to sustain them when they encounter setbacks and can reinforce their sense of connection to the discipline. Consider collecting testimonials from students who have taken your course in the past, preferably stories

179

that convey both the challenges of the course and the benefits of working through them. Sharing such testimonials with current students helps to convey that struggle is natural and productive, and not a sign that they do not belong. Finally, discuss your own journey in the field, including setbacks and challenges you yourself overcame. For instance, you might show how many drafts of a manuscript you had to generate before it was published. Self-disclosure helps to disabuse students of the notion that success should always come easily. (Note: We recognize that for women and minoritized faculty members who often have to work harder than male or majority counterparts to demonstrate credibility and prove that they themselves belong in the academy, showing vulnerability can be a double-edged sword. Thus, considering where and when self-disclosure is productive would be especially important for faculty in these groups.)

Ask a Colleague to Observe Your Course We are not always conscious of behaviors we engage in that might send subtle messages about belonging. For instance, we might inadvertently call on some students more than others, ask some students less challenging questions, respond to some students more positively, or interrupt some students more frequently or impatiently. Sometimes these behaviors correlate to the groups students belong to and unconscious biases we may possess. To explore this issue, start by replacing defensiveness with curiosity. We all have unconscious biases; the trick is to make them conscious so we can confront them. Then ask a trusted third party (a TA, a teaching center consultant, a colleague) to sit in on your class, observe your interactions with students, and collect data on the number and type of interactions with students from different demographic groups (How often do you call on White students versus students of color? How do you respond to questions from students of different genders?), looking for patterns you may not be aware of yourself. The data might show that you have been equitable all along, or it may point to potential areas for improvement.

Strategies to Ensure That Course Tone Is Positive and Supportive

Use the Syllabus and First Day of Class to Set the Tone First impressions color all subsequent interactions. Your students will quickly form impressions about you and your course, so use the syllabus and first day (or introduction module) of class to set the tone that you want to permeate the course. Make sure your syllabus conveys warmth and accessibility and makes clear to students how they can contact you or get help if they are struggling. Plan how you can use your first day of class, whether virtual or in-person, to quickly establish competence and authority on one hand and supportiveness and approachability on the other. Use activities on the first day that immediately establish a culture of participation and active engagement, and do not let students develop a habit of passivity. In online courses (or your face-to-face courses), use an introductory video or a welcome email to introduce yourself to students and immediately establish a sense of presence and immediacy.

Establish Ground Rules for Interaction Explain that discourse, debate, and disagreement can be opportunities for learning, while making it clear that you will not tolerate disrespect from anyone in the class. Establishing ground rules for discussion can help to ensure that students are inclusive and respectful of one another. To generate deeper thought as well as buy-in, consider involving students in the process of creating ground rules (see Appendix B on ground rules). Be aware as you create your ground rules that common guidelines, such as "speak from your own experience" and "assume good intentions," can sometimes inadvertently reinforce dominant social hierarchies by allowing students to speak from ignorance or cause pain to others with impunity. Sensoy and DiAngelo (2014) provide an alternative set of ground rules for discussion, rules that encourage students to strive for intellectual humility, notice their own defensive reactions, look beyond individual anecdotal experience to search for broader social patterns, subject assumptions to scrutiny, and distinguish between safety—which is essential for learning—and comfort—which is not essential for and may sometimes impede learning.

Revisit Ground Rules Periodically It is not sufficient simply to set ground rules and call it a day. You will likely need to revisit your ground rules periodically. For instance, you might do so at the midpoint of a course, before a discussion you think will be particularly difficult or emotional, or after a discussion that proved more complicated or uncomfortable than you anticipated. Revisiting ground rules once the course has begun can be an opportunity for more contextualized and meaningful discussion than at the beginning of the course, when such guidelines are still largely theoretical, and can serve as the occasion to refine or operationalize ground rules that are not fully serving their purpose. Let students know at the beginning of the class that you will periodically review the ground rules together to ensure that they are understood and are being followed, and to make adjustments as needed. In addition to establishing ground rules, you will need to model them. You should also think through in advance how you will respond if students violate these rules.

Model Inclusive Language, Behavior, and Attitudes When you as the instructor model inclusiveness, it provides a powerful learning experience for students. There are many ways to do this. When using American idioms, explain them for the benefit of non-native English speakers. Use respectful language when speaking to students. Use students' pronouns when they are provided, and consider providing your own, but avoid asking students to offer their pronouns as a matter of course. Doing so puts people on the spot and can exacerbate feelings of vulnerability or alienation (Poore-Pariseau, 2021). Demonstrate humility, authenticity, and curiosity so that students who encounter microaggressions in or outside your classroom feel comfortable coming to you to talk about it. Your behavior sets the tone for the class.

Provide Opportunities for Anonymous Feedback No matter how many immediacy behaviors you demonstrate and how accessible you are, students may not feel comfortable bringing up concerns they have about your course, simply because you have power over their grades. To make sure there is an open channel of communication, consider providing a way for students to give regular, anonymous feedback, for example through a short survey that students can complete whenever and as often as they like. The survey can be structured to focus on specific questions you have about course climate (e.g., How comfortable do you feel sharing your perspectives and experiences in this course?) or it can be unstructured to allow students to share whatever they want (e.g., What's on your mind?). Periodically report back to the class about what you have been learning so that students know that you are paying attention and care what they have to say.

Conduct an Early Course Evaluation Find out about potential problems early by conducting an early course evaluation (three to four weeks into the course is generally appropriate) or midterm course evaluations (about mid-semester). Include questions that explicitly address belonging, climate, and the atmosphere of your classroom. Share the results with the class, making sure you clearly address issues about climate and belonging. Pay particular attention to how you share the results and avoid any tendency to be dismissive or defensive. Rather, be authentic and sensitive to the honest feedback students have provided, so they will feel comfortable offering other feedback to you in the future.

Prepare for Potentially Sensitive Issues As instructors, we can usually—though certainly not always—anticipate topics that will be controversial or emotional for students. For instance, a discussion of how different cultures control reproduction or end pregnancies might spark strong feelings. To ensure that students are prepared to learn from these opportunities (and do not simply flare up or shut down), make sure they know what to expect; do not simply spring the conversation on them. Frame the discussion thoughtfully as well. For instance, you might acknowledge that the topic could have personal significance for some students and explain *why* you have chosen to include it, perhaps providing an "opt out" for students who find it painful. You may also want to set ground rules to ensure a civil discussion (see Appendix B on ground rules).

Address Tensions Early What should you do if students make offensive comments in class or in asynchronous online interactions, intentionally "press buttons," or silence or marginalize other students? Address the situation immediately. In some situations, that might require stopping class long enough to call attention to a problematic turn of phrase or microaggression (e.g., "Serena, the term *illegals* dehumanizes whole groups of people. We're not going to use that term here."). However, it can sometimes be tricky to address a poorly phrased comment during class without making the situation worse for students already in a vulnerable position. In such cases, a better course of action might be to briefly signal your recognition of the problem with a pointed look or comment in the moment (e.g., "Tom, let's talk after class), then call the offending student aside after class for more discussion. When explaining to a student that a comment made during class was problematic, be sure to differentiate intent from impact; in other words, comments can be painful to others whether or not the speaker intended them to be. College students do not always know how to express themselves appropriately or to manage their emotions, so be gentle and allow room for growth while at the same time not giving a pass to offensive or hurtful comments. Remember that such comments add to and reinforce larger injustices and harms, particularly those experienced by students from marginalized groups, so be sure not to let them slide. Perhaps most important, monitor your own behavior. If you say something unintentionally alienating, apologize sincerely. Modeling self-review and genuine contrition can be a powerful example in its own right.

Turn Discord and Tension into a Learning Opportunity Debate, tension, discord, disagreement, and cognitive dissonance are all opportunities to expand one's perspective, delve deeper into a topic, better understand opposing views, and so on. Hence, we need not avoid them. Students do not always recognize that, however. Moreover, because they are still developing social and emotional skills, these can often overshadow intellect, logic, and rational thinking. As a result, we need to work to continually shape our classroom climate. So do not foreclose a discussion just because tensions are running high; rather, funnel those emotions into useful dialogue. For example, you might ask students to take on another perspective using a role-play, take a time out (e.g., write their reactions down so that they are more useful and constructive), or simply explain how and why discomfort and tension can be a valuable part of learning.

Help Students Develop Active Listening Skills Sometimes tensions arise because students do not hear what others are saying or are intentionally distorting one another's words to battle a straw man or score points. To build stronger listening skills, you might ask one student to paraphrase what another student has said, following up with questions that encourage exploration of nuance ("Is that what she actually said or what you're extrapolating from what she said?"). You can then ask the original speaker if the paraphrase was accurate. You can also model active listening yourself by periodically summarizing a student's response and then asking whether you captured their perspective accurately.

Be Authentic Well-meaning instructors can make complicated situations worse by trying too hard to be perfect. Instead of endeavoring to be on top of every situation, try to maintain a posture of humility, openness, and authenticity. Acknowledge that—like everyone—you are still learning and ask for feedback and forbearance as you do. Tell students that you want to hear from them if you say or do something that troubles or upsets them. Sincerely thank those who offer you input, and take it to heart in the spirit of learning and improvement, not self-recrimination or shame.

Strategies to Make Course Content More Inclusive

Do an Inclusivity Audit of Your Course Materials Think about the materials you assign for your course. Are almost all the readings by White authors? By men? If so, see if you can incorporate authors of more diverse identities and backgrounds. Also consider what issues relevant to your field are and are not included. Is poverty glossed over in a political science course? Does a medical policy course neglect health disparities? Are discussions of race framed only in terms of a Black-White binary? The people and perspectives we include or neglect in our courses convey who and what we regard as central versus marginal in our subject areas. These choices, in turn, send powerful messages to students that can affect their sense of belonging. Do an audit of your courses and see whether there are opportunities for the content to be more inclusive.

Incorporate Diverse Examples Incorporate examples and cases that reference different communities and life experiences. This helps to ensure that no single group's experience is taken as the unspoken norm and students from a range of backgrounds feel seen and included in the course content. For instance, if teaching about app design, you might highlight innovative apps developed by or targeted to the needs of the disabled community. Or when teaching business communication, you might feature cases from Black- or Hispanic-owned businesses. Be sure that the examples you use represent diverse experiences but be careful not to perpetuate stereotypes. Think about the names used in case studies, for example, and what they convey about identity in relation to the issues raised in the case. Are the people in a medical case study of substance use named Leticia and Jose while the people in a business case study of successful entrepreneurship are named Katie and Travis? These small details can undermine a sense of belonging and trigger stereotype threat.

Strategies to Foster a Sense of Presence

Work to Build Connection and Community, Particularly in Online Courses Because distance courses can feel, well, *distancing*, it is important for online instructors to work proactively to create a sense of connection and community within their courses. To foster *social presence,* spend time at the beginning of the course on introductions. There are a host of easy, free, media-enabled online tools to facilitate this. Give students ample opportunity to interact with one another throughout the course. Assign online discussion prompts that invite perspective sharing and genuine exchange and use well-designed small-group tasks to encourage different modes of interaction and collaboration. Use ice breakers at the beginning of synchronous class sessions; the chat function enables this well. Also, build a strong sense of *instructor presence*. Record informal video introductions for modules so students know your face and feel connected to you. Check in regularly with students, for example by sending links to course-relevant news articles and reminding them about upcoming deadlines. Hold informal online office hours. Participate in online discussions yourself so students know that their involvement matters to you and you care what they have to say. If possible given your class size, consider sending personalized messages to individual students, asking how the course is going for them, what they're finding most interesting, and where they could use additional support.

Reduce Anonymity When students feel recognized and appreciated as individuals, they are more invested in their learning. Come to class a little early and stay a little late so you can chat with students informally. Use short ice breakers at the beginning of virtual class sessions (chat is a powerful tool for doing this both quickly and well). Hold office hours, and encourage students to attend. When possible, find ways to connect with students outside the classroom. Spend time and be visible in the spaces on campus that students frequent: dining halls, libraries, bookstores, and so on. This provides opportunities for incidental interactions that can help to reduce distance and create a sense of community. Make an effort to learn your students' names and pronounce them correctly. Use software that allows you to collect audio snippets of students pronouncing their own names so you can practice saying them correctly. Take time to make sure students can pronounce your name. If you occasionally get pronunciation wrong, make an honest effort to correct yourself, apologize, and move on. Perfection is not required, but an effort is. Share your audio roster with your students so they can learn and practice each other's names. When it comes to names, encourage students to have grace and patience with each other and work toward the common goal of showing respect.

SUMMARY

In this chapter, we have argued that, because students are social and emotional as well as intellectual beings, it is our responsibility as instructors to take seriously the need to foster an environment in which all students feel that they belong and can thrive. Our hope is that instructors can be more intentional in how they shape their course's climate and, consequently, student learning.

CHAPTER 8

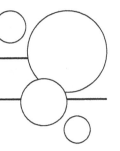

How Do Students Become Self-Directed Learners?

The A Student

I was exhausted from reading and grading 25 papers over the past weekend, but I was glad to be able to hand them back so quickly. It was the first big assignment in my freshman seminar on immigration, and it required students to state an argument and support it with evidence from course readings and supplemental documents. After class, one of the students, Melanie, approached me and insisted that she needed to talk with me immediately about her grade (not about her paper, mind you!). Hers was a typical first paper in this course: it lacked a clearly articulated argument—instead introducing the topic with flowery narrative—and there was only weak evidence to support her contentions. As we walked across campus toward my office, she began explaining that she was a "gifted" writer who had always received As on her high school English papers. She made it clear to me that there must be some mistake in this paper's grade because she had sent a copy to her mother, a high school English teacher, who thought it was wonderful. Melanie admitted that she had started this assignment the night before it was due, but insisted that she worked best under pressure, saying, "That's just how my creative juices flow."

Professor Sarafina Yang

The Hamster Wheel

After I saw John's grade on the second modern chemistry exam, I couldn't help but ask myself, "How can someone attend every single lecture—sitting attentively in the front row—and go to every recitation and lab, no less, and still do so poorly on my exams?" I had explicitly told the students that my exams are designed to test conceptual understanding, and yet John seemed to be thrown for a loop. His first exam score had also been pretty low, but he wasn't alone in that, given students' first-exam jitters. By this time, however, I thought he would have learned what to expect. I asked John what had happened, and he too seemed perplexed. "I studied for weeks," he said, flipping open his textbook. I could hardly believe how much of the text was highlighted. The pages practically glowed with neon yellow. He went on to describe how he had reread the relevant chapters multiple times and then memorized various terms by writing their definitions on flashcards. I asked where he had learned this approach to studying, and he explained that it had always worked for him when he used to prepare for his science tests in high school.

Professor Gar Zeminsky

WHAT IS GOING ON IN THESE TWO STORIES?

On the surface, these stories seem quite different: Melanie starts her history paper at the last minute, whereas John studies hard (and harder) for weeks before his chemistry exams. However, both students perform well below their expectations without understanding why. As we analyze the details of each story, other issues emerge. We see that John has a set of study strategies—mostly involving rote memorization of facts and definitions—that may have been sufficient in his high school classes but were proving ineffective for the intellectual demands of a college course. Rather than changing his approach after a poor performance on the first exam, however, John doggedly redoubles his efforts only to find that more of the same does not help. Melanie also enlists strategies that worked for her in the past, but she fails to recognize important differences—in both disciplinary approach and level of sophistication—between the kinds of writing valued in high school English classes and the kinds of writing expected in her college history course. Furthermore, she is so invested in a conception of herself

188

as a talented writer that she is unable to process critique, seeing it as an attack on her identity rather than an opportunity to improve her skills. Both Melanie and John are encountering new sets of intellectual challenges. Unfortunately, neither of them recognizes the shortcomings in their strategies, and they fail to develop new ones. To complicate matters, Melanie holds beliefs about her own abilities, based in part on past performance, that make her unwilling to admit that there is anything wrong with her current approach.

WHAT PRINCIPLE OF LEARNING IS AT WORK HERE?

Although these two students are struggling with different tasks in distinct courses, their difficulties point to similar shortcomings in metacognition. Metacognition refers to "the process of reflecting on and directing one's own thinking" (National Research Council, 2001, p. 78). Both Melanie and John have trouble accurately assessing their own learning and performance, and they fail to adapt their approaches to the current situation. As a result, both students' learning and performance suffer. In other words, when it comes to applying metacognitive skills to direct their own learning—the focus of this chapter— Melanie and John fall short.

> **Principle:** *To become self-directed learners, students must learn to assess the demands of the task, evaluate their own knowledge and skills, plan their approach, monitor their progress, and adjust their strategies as needed.*

This principle lays out the key metacognitive skills that are critical to being an effective self-directed (also called *self-regulated* or *lifelong*) learner, skills also associated with cultural competence (Ang et al., 2015; Cho & Kim, 2022) and critical thinking (Bernal et al., 2018). Metacognitive skills arguably become more and more important at higher levels of education and in professional life as one takes on more complex tasks and greater responsibility for one's own learning. For example, compared to high school, students in college are often required to complete larger, longer-term projects and must do so rather independently. Such projects often demand that students recognize what they already know that is relevant to completing the project, identify what they still need to learn, plan an approach to learn that material independently, potentially redefine the scope of the project so they can realistically accomplish it, and monitor and adjust their approach along the way. Given all this, it is not surprising that one of the major intellectual challenges students face on entering college is managing their own learning (Pascarella & Terenzini,2005).

Unfortunately, these metacognitive skills tend to fall outside the content area of most courses, and consequently they are often neglected in instruction. However, helping students to improve their metacognitive skills can hold enormous benefits. The benefits include not only intellectual habits that are valuable across disciplines (such as planning one's approach to a large project, considering alternatives, and evaluating one's own perspective) but also more flexible and usable discipline-specific knowledge. Imagine if John and Melanie had learned to evaluate the demands of the tasks that they were given and had been able to adjust their approaches to learning accordingly. By the second exam, John might have shifted from highlighting his textbook and memorizing facts to concentrating on the conceptual underpinnings of chemistry, perhaps creating a concept map to test his understanding of key ideas and the causal relationships between them. Melanie might have switched to a new writing strategy that centered on articulating a clear argument and supporting it with evidence, rather than persisting with the descriptive approach she probably used in high school. In other words, better metacognitive skills would have helped both John and Melanie learn more, which would have been reflected in improved performance.

WHAT DOES THE RESEARCH TELL US ABOUT METACOGNITION?

Researchers have proposed various models to describe how learners would ideally apply metacognitive skills to learn and perform well (Brown et al., 1983; Butler, 1997; Pintrich, 2000; Winne & Hadwin, 1998). Although these models differ in their particulars, they share the notion that learners need to engage in a variety of processes to monitor and control their learning (Zimmerman, 2001). Moreover, because the processes of monitoring and controlling mutually affect each other, these models often take the form of a cycle. Figure 8.1 depicts a cycle of basic metacognitive processes in which learners can do the following:

- Assess the task at hand, taking into consideration the task's goals and constraints
- Evaluate their own knowledge and skills, identifying strengths and weaknesses
- Plan their approach in a way that accounts for the current situation
- Apply various strategies to enact their plan, monitoring their progress along the way
- Reflect on the degree to which their current approach is working so that they can adjust and restart the cycle as needed

In addition to the many ways in which these processes can overlap and interact with each other, students' beliefs about intelligence and learning (such as whether intelligence is fixed or malleable and whether learning is quick and easy or slow and effortful) represent a factor that can influence the whole cycle in a variety of ways (see the center of Figure 8.1). In the following sections, we

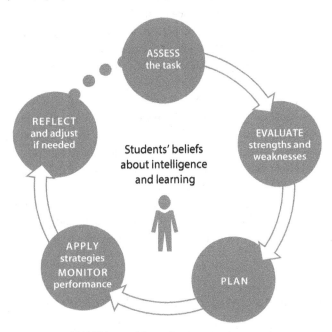

Figure 8.1. Cycle of Self-Directed Learning

191

examine key research findings related to each process in this cycle, as well as to students' beliefs about intelligence and learning.

Assessing the Task at Hand

When students submit work that misses the point of an assignment, faculty members often ask themselves in bewilderment: "Did they even read the assignment?" In fact, your students may not have or, if they did, they may have failed to accurately assess what they were supposed to do, perhaps making assumptions about the task based on their previous educational experiences. In one research study investigating students' difficulties with college writing assignments, Carey and others (1989) found that half of the college students they observed ignored the instructor's articulation of the writing assignment and instead used a generic writing-as-knowledge-telling strategy that they had used in high school. These students consequently presented everything that they knew about the paper's topic without regard to the specific goal or purpose of the assignment.

This research suggests that the first phase of metacognition—assessing the task—is not always a natural or easy one for students. We see this in the stories at the beginning of the chapter. Even though Professor Yang's assignment specified that students' papers should present an argument with supporting evidence, Melanie fell back on strategies that she had learned in her high school English class. John also ignored—or misunderstood—his professor's statement about the purpose of the exam (to test conceptual knowledge) and assumed that he knew how to study based on his high school experiences (memorize facts rather than identify key ideas and their relationships). In both cases, the student inappropriately assessed the task despite the instructor's efforts toward giving clear directions.

Given that students can easily misassess the task at hand, it may not be sufficient simply to remind students to "read the assignment carefully." In fact, students may need to (1) learn how to assess the task, (2) practice incorporating this step into their planning before it will become a habit, and (3) receive feedback on the accuracy of their task assessment before they begin working on a given task.

Evaluating One's Own Strengths and Weaknesses

Even if students can adequately assess an assignment—that is, they manage to determine what needs to be done to effectively complete the assignment—there is still a question of how well prepared they are to meet the task at hand. Research has found that people in general have great difficulty recognizing their own strengths and weaknesses, and students appear to be especially poor judges of their own knowledge and skills.

Students' poor ability to self-assess has been amply documented in a variety of contexts and cultures (Coutinho et al., 2020; Dunning, 2007). For example, when nursing students were asked about their proficiency in performing several basic procedures (such as inserting an IV), the majority of them overestimated their abilities relative to their actual performance. Moreover, research suggests that the students with weaker knowledge and skills are less able to assess their abilities than students with stronger skills. For instance, when asked to predict their performance both before and after completing a test, students in an undergraduate psychology course showed different levels of accuracy in their estimates, based on their actual performance: the highest-performing students were accurate in their predictions and postdictions (and became more accurate over subsequent tests), but the poor students grossly overestimated their performance both before and after taking the test and showed little improvement in their estimates over time (Hacker et al., 2000).

This tendency—especially among novices—to inaccurately assess one's knowledge and skill relative to a particular goal is particularly troubling because it has serious consequences for one's ability to achieve that goal. For example, students who inaccurately assesses their skills for a particular task might seriously underestimate the time it will take to effectively complete the given assignment, or just as unfortunately, they may fail to seek the additional help and resources they need (Aleven et al., 2003; Ryan et al., 2001).

In addition to inaccuracy in assessing their own knowledge and skill, students also tend to be inaccurate in assessing what helps them best learn (Deslauriers et al., 2019; Kornell & Bjork, 2008; see the discussion of learning styles in Chapter 1 on individual differences). For example, Kornell and Bjork (2008) conducted an experiment in which students learned about different artists' painting styles via either massed study (where paintings from each artist were studied consecutively) versus spaced study (where paintings from a given artist were interleaved with other artists' paintings). Researchers collected direct measures of students' learning under each method as well as their judgments of which method worked best. In most cases, the direct measures and judgments did not match. Indeed, most of the students thought that they learned best via massed study, but this was true for only about 20% of them.

The inability to self-assess—either one's knowledge and skills or what works best for one's learning—is apparent in both stories from the beginning of the chapter. Melanie believes that she is a gifted writer and considers her strength to be writing under pressure. As a result of this overconfidence, she begins her history paper at the last minute. John, too, is proud of his meticulous reading and relentless highlighting of his chemistry textbook, and despite evidence to the contrary, he seems to maintain the belief that this is a good way for him to study. Without proper assessment of how he is learning the material, he spends lots of effort for little gain. If these students had managed to evaluate their abilities and learning strategies more realistically, they might have engaged more appropriate approaches that, in turn, could have produced better outcomes.

Planning an Appropriate Approach

Given students' difficulties in assessing the task and their own abilities, it follows that their capacity to plan effectively would also be compromised. In the stories at the beginning of the chapter, we see two ways student planning can go awry: (1) simply not planning enough, especially for a complex task and (2) planning inappropriately for the current situation. Melanie exemplifies the first problem by starting her paper the night before and spending little or no time thinking ahead about what (and how) she needs to write for this assignment. John definitely plans how he will study for his chemistry test; however, his plan is poorly suited to the kind of exam Professor Zeminsky gives. Research on students' planning behavior provides evidence for both of these planning problems.

Melanie's lack of planning is consistent with a body of research that shows students tend to spend too little time planning, especially when compared to more expert individuals. For example, in one study, physics experts (graduate students and faculty members) and novices (students in introductory courses) were asked to solve various physics problems. Not surprisingly, the experts solved the problems more quickly and more accurately than the novices. However, the intriguing result was that the experts spent proportionately much more time than novices planning their approach. Novices, conversely, spent almost no time planning and instead started each problem by applying various equations to try to find a solution. This lack of planning led the novices to waste much of their time because they made false starts and took steps that ultimately did not lead to a correct solution (Chi et al., 1989). Similar effects have been found in other disciplines, such as writing and math (Hayes & Flower, 1986; Schoenfeld, 1987).

In other words, even though planning one's approach to a task can increase the chances of success, students tend not to recognize the need for it.

Research also shows that when students do engage in planning, they often make plans that are not well matched to the task at hand. For example, one research study analyzed the planning approaches of experts (college writing teachers) and novices (students) and then used independent judges to rate the quality of the final written texts. Results showed that all writers' plans addressed the content of what they intended to write, but only the most successful writers (based on final texts) considered the audience and overall purpose of the writing task they had been assigned (Carey et al., 1989).

Applying Strategies and Monitoring Performance

Once students have a plan and begin to apply strategies that implement their plan, they need to monitor their performance. In other words, students need to ask themselves, "Is this strategy working, or would another one be more productive?" Without effectively monitoring their own progress, students like John in the story at the beginning of the chapter may continue to apply an ineffective strategy and consequently waste time and achieve poor outcomes.

Research on the effects of students' self-monitoring activities has highlighted two important findings. First, students who naturally monitor their own progress and try to explain to themselves what they are learning along the way generally show greater learning gains as compared to students who engage less often in self-monitoring and self-explanation activities. For example, in one study, students were asked to talk aloud while they studied an introductory science topic in a textbook. After studying, the students took a problem-solving test that measured how much they had learned. The researchers analyzed the students in two groups according to their problem-solving performance—the good problem solvers and the poor problem solvers—and then looked at the talk-aloud protocols to see whether there were any differences in how students in the two groups had studied the textbook. A key difference they found was that the good problem solvers were far more likely to have monitored their understanding while they studied, that is, continually stopping themselves as they were reading to ask whether they were understanding the concepts just presented (Chi et al., 1989).

Although this research shows a positive relationship between natural self-monitoring behaviors and learning effectiveness, the question of real

195

interest for instructors is whether prompting students to self-monitor actually improves students' learning. Research in multiple science domains indicates that the answer is yes. Students who were taught or prompted to monitor their own understanding or to explain to themselves what they were learning had greater learning gains relative to students who were not given any monitoring instruction (Bielaczyc et al., 1995; Chi et al., 1994). In addition, research has shown that when students are taught to ask each other a series of comprehension-monitoring questions during reading, they learn to self-monitor more often and hence learn more from what they read (Palinscar & Brown, 1984).

Reflecting On and Adjusting One's Approach

Even when students monitor their performance and identify failures or short-comings in their approach, there is no guarantee that they will adjust or try more effective alternatives. They may be resistant, for any number of reasons, to change their current method, or they may lack alternative strategies. Melanie, for example, is reluctant to deviate from a style of writing that won her praise in high school. But even if she were able to recognize deficits in her analytical writing, she might not know how to write differently. John, too, may not know any other ways to study for an exam.

Research has shown that good problem solvers will try new strategies if their current strategy is not working, whereas poor problem solvers will continue to use a strategy even after it has failed (National Research Council, 2001, p. 78). Similarly, good writers will evaluate their writing from their audience's perspective and revise the parts of their work that do not convey the desired meaning (Hayes & Flower, 1986). However, these kinds of adjustments tend not to occur if the perceived cost of switching to a new approach is too high. Such costs include the time and effort it takes to change one's habits as well as the fact that new approaches, even if better in the long run, tend to underperform at first. So, busy or procrastination-prone students may be unwilling to put in an upfront invest-ment in making a change. In fact, research shows that people will often continue to use a familiar strategy that works moderately well rather than switch to a new strategy that would work better after some experience (Fu & Gray, 2004). This suggests that students will tend not to adopt newly learned strategies unless the perceived benefits clearly outweigh the perceived costs, especially the costs of effort and time.

Beliefs About Intelligence and Learning

At the beginning of this chapter, we indicated that students' beliefs about intelligence and learning can have a pervasive influence on metacognitive processes. Examples of such beliefs include whether students view learning as fast and easy or slow and difficult, and whether they perceive intelligence as fixed or malleable. Other examples include students' beliefs about their own abilities (in either direction) and their special talents.

Research shows that students' beliefs in these areas are associated with their learning-related behaviors and outcomes, including course grades and test scores (Schommer, 1994). For example, in one study, researchers collected a variety of measures, including students' beliefs about whether intelligence was fixed (there is nothing one can do to improve it) or incremental (one can work to develop greater intelligence), sense of self-efficacy, motivation, time spent studying, study strategies, and learning behaviors. By applying various statistical techniques to sort out the relationships among all these variables, the researchers found a pattern that linked students' beliefs about intelligence with their study strategies and learning behaviors (Henderson & Dweck, 1990). This connection makes intuitive sense in that students who believe intelligence is fixed have no reason to put in the time and effort to improve because they believe their effort will have little or no effect. Having put in relatively little effort, such students are less likely to learn and perform well. By contrast, students who believe that intelligence is incremental (i.e., skills can be developed that will lead to greater academic success) have a good reason to engage their time and effort in various study strategies because they believe this will improve their skills and hence their outcomes. Having put in relatively more effort—especially after facing difficulty—such students are more likely to learn and perform better.

The first story from the beginning of the chapter illustrates how beliefs about one's own abilities can also have an impact on metacognitive processes and learning. Melanie has beliefs about herself—"I'm a good writer" and "I always get As on my papers"—that influence her approach to Professor Yang's assignment. She starts her paper late, assuming that her innate talent for writing and her ability to work under pressure will carry her through. When the result—mainly her poor grade—does not match her beliefs and expectations, Melanie attributes the outcome to inaccurate grading rather than to her own conceptualization of the task, her skills, or the effort that she invested. If Melanie maintains these beliefs, it seems likely that she will not change her approach or try to refine her writing skills, even if she is given other opportunities to practice writing in this course.

197

By the converse line of reasoning, students who have negative beliefs about their abilities in particular contexts (e.g., "I'm no good at math") may feel defeated from the outset and consequently not bother to plan or implement effortful strategies because of the belief that any time and effort expended will do little good. Unfortunately, therefore, a belief in one's own abilities in either direction—strong or weak—can seriously impede one's metacognitive processes and hence learning and development.

What can be done to help students acquire more productive beliefs about learning? Although a common finding is that beliefs and attitudes are difficult to change, research offers some hope for modifying students' beliefs and consequently improving their learning. In a study of Stanford University students (Aronson et al., 2002), half of the students were given a short information session that promoted a *growth mindset*—belief in intelligence as malleable, that is, something that develops with practice and hard work. The other half received training that promoted a *fixed mindset*; these students were told that intelligence comprises multiple components (e.g., verbal, logical, interpersonal) and that people need to discover which of these fixed attributes is their particular talent in order to leverage their strengths. Both groups then participated in three sessions in which they were told to write letters to academically struggling high school students. In these letters, the study participants were encouraged to discuss the view of intelligence they had been taught in their information session as a means of encouraging their high school pen pals (who, in fact, did not exist). Follow-up assessments found that students in the growth mindset session showed more change in their views on intelligence and endorsed the malleable perspective more strongly than the fixed group and another control group of students who received no training. Over time, the malleable group showed an even stronger endorsement of the malleable position whereas the fixed and control groups did not. Perhaps most important, students in the growth mindset group rated their enjoyment of academics higher and showed a grade advantage the following quarter compared to the fixed and control groups.

As research on mindset has expanded into new study populations, it has led both to new insights and new critiques. In the former category, recent studies have demonstrated the relevance of mindset in discussions of educational disparities. For instance, one study showed that faculty members with fixed mindsets can inadvertently depress the motivation of students from groups underrepresented in STEM (Canning et al., 2019). Another study, conducted in Chile, suggested that a growth mindset can help to buffer students academically from the deleterious effects of poverty (Claro et al., 2016). At the same time, however, some researchers have been critical of mindset scholarship. Finding the results of earlier studies difficult to replicate (Burgoyne et al., 2020; Fletcher-Wood, 2022; Li & Bates, 2019; Macnamara, 2018), these scholars have questioned whether the effects of mindset have been overstated and suggest that factors other than mindset, for instance self-efficacy, might better explain the outcomes attributed to mindset (Burgoyne et al., 2020; Fletcher-Wood, 2022). Such critiques deserve consideration. At the same time, it should be pointed out that dozens of studies, some quite large (Yeager, 2019), continue to support the broader conclusions of mindset research (Rege et al., 2020; Yeager et al., 2019; Zhu et al., 2019). Moreover, the research is evolving, with studies focused less on *whether* mindset effects and interventions are significant and are instead moving toward exploring the *contexts* in which they are and the *mediators* that affect their salience (Yeager & Dweck, 2020). Some studies have explored the (not always intuitive) influence of culture on beliefs about learning and intelligence and thus the effects of mindset effects in different cultural milieus (Li & Bates, 2019; Osborn et al., 2020; Rege et al., 2020). Others are investigating how the contexts in which mindset interventions are administered function as critical mediators in their effects. As Yeager and Dweck (2020) point out, the questions for researchers going forward are when and where mindset effects are most salient and the interventions most powerful.

Implications of This Research

Perhaps the simplest summary of the research presented in each of the preceding six sections is to say that students tend not to apply metacognitive skills as well or as often as they should. This implies that students will often need our support in learning, refining, and effectively applying basic metacognitive skills. To address these needs, then, requires us as instructors to consider the advantages these skills can offer students in the long run and then, as appropriate, to make the development of metacognitive skills part of our course goals.

In the case of assessing the task at hand and planning an appropriate approach, students not only tend to generate inappropriate assessments and plans but also sometimes completely fail to consider these critical steps. This suggests that students may need significant practice at task assessment and planning even to remember to apply those skills.

199

In the case of monitoring one's progress and reflecting on one's overall success, research indicates that explicitly teaching students to engage in these processes is beneficial. Nevertheless, students will probably need considerable practice to apply these skills effectively.

Finally, some of the research—for example, on students' ability to evaluate their own strengths and weaknesses, their ability to adjust their strategies, and the impact of their beliefs about learning and intelligence—indicates somewhat larger obstacles to be overcome. In these cases, the most natural implication may be to address these issues as directly as possible—by working to raise students' awareness of the challenges they face and by considering some of the interventions that helped students productively modify their beliefs about intelligence—and, at the same time, to set reasonable expectations for how much improvement is likely to occur.

WHAT STRATEGIES DOES THE RESEARCH SUGGEST?

In this section, we list strategies for promoting each of the aspects of metacognition discussed in the chapter. In addition, we present two strategies that can be useful in helping students develop metacognitive skills in general.

Strategies to Promote Assessing the Task at Hand

Be More Explicit About the Goals of an Assignment Than You May Think Necessary Although it is natural to assume that a basic description of an assignment is sufficient, students may have assumptions about the nature of the task that are not in line with yours. For example, students in a design course might assume from previous experiences that the goal of any project is simply getting a finished product that they like. With this in mind, they might focus solely on the final design or presentation. However, if the instructor's objective is for students to develop more sophisticated process skills (e.g., researching relevant design ideas to spur their creativity, recording their exploration of multiple concepts, and explaining their design choices and revisions along the way to a final product), expressing these goals explicitly can have a positive impact on students' perceptions and learning, especially those from underrepresented groups (Winkelmes et al., 2016). It may also help to explain to students why these particular goals are important (e.g., "Developing strong process skills will help you become more consistent and more able to handle complex tasks") and to articulate what students need to do to meet the assignment's objectives (e.g., keeping a process journal in which they document their design iterations and explain their thought processes).

Tell Students What You Do Not Want In addition to clearly articulating your goals for an assignment, it can be helpful to identify what you do not want by referring to common misinterpretations students have shown in the past or by explaining why some pieces of work do not meet your assignment goals. For example, in the case of writing, it is often helpful to share writing samples that are annotated to highlight strong or weak features. Such samples can also be used to give students practice at recognizing some of the components you want them to include in their work (e.g., identifying an argument and its supporting evidence).

Check Students' Understanding of the Task To make sure that students are accurately assessing the task at hand, ask them what they think they need to do to complete an assignment or how they plan to prepare for an upcoming exam. Then give them feedback, including suggestions of alternatives if their strategies do not map onto the requirements of the task. For complex assignments, ask students to rewrite the main goal of the assignment in their own words and then describe the steps that they feel they need to take in order to complete that goal. Note that it can also be helpful (and eye-opening!) after introducing in-class group work to ask students to summarize the task they are about to do. This enables you to correct misconceptions before they break into groups—especially important online, where you may not have visibility into their work in breakout rooms. Moreover, if done regularly, this strategy encourages students to listen more carefully to task instructions in anticipation of having to explain the task themselves.

Provide Performance Criteria with the Assignment When distributing an assignment, clearly articulate the criteria that will be used to evaluate students' work. This can be done as a checklist that highlights the assignment's key requirements (see Appendix F on learner checklists), such as content, structural features, and formatting details. Encourage students to refer to the checklist as they work on the assignment and require them to submit a signed copy of it with the final product. With further practice on similar assignments, such checklists can be phased out as students begin to check their work on their own.

Your criteria could also be communicated to students through a performance rubric that explicitly represents the component parts of the task along with the characteristics of each component at varying levels of mastery (see Appendix E on rubrics). Distributing the rubric with the assignment description—instead of only with the graded assignment—helps students assess the task more accurately. In addition to helping students size up a particular assignment, rubrics can help students develop other metacognitive habits, such as evaluating their own work against a set of criteria. Over time, these metacognitive skills should become internalized and automatic.

Strategies to Promote Evaluating One's Own Strengths and Weaknesses

Give Early, Performance-Based Assessments Provide students with ample practice and timely feedback to help them develop a more accurate assessment of their strengths and weaknesses. Do this early enough in the semester so that they have time to learn from your feedback and adjust as necessary. Identify the particular skills that questions and assignments target (e.g., "These first five questions ask you to define terms and concepts while the second set of five requires a more sophisticated synthesis of theoretical approaches") so that students can see how well they do on a range of skills and can focus their energies on improving weaker skills. These formative assessments should help students detect the knowledge gaps they need to overcome.

Incorporate Polls, Clicker Questions, and Low-Stakes Quizzes to Build Self-Assessment Skills Whether teaching face-to-face or virtually, it is beneficial to incorporate frequent knowledge checks to help students assess their understanding and calibrate their study strategies and help-seeking decisions accordingly. This can be done synchronously through the incorporation of polls or clicker questions during virtual or face-to-face class sessions or asynchronously with the incorporation of knowledge-check questions in digital platforms to accompany readings, videos, or other asynchronous content. Ungraded pre-assessments—questions administered to students *before* providing content—can also help students identify knowledge gaps, motivating further learning while also building metacognitive skills. It should be noted that many digital platforms make it possible to integrate auto-graded self-assessments that do not add additional grading work for instructors. For more information on self-assessments, see Appendix C.

Provide Practice Exams for Self-Assessment Consider giving students practice exams that replicate the kinds of questions that they will see on real exams and then provide answer keys so that students can check their own work. When doing so, it is important to emphasize to students that the true benefits come from doing the activity—that is, writing answers to sample essay questions or solving problems—and reflecting on the experience rather than simply looking over the answers provided. This is important because looking at a solution or model answer without first working through the problem can lead students to believe that they know how to generate answers when they only know how to recognize a good answer when it is given to them.

Leverage Technology to Help Students Assess Their Strengths and Areas for Improvement New technologies and platforms can provide students with insights on their learning that can help them build stronger self-assessment skills. Knowledge checks and formative assessments embedded in videos and online lessons can provide students with immediate feedback on their understanding. Learning analytics and student dashboards can help students assess their strengths and weaknesses relative to stated learning objectives. In addition, opportunities for reflection and future planning can be built into online content, encouraging reflective habits of mind.

Strategies to Promote Planning an Appropriate Approach

Have Students Implement a Plan That You Provide For complex assignments, provide students with a set of interim deadlines or a timeline for deliverables that reflects the way that you would plan the stages of work—in other words, a model for effective planning. For example, for a semester-long research paper, you could ask students to submit an annotated bibliography of the sources they anticipate using by week 4, a draft of their thesis statement in week 6, evidence supporting their thesis in week 8, a visual representation of their paper's structure in week 10, and a draft that has been reviewed by at least three peers and revised accordingly in week 12. Although requiring students to follow a plan that you provide does not give them practice developing their own plan, it does help them think about the component parts of a complex task, as well as their logical sequencing. Remember that planning is extremely difficult for novices. As students gain experience, this kind of explicit modeling can be removed gradually and students can be required to develop and submit their own plan for approval.

Have Students Create Their Own Plan When students' planning skills have developed to a degree that they can make plans more independently, you can require them to submit a plan as the first deliverable in larger assignments. This could be in the form of a project proposal, an annotated bibliography, or a time line that identifies the key stages of work. Provide feedback on their plan, given that this is a skill that they should continue to refine. If students perceive that planning is a valued and assessed component of a task, they will be more likely to focus time and effort on planning and, as a result, benefit from their investment.

Make Planning the Central Goal of the Assignment If you wish to reinforce the value of planning and help students develop the skills of generating and revising their own plans, assign some tasks that focus solely on planning. For example, instead of solving or completing a task, students could be asked to plan a solution strategy for a set of problems that involves describing how they would solve each problem. Such assignments enable students to focus all of their energy on thinking the problem through and planning an appropriate approach. They also make students' thought processes explicit, rather than requiring you to intuit them from a final product. Follow-up assignments can require students to implement their plans and reflect on their strengths and deficiencies.

Teach Students How to Use General-Purpose Planning Tools Project management tools encourage students to break down complex tasks and evaluate the time and resources needed to complete them. This can help with both task assessment and planning. Consider building the use of these tools explicitly into assignments. For example, one milestone or interim deliverable in a project might be to submit a Gantt chart or other planning document. This gives students both a designated opportunity to plan and the chance to get early feedback. Bear in mind that, as technologically savvy as they are, students may not know how to use these tools, so you may need to demonstrate each tool's functions and explain its learning benefits.

Strategies to Promote Applying Strategies and Monitoring Performance

Provide Simple Heuristics for Self-Correction Teach students basic heuristics for quickly assessing their own work and identifying errors. For example, encourage students to ask themselves, "Is this a reasonable answer, given the problem?" If the answer is unreasonable—such as a negative number for a quantity measuring length—the students know that they did something wrong and can reconsider their reasoning or recalculate. There are often disciplinary heuristics that students should also learn to apply. For example, in an anthropology class, students might ask themselves, "What assumptions am I making here, and to what extent are they appropriate for cross-cultural analysis?" Similarly, instructors can provide more practical guidelines for assignments, such as how long it should take to complete an assignment. If students find that they are taking far longer to complete the task than is reasonable, they know to either try a different approach or to seek help.

Have Students Do Guided Self-Assessments Require students to assess their own work against a set of criteria that you provide, for example a rubric or a checklist. Exercises in self-assessment can raise students' awareness of task requirements, hone their ability to recognize the qualities of good as well as poor work, and teach them how to monitor their own progress toward learning goals. However, students may not be able to accurately assess their own work without first seeing this skill demonstrated or getting some explicit instruction and practice. For example, some instructors find it helpful to share annotated samples of student work, in which good and poor qualities of the work are highlighted, before asking students to assess their own work.

Require Students to Reflect On and Annotate Their Own Work Require as a component of the assignment that students explain what they did and why, describe how they responded to various challenges, and so on. This can be done in various ways for different disciplines. For example, engineering students can annotate problem sets, sociology students can answer reflective questions about their methodological decisions or assumptions, and architecture students can keep process logs in which they record various iterations of a design and explain their choices. Requiring reflection or annotation helps students become more conscious of their own thought processes and work strategies and can lead them to make more appropriate adjustments.

Use Peer Review/Reader Response Have students analyze their classmates' work and provide feedback. Reviewing one another's work can help students evaluate and monitor their own work more effectively and then revise it accordingly. However, peer review is generally only effective when you give student reviewers specific criteria about what to look for and comment on (e.g., a set of questions to answer or a rubric to follow). For example, you might ask student reviewers to assess whether a peer's writing has a clearly articulated argument and corresponding evidence to support the argument. Similarly, you might ask students to document or evaluate how a classmate has solved a math problem and provide their own recommendations for a more effective strategy. For more information on peer reviews/reader responses, see Appendix I.

205

Strategies to Promote Reflecting On and Adjusting One's Approach

Provide Activities That Require Students to Reflect on Their Performances Include as a component of projects and assignments—or across projects and assignments—a formal requirement that students reflect on and analyze their own performance. For example, they may answer questions such as, What did you learn from doing this project? What skills do you need to work on? How would you prepare differently or approach the final assignment based on feedback across the semester? How have your skills evolved across the last three assignments? Requiring this self-reflective step can give students a valuable opportunity to stop and assess their own strengths and weaknesses and to build their metacognitive skills.

Prompt Students to Analyze the Effectiveness of Their Study Skills When students learn to reflect on the effectiveness of their own approach, they are able to identify problems and make the necessary adjustments. A specific example of a self-reflective activity is an "exam wrapper," which are typically short handouts that students complete when an exam is returned to them; exam wrappers guide students through a brief analysis of their own performance on an exam and then ask students to relate their performance to various features of how they studied or prepared. For example, an exam wrapper might ask students (1) what types of errors they made (e.g., mathematical versus conceptual), (2) how they studied (e.g., "looked over" problems the night before versus worked out multiple problems a week prior to the exam), and (3) what they will do differently in preparation for the next exam (e.g., rework problems from scratch rather than simply skim solutions). When students complete and submit exam wrappers after one exam, their responses can be returned to them before the next exam so they have a ready reminder of what they learned from their prior exam experience that can help them study more effectively. For more information on exam wrappers, see Appendix J.

Present Multiple Strategies Show students multiple ways that a task or problem can be conceptualized, represented, or solved. One method for doing this in the arts is through public critiques in which students share different ways that they approached the problem, thus presenting one another with a range of possible solutions. In this way, students get exposure to multiple methods and can consider their pros and cons under a variety of circumstances. In other courses, students might be asked to solve problems in multiple ways and then discuss the advantages and disadvantages of the different methods. Exposing students to different approaches and analyzing their merits can highlight the value of critical exploration.

Create Assignments That Focus on Strategizing Rather Than Implementation Have students propose a range of potential strategies and predict their advantages and disadvantages rather than actually choosing and carrying one through. For example, students might be asked to assess the applicability of different formulas, methodologies, or artistic techniques for a given problem or task. By putting the emphasis of the assignment on thinking the problem through, rather than solving it, students get practice evaluating strategies in relation to their appropriate or fruitful application.

Strategies to Promote Productive Beliefs About Intelligence and Learning

Broaden Students' Understanding of Learning Students often believe that "you either know something or you don't know it." In fact, learning and knowledge can operate on multiple levels, from the ability to recall a fact, concept, or theory (declarative knowledge) to knowing how to apply it (procedural knowledge) to knowing when to apply it (contextual knowledge) to knowing why it is appropriate in a particular situation (conceptual knowledge). In other words, you can know something at one level (recognize it) and still not know it (know how to use it). Consider introducing students to these various forms of knowledge so that they can more accurately assess a task (e.g., "This calls for me to define x and explain when it is applicable"), assess their own strengths and weaknesses in relation to it (e.g., "I can define x but I don't know when to use it"), and identify gaps in their education (e.g., "I've never learned how to use x"). You might also point out to students that different kinds of knowledge are required for different tasks—for example, solving problems, writing poetry, designing products, and performing on stage. Asking students to consider diverse types and dimensions of knowledge can help expand their beliefs about intelligence and ability in ways that enhance their metacognitive development (see types of knowledge in Chapter 2 on prior knowledge).

Directly Address Students' Beliefs About Themselves and Their Learning Even if it is not directly germane to the disciplinary content of your course, consider discussing the nature of learning and intelligence with your students to disabuse them of unproductive beliefs (e.g., "I can't draw" or "I can't do math") and to highlight the positive effects of practice, effort, and adaptation. Some instructors like to point out that the brain is like a muscle that requires exercise or to make the analogy between the ongoing practice required by musicians, dancers, and athletes to achieve excellence and the mental discipline and practice necessary for developing intellectual skills. The message "this course will require real mental effort, but you can do it and you will come out the other side stronger for it" is empowering and can help cultivate students' growth mindset.

Normalize That Learning Is Effortful An attribute of fixed mindset is that students believe that if learning is difficult or effortful, something is wrong. In fact, it is often the act of struggling to learn something that makes knowledge stick in long-term memory, a key aspect of Bjork's notion of "desirable difficulties" (Bjork & Bjork, 2020; see Chapter 6 on practice feedback). To help students see that effort is productive rather than a sign of trouble, it can be helpful to talk explicitly about how working hard on an upcoming assignment makes the learning itself more robust and meaningful. Some instructors give their students a range of time it will likely take to, say, finish a given problem set. This can help students calibrate their expectations of reasonable effort (so they don't give up too quickly) and also indicate when students may be spinning their wheels (and could use more/different strategies to apply their effort more effectively).

Help Students Set Realistic Expectations Give students realistic expectations for the time that it might take them to develop particular skills. It can be helpful to recall your own frustrations as a student and to describe how you (or famous figures in your field) overcame various obstacles. Seeing that intelligent and accomplished people sometimes struggle to gain mastery—and that learning does not happen magically or without effort—can prompt students to revise their own expectations about learning and their views of intelligence and to persevere when they encounter difficulty. It can also help students avoid unproductive and often inaccurate attributions about themselves (e.g., "I can't do it; I must be dumb," "This is too hard; I'm not cut out for science") or the environment (e.g., "I still haven't learned it; this instructor is no good," "I failed; the test was unfair") and instead focus on aspects of learning over which they have control: their effort, concentration, study habits, level of engagement, and so on.

Promote Help-Seeking as a Positive Learning Strategy For a number of reasons, students may be reluctant to approach their instructors for help. They may be intimidated by the power differential, afraid of admitting confusion, or hesitant to impose on the instructor's time. They may also not realize the extent to which good advice at early stages of a project or paper could save them time and prevent mistakes later. It is important to combat this reluctance to seek help by actively promoting help-seeking. Tell students explicitly that seeking help is a critical part of effective learning and a normal part of academic growth. Make sure they know how to contact you if they are struggling and how quickly they can expect a response. Share information about university support centers (e.g., writing center, academic support unit, disability services) and explain how other students have found them helpful to help demystify their services and reduce negative perceptions associated with their use. Encourage students to come to your office hours when they need help or simply want to talk about course material. Some instructors even give students bonus points for attending office hours early in the semester. When students do reach out, welcome them warmly and commend them for taking the initiative.

Model a Growth Mindset The best way to encourage a growth mindset in your students is to model a growth mindset yourself. Acknowledge when you do not have all the answers ("That's a great question. I'll look into it and let you know in the next class."). Share your own intellectual growth with your students by discussing how your thinking, research strategies, approaches to collaboration, and so on, have changed over time. Thank students when they teach you things you did not know. Modeling a cognitive orientation focused on learning, self-reflection, and humility (as opposed to performance, achievement, and ego) creates the conditions for students to do the same.

Provide Opportunities to Reflect on Values Researchers have found that focusing student attention on the core values that guide them can serve as a type of inoculation from discouragement when they encounter failures or setbacks (Broda et al., 2018; Hecht et al., 2021; Shnabel et al., 2013). This is particularly true for students in groups vulnerable to social identity threats (Cook et al., 2012; Wu et al., 2021). Thus, if appropriate for a given course, it can be helpful to incorporate opportunities for students to write about their values and reflect on how those values drive and sustain them, particularly in relation to the course content. For instance, one student might write about how her commitment to addressing health problems in her community brought her into medicine and sustains her when she is feeling defeated or insecure. Another might write about how his family's strong orientation to social justice has led him to pursue education and why contributing to the next generation is important to him. Reflecting on core values can serve as an anchoring point to stabilize and bolster students through times of adversity.

General Strategies to Promote Metacognition

Beyond these strategies that target individual processes of the metacognitive cycle, there are additional strategies that are useful for supporting a variety of metacognitive skills. These strategies can be employed to promote the development of multiple metacognitive skills at once or to concentrate on a particular one.

Model Your Metacognitive Processes Show students how you yourself would approach an assignment and walk them through the various phases of your metacognitive process. Let them hear you talk out loud as you describe the way you would assess the task ("I like to begin by asking what the central problem is and considering the audience") and assess your own strengths and weaknesses in relation to the task ("I have a pretty good handle on the basic concepts, but I don't yet know what recent research has been done on the subject"). Then lay out your plan of action explicitly, articulating the various steps that you would undertake to complete the assignment ("I would start by browsing the relevant journals online, then create a set of exploratory sketches, then . . ."). You could also include in your modeling some discussion of how you evaluate and monitor your progress—for example, by mentioning the kinds of questions you ask yourself to ensure that you are on the right path ("Could I be solving this problem more efficiently?" or "Am I making any questionable assumptions here?"). It is especially helpful for students to see that even experts—in fact, especially experts—constantly reassess and adjust as they go. Finally, you can show your students how you would evaluate the finished product ("I would revisit the original goal of the project and ask myself whether I satisfied it" or "I would ask a friend of mine with some knowledge of the subject matter to read my essay and point out logical inconsistencies").

A variation on, or potentially a second stage of, this modeling process is to lead students through a given task with a series of questions they can ask themselves each step of the way (e.g., How would you begin? What step would you take next? How would you know if your strategy is working? Is there an alternative approach?).

Scaffold Students in Their Metacognitive Processes Scaffolding refers to the process by which instructors provide students with cognitive supports early in their learning, and then gradually remove them as students develop greater mastery and sophistication. There are several forms of scaffolding that can help students develop stronger metacognitive skills. First, instructors can give students practice working on discrete phases of the metacognitive process in isolation before asking students to integrate them. (Some examples of this were discussed in relation to specific phases of metacognition.) Breaking down the process highlights the importance of particular stages, such as task assessment and planning, that students often undervalue or omit while giving them practice with and feedback on each skill individually. After giving students practice with particular skills in isolation, it is equally important to give students practice synthesizing skills and using them in combination. Ultimately, the goal of this form of scaffolding is to progress toward more complexity and integration.

A second form of scaffolding involves a progression from tasks with considerable instructor-provided structure to tasks that require greater or even complete student autonomy. For example, you might first assign a project in which students must follow a plan that you devise—perhaps including a breakdown of component tasks, a timetable, and interim deadlines for deliverables—and then in later projects, relegate more of these planning and self-monitoring responsibilities to the students themselves.

SUMMARY

Faculty members almost invariably possess strong metacognitive skills themselves, even if they are not explicitly aware of using them. They may, as a result, assume that students also possess these skills or that they will develop them naturally and inevitably. Consequently, faculty members may both overestimate their students' metacognitive abilities and underestimate the extent to which these skills and habits must be taught and reinforced through thoughtful instruction. Indeed, the research cited in this chapter suggests that metacognition does not necessarily develop on its own and that instructors can play a critical role in helping students develop the metacognitive skills that they need to succeed: assessing the task at hand, evaluating one's own strengths and weaknesses, planning, monitoring performance along the way, and reflecting on one's overall success.

Conclusion:
Applying the Eight
Principles to Ourselves

By now, the power of the principles described in the book should be apparent. These principles explain and predict a wide range of learning behaviors and phenomena and hence aid the design of courses and classroom pedagogy, support the development of meaningful learning activities and assessments, and guide the diagnosis of many teaching problems. Their interconnectedness should also be evident. Many of the problems students encounter when learning stem from an interaction of intellectual, social, and emotional factors. Therefore, their pedagogical solutions should ideally address all these facets at once. This is achievable precisely because our principles work together to provide solutions. It also means that the number of strategies we must master to be effective teachers is not infinite. In fact, although the specific strategies throughout this book vary from chapter to chapter, there are recurring themes among the strategies, such as collecting data about students, modeling expert practice, scaffolding complex tasks, and being explicit about objectives and expectations. These basic themes jointly address cognitive, motivational, and developmental goals. For instance, being explicit about one's learning objectives and grading criteria helps students see the component parts of a complex task and thus enables them to target their practice and move toward mastery. It also serves a motivational function because it increases students' expectations of success at the task, and it even affects the learning climate by fostering a sense of fairness.

What is perhaps less evident is that these principles of learning apply to instructors as well because, when it comes to teaching, most of us are still learning. Teaching is a highly complex activity, and yet most of us have not received formal training in pedagogy or the scholarship that informs our understanding of the mechanisms by which students process information and learn. Furthermore, teaching is a highly contextualized activity because it is shaped by the students we have, advancements in our respective fields, changes in technology, national or global disasters, and so on. Therefore, our teaching and our role as teachers must constantly adapt to changing parameters. Although this realization can be overwhelming for some, it can also help us reframe our approach to improving our teaching because it means that we need not expect a static perfection but rather a developing mastery of teaching. Learning to improve one's teaching is a process of progressive refinement, which, like other learning processes, may be productively informed by the learning principles set forth in this book. This concluding chapter thus applies our eight learning principles to the process of learning about teaching. We highlight each principle's implications to learning about teaching. Just as in the previous chapters, we consider each principle individually for ease of exposition, but the ideas stemming from the eight principles are all interrelated.

Just like we did for the students, we start by acknowledging our individuality as educators. As Parker Palmer noted in *The Courage to Teach* (2017), good teaching cannot be reduced to technique. Instead, "good teaching comes from the identity and integrity of the teacher" (p. 10). Our histories, personalities, intersectional identities, and aspirations have shaped how we approach teaching. Our identities might be points of connection with some students but not with others. Whether we are seen by our students as approachable or aloof, easy or harsh graders, authoritarian or democratic, gatekeeping or uplifting, our teaching style is the synthesis of our unique experiences. At the same time, our current situation is not our pedagogical destiny. We all possess the ability to evolve as teachers, and just like our students, we go through developmental processes ourselves. We have described the *intellectual development* process for our students, and something analogous happens for educators as well. We might begin at a stage where we are looking for the "right answer," the pedagogical magic bullet that will, say, achieve full student participation during classroom discussion. At some other stages, we might regard teaching solely as a matter of personal style and believe there is no better or worse way to go about it. At later stages we might realize that teaching is highly contextualized and think about the many decisions we need to make as educators in terms of student learning. In addition, our *identity* as instructors also goes through developmental stages. We have to work to develop a sense of competence, autonomy, and purpose as educators, a productive way to relate to the students, and appropriate ways to express our emotions in the classroom. In advanced stages of intellectual and identity development, we might develop trust in our own style while being open to improvement. Our developing *social identities* also shape our teaching. Our experiences with privilege and marginalization can instill us with a broader sense of purpose, even as we struggle to rework what that might mean in practice. At the same time, our identities can complicate our experience as educators, and like our students, we may need to seek help and build support networks for advocacy and allyship.

Like students, we possess considerable *prior knowledge* on which we draw consciously and unconsciously when we teach, and this prior knowledge affects further learning and performance. But as we have seen, prior knowledge can be insufficient, inaccurate, or inappropriate, in which case it will hinder further learning. For instance, as experts in our respective fields, we possess a wealth of content knowledge, but this alone is insufficient for effective teaching. Some of us also possess the misconception that good teaching is all about entertainment and personality, and that to be a good teacher one must be outgoing and funny. Not only is this notion inaccurate, but also it is problematic because it locks both introvert and extrovert teachers into narrow and rigid roles without much room for growth. Finally, although it is helpful to be mindful of our own experiences as learners, it would be inappropriate to presume that all our students will share the same experiences we do and that therefore whatever teaching methods worked for us should work for our students as well. As pointed out repeatedly throughout this book, we are different from our students in many important ways. One of the recurring strategies emphasized in this book involves collecting data about students to help inform our teaching practice. Seen in this light, learning about our students is a way to build on our prior knowledge by learning more about our current instructional context and using this information to tailor our teaching to our audience.

Of course, in conjunction with the knowledge we possess about teaching, we need to think about the *organization* of that knowledge. Many of us started our careers without a rich, integrated, and flexible network of knowledge about teaching. For example, it is fairly common to keep one's knowledge of teaching compartmentalized by course: these are the kinds of assignments that work better for this course, these are the kinds of policies that are necessary when teaching first-year students, this is how to teach an online course, and so on. This organization is born out of experience, but it does not make for a flexible and systematic way to think about teaching because it centers on surface features of the course. The principles of learning presented in this book offer a deeper, more meaningful structure for organizing one's knowledge of teaching and learning and for building on that knowledge. This can help, for instance, when planning a new course for a new audience or offering a course in a new modality.

But refining our teaching is not solely a cognitive process. It is also important to consider our *motivation* to learn (and continue to learn) about teaching. Given our other professional responsibilities and constraints, what will sustain our efforts to improve our teaching? As we have seen, motivation is broadly determined by value and expectancy. One thing that most instructors value is efficiency. We are all busy, with multiple demands on our time. Working on our teaching further taxes that limited resource. Therefore, it is important that our time investment pays off. Several of the strategies we offer in this book require a time investment up front, but they yield time savings later on, especially for future iterations of the same course. For instance, creating a rubric can be time-consuming, especially the first time, but it also saves time later by streamlining the grading process and reducing student complaints—in addition to the learning benefits for students. On the expectation side, we are more likely to stay motivated if we set teaching goals for ourselves that are realistic, so that we are more likely to maintain confidence in our ability to achieve those goals. This may, for example, mean that we should concentrate on improving one or two aspects of our teaching in a given semester, rather than trying to address everything simultaneously. It also might mean that instead of making radical changes to a course, we attempt more incremental changes, reflecting on those changes as we go. Many successful, experienced instructors maintain that it takes at the very least three years of progressive refinement to build an effective course.

Realistic expectations are especially important because teaching is an immensely complex skill. To develop *mastery* in teaching, we need to acquire its component skills, integrate them, and apply them appropriately. Of course, this requires that we first unpack the multifaceted task of teaching. For example, the ability to facilitate productive and engaging discussions requires multiple subskills: the ability to pose appropriate questions, listen empathetically, maintain flow, respectfully correct misconceptions, navigate the classroom technology, monitor the classroom tone, manage time effectively, and many more. Putting all these skills together is the ultimate multitask. We need to acquire fluency in each of the component parts in order to develop automaticity, which reduces the cognitive load that any one subskill requires. Moreover, as with the development of mastery in any other domain, teaching requires learning when and where various teaching strategies and instructional approaches are applicable; for example, when one's learning objectives would be best served by group projects or case studies and when they would not, or when a multiple choice test is warranted and when it is not. In other words, refining our teaching practice requires that we

215

transfer what we learn about teaching from one context to another, making adjustments as our courses, our students, our fields—and, indeed, ourselves—change. Perhaps most importantly, we need to be constantly on the lookout for situations in which our expert blind spot prevents us from accurately gauging where our students are and what they need from us in order to progress.

Developing mastery in teaching is a learning process, and as such it requires the coupling of *practice and feedback*. As we have seen, for practice to be maximally effective, it should be focused on clear goals. In order to set appropriate goals for our teaching, we can be guided by timely and frequent feedback on what aspects of our courses are and are not working. Most institutions mandate end-of-semester evaluations in which students can give instructors feedback about their teaching, but that kind of feedback is not the most useful for direct improvement of our teaching practice because it happens at the end of the term. The best feedback is formative feedback throughout the semester. This feedback can come from sources such as early course evaluations, student management teams, colleagues, and teaching center staff. So, for instance, if students raise concerns about the organization of our lectures, this can help us focus our efforts on a particular goal to improve. Just as many of our students do not think of homework as practicing specific skills, most of us do not think of our teaching as "practice." However, like our students, we learn most efficiently when we exercise the skills we most need to develop. If we think of teaching as deliberate, focused practice, in the previous hypothetical situation we could decide to cultivate specific practices such as having an agenda for every lecture or making transitions between subtopics more explicit, and then we can seek feedback on how those practices worked.

Thinking of teaching as progressive refinement raises the issue of *climate*, because climate affects our ability to learn and grow just as it does our students' ability. Like our students, we are social and emotional—and not merely cognitive—beings. Working in a department that values and supports teaching, where learning principles and teaching strategies are regularly discussed, and where we feel comfortable sharing challenges and seeking advice, is energizing and conducive to learning. Conversely, it is isolating and demoralizing to work in a department or institution that does not adequately support efforts to improve teaching. Continuing to expand our skills and insights as teachers in such an environment is difficult. Even in departments that value teaching and promote professional development, faculty members from underrepresented groups can feel marginalized—their sense of belonging eroded—if the programming offered does not represent their own teaching experiences. These experiences can be shaped as much by students as they are by departments, institutions, and colleagues. Indeed, faculty members from minoritized groups may encounter far more microaggressions and disrespect in the classroom than their majority counterparts, factors that influence the teaching climate in profoundly negative ways. Departments that want both their faculty members and their students to thrive would be wise to create spaces where these issues can be discussed openly, along with mechanisms to identify and remediate them. We have options to consider individually as well. If our immediate environment does not support our growth and well-being as teachers, we can seek more supportive climates by broadening our reach to colleagues in other departments, to the education section of the various professional associations, to the teaching center on campus, or to colleagues at other institutions. These supportive networks can also help neutralize the dispiriting challenges higher education faces on the broader societal and national levels (see Preface).

In this chapter, we have highlighted various aspects of learning about teaching using the learning principles as lenses of analysis. In general, all these principles can help us be more reflective—that is, metacognitive—about our teaching. As shown in this book, *self-directed learning* (metacognition) requires engaging in a cyclical process with several phases. Specifically, we need to carefully consider our own strengths and weaknesses in relation to our teaching, not only so we can play to our strengths but also so we can challenge ourselves to develop in areas in which we may need work. Moreover, because the task of teaching constantly changes (as our student population changes, as we teach new courses, as we revise old courses to include new material, and as we try new approaches), we must continually reassess the task, plan an effective approach, monitor our progress, evaluate, and adjust. Just as many students do not naturally think of planning before they get started on a task, many instructors do the same with their courses. For instance, they construct the assessments for a course as an afterthought, instead of planning them—from the start—to be in alignment with the course's learning objectives and instructional strategies. Knowing that we are likely to skip some of the steps in the metacognitive cycle can help us be mindful of this tendency and compensate for it.

Finally, refining our teaching practice requires being aware of our core beliefs about teaching and learning. For instance, what do we believe is the purpose of our teaching? What do we believe about intelligence, ability, and learning? All these beliefs will affect our metacognitive cycle. For instance, if we think of teaching skill as a talent that one either has or lacks, we may not engage in the kinds of behaviors (e.g., self-reflection, comparing strategies with colleagues, seeking professional development, and reading this book!) that might help us improve. Conversely, if we think of teaching as a set of skills one can develop and refine, it makes sense to engage in progressive refinement and in the whole meta-cognitive cycle. This book is a start in that process and an invitation to keep thinking and learning about teaching. We hope that the ideas presented here will be generative of more insights and more strategies as readers apply and refine them over time.

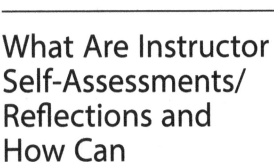

What Are Instructor Self-Assessments/ Reflections and How Can We Use Them?

A s humans, we all operate under a set of assumptions that help us deal with the complexities of life, including the classroom setting. Some of the assumptions we hold are more conscious than others, and some turn out to hold true more often than others. Nevertheless, it is often productive to uncover and question our assumptions because they can have a large impact on the way we interact with our students, and hence, on their learning. The Pygmalion Effect (Rosenthal & Jacobson, 1992) documents this phenomenon. Here is a set of questions to help us reflect on our assumptions. The list is adapted from the Derek Bok Center for Teaching and Learning (n.d.). The original list has been updated and expanded, and organized in broad categories.

ASSUMPTIONS ABOUT EXPERIENCE/KNOWLEDGE

All too often we unconsciously assume other people have our same frames of reference, and we speak and behave as if everyone is familiar with them. We might not realize that the terms we use, or the examples we choose, do not speak as powerfully to other people, which makes our explanations less meaningful. Some students might also feel marginalized by our language. Here are some examples of questions we might ask ourselves.

- Do I expect my students to share my cultural and political perspectives?
- Do I expect most students to come from "comfortable" backgrounds?
- Do I expect most students to share my historical, popular culture, religious, or literary references?
- Do I expect most students to come from traditional families?
- Do I fail to recognize that members of the dominant group have benefited from the privileges that come from membership in that group?
- Do I expect most students of color to come from lower-income families or have weaker academic preparation?
- Do I expect minority students to be first-generation college students?
- Do I expect African Americans, Latinos, Asians, or other students of color to be all alike within their group?

ASSUMPTIONS ABOUT ABILITY

This set of assumptions pertains to our expectations about students. Instructor's expectations are powerful determinants of motivation and performance because students tend to conform to the expectations placed on them, or instructors might inadvertently discount information that is contrary to their expectations. These phenomena are amply documented in theory and research about internalized expectations, self-efficacy, stereotype threat, Pygmalion complex, and confirmation bias. Here are some examples of questions we might ask ourselves.

- Do I expect minority students to need extra help?
- Do I imagine that Latinos or Blacks will express their opinion in non-academic language?
- Do I expect that Asian students will do better than other students, especially in math?
- Do I expect women in scientific fields to struggle more?
- Do I expect students from certain majors to have weaker intellectual skills?
- Do I assume international students have less language skills?
- Do I link certain individual characteristics with levels of intelligence and ability (e.g., political or religious beliefs, tattoos and piercings, athletic or Greek system membership)?

ASSUMPTIONS ABOUT IDENTITY AND VIEWPOINT

Some aspects of our identity are readily visible, others are invisible, and others yet are deceiving. It is easy to focus only on the visible aspects, but this might alienate some students who don't see themselves represented in your language or in the course curriculum. Students who feel marginalized in a course are likely to experience a decrease in their intrinsic motivation to learn the material. Here are some examples of questions we might ask ourselves.

- Do I treat students as if they are all heterosexual?
- Do I treat students as if they are all Christian?
- Do I think all students look like the gender or race they identify as?
- Do I think I know my students' pronouns?
- Do I think I can tell which students have physical or mental/learning disabilities?
- Do I think I can tell the political affiliation of my students?
- Do I think all students can easily meet in groups out of class?

ASSUMPTIONS INFLUENCING ATTRIBUTIONS

When faced with certain events in the classroom (a student's question, a request for an extension, a suspicious paper) we make attributions about what explains that event, and we react accordingly. A lot of our attributions are colored by assumptions; therefore, it is worth reflecting on them. Here are some examples of questions we might ask ourselves.

- Do I ascribe confident-sounding (as opposed to tentative) language to intellectual strength (as opposed to weakness)?
- Do I link less-than-fluent English skills (speaking and writing) to weaker preparation?
- Do I believe that certain cultural communication styles (e.g., those that never seem to get to the point or take a position) betray a low level of preparedness or confidence?
- Do I assume that students who don't participate in discussions have not done the readings?

- Am I inclined to believe that "good" students requesting an extension probably have a good reason, whereas "bad" students doing the same are just lazy?
- If content and materials are not diverse, was there a deliberate choice to limit the diversity of the materials and does that choice truly serve the course's teaching and learning aims?

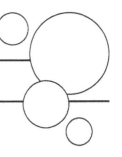

What Are Ground Rules and How Can We Use Them?

Ground rules help to maintain a productive and welcoming classroom climate by clearly articulating a set of expected behaviors for classroom conduct, especially for discussions. Ground rules can be set by the instructor or created by the students themselves (some people believe that students adhere more to ground rules they have played a role in creating). Ground rules should reflect the objectives of the course. For example, if an objective of the course is for students to enlist evidence to support an opinion, a ground rule could reinforce that goal; if a goal is for students to connect content material to personal experiences, then ground rules that protect privacy and create a safe environment for sharing personal information are important.

Ground rules should be established at the beginning of a course, and the instructor should explain the purpose they serve (e.g., to ensure that discussions are spirited and passionate but not combative, that everyone is respected and every voice heard, and that participants work together toward greater understanding rather than contribute disjointed pieces). Some instructors ask students to sign a contract based on the ground rules; others simply discuss and agree to the ground rules informally. It is important for instructors to remind students of these ground rules periodically, particularly if problems occur (e.g., students cutting one another off in discussion or making inappropriate personal comments). Instructors should also be sure to hold students accountable to these rules, for example, by exacting a small penalty for minor infractions (this can be done in a lighthearted way, perhaps by asking students who violate the rules to contribute a dollar to a class party fund), by factoring conduct during discussions into a participation grade for the course, and by responding immediately and unequivocally to behavior that marginalizes or belittles others in the class.

For sample ground rules, see Exhibit B.1, and for a method for helping students create their own ground rules, see Exhibit B.2.

Exhibit B.1. Sample Ground Rules

For Face-to-Face Discussions

Listen actively and attentively.
Ask for clarification if you are confused.
Do not interrupt one another.
Recognize that your classmates have different lived experiences.
Treat your classmates' comments and questions with respect.
Critique ideas, not people.
Do not offer opinions without supporting evidence.
Avoid put-downs (even humorous ones).
Take responsibility for the quality of the discussion.
Build on one another's comments; work toward shared understanding.
Always have your book or readings in front of you.
Make space for others; do not monopolize discussion.
Speak from your own experience without generalizing.
Consider anything that is said in class strictly confidential.

Additional Ground Rules for Online Discussions

NO YELLING!!!
If you wouldn't say it in person, don't say it here.
Double-check clarity, spelling, and grammar before posting.
Read the entire thread before commenting.
Make substantial contributions to the discussion ("I agree" is fine but not sufficient).
Bear in mind that nuance can get lost in the absence of facial expressions and be mindful of tone.

For Face-to-Face Lectures

Arrive on time.
Turn your cell phone off.
Use laptops only for legitimate class activities (note-taking, assigned tasks).
Do not leave class early without okaying it with the instructor in advance.
Ask questions if you are confused.
Try not to distract or annoy your classmates.

(Continued)

Exhibit B.1. (Continued)

Additional Ground Rules for Online Lectures

Close browser windows and apps to minimize distractions.
Activate your webcam if possible (we know it isn't always possible).
Raise your digital hand or indicate in chat if you have questions.
Minimize backchat (private chat).

Exhibit B.2. A Method for Helping Students Create Their Own Ground Rules

- Ask students to think about the best group discussions in which they have participated and reflect on what made these discussions so satisfying.
- Next, ask students to think about the worst group discussions in which they have participated and reflect on what made these discussions so unsatisfactory.
- For each of the positive characteristics identified, ask students to suggest three things the group could do to ensure that these characteristics are present.
- For each of the negative characteristics identified, ask students to suggest three things the group could do to ensure that these characteristics are not present.
- Use students' suggestions to draft a set of ground rules to which you all agree, and distribute them in writing.
- Periodically ask the class to reflect on whether the ground rules established at the beginning of the semester are working, and make adjustments as necessary.

SOURCE: Brookfield and Preskill (2005).

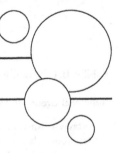

APPENDIX C

What Are Student Self-Assessments and How Can We Use Them?

One way to gather information on students' prior knowledge and skills is to ask them to assess their own level of knowledge or skill. The objective is to get an idea of the range of abilities and experience of the class as a whole, not to evaluate individuals. Questions can focus on knowledge, skills, or experiences that you assume students have acquired and are prerequisites to your course, things that you believe are valuable to know but not essential, and topics and skills that you plan to address in the course. Students' responses to questions can help you calibrate your course appropriately or help you direct students to supplemental materials that will help them fill in gaps or weaknesses in their existing skill or knowledge base that may hinder their progress. The questions also help students identify and focus on the most important knowledge and skills addressed by your course and access information from prior courses or experiences that apply to your course.

The advantage of a self-assessment instrument is that it is relatively easy to construct and score and, because it can be administered anonymously, is very low stakes and is low anxiety for the student. The weakness of the method is that students may not be able to accurately assess their abilities. Generally, people tend to overestimate their knowledge and skills, especially among those with lower levels of skill. However, accuracy improves when the response options are clear and tied to specific concepts or behaviors that students can reflect on or even mentally simulate, such as being able to define a term, explain a concept, or recall specific kinds and qualities of experience, such as building or writing or performing in a specific context.

These student self-assessments can be administered using the survey functionality in a learning management system (LMS) or with one of the easy-to-use and readily available online survey tools.

Exhibit C.1 presents some examples of questions and response items.

Exhibit C.1. Sample Self-Assessments

How familiar are you with "Karnaugh maps"?

a. I have never heard of them.
b. I have heard of them but don't know what they are.
c. I have some idea of what they are but don't know when or how to use them.
d. I have a clear idea of what they are but haven't used them.
e. I can explain what they are and what they do, and I have used them.

Have you designed or built a digital logic circuit?

a. I have neither designed nor built one.
b. I have designed one but have never built one.
c. I have built one but have not designed one.
d. I have both designed and built a digital logic circuit.

What do you know about a "t-test"?

a. I have never heard of it.
b. I have heard of it but don't really know what it is.
c. I have some idea of what it is but am not too clear.
d. I know what it is and could explain what it's for.
e. I know what it is and when to use it and could use it to analyze data.

In the past, have you participated in or done any of the following in a college-level course?

	Yes	No
Participated in an online course		
Participated in an online discussion board		
Submitted an assignment through an LMS like Canvas or Blackboard		
Taken an online exam		
Been a part of a group project in an online course		

(Continued)

Exhibit C.1. (Continued)

How familiar are you with Photoshop?

a. I have never used it, or I have tried it but couldn't really do anything with it.
b. I can do simple edits using preset options to manipulate single images (e.g., standard color, orientation, and size manipulations).
c. I can manipulate multiple images using preset editing features to create desired effects.
d. I can easily use precision editing tools to manipulate multiple images for professional quality output.

For each of the following Shakespearean plays, place a check mark in the cells that describe your experience.

Play	Have seen a TV or movie production	Have seen a live performance	Have read it	Have written a college-level paper on it
Hamlet				
King Lear				
Henry IV				
Othello				

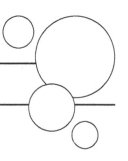

APPENDIX D

What Are Concept Maps and How Can We Use Them?

Concept maps are graphical tools for organizing and representing knowledge (Novak & Cañas, 2008). They are drawn as nodes and links in a network structure. Nodes represent concepts, usually enclosed in circles or boxes, and links represent relationships, usually indicated by lines drawn between two associated nodes. Words on the line, referred to as linking words or linking phrases, specify the relationship between the two concepts. Concept maps can be generated by hand or by using any number of digital applications. An online search for "concept mapping tools" will produce a variety of options for useful online tools to help your students create and share concept maps.

There are many ways to use concept maps. For instance, you might ask students to create a concept map representing what they already know about a particular domain or question (i.e., their current knowledge organization). You can then use that information to direct your teaching. You can also use concept maps to see how students' knowledge and understanding grows over time (i.e., their evolving knowledge organization). For example, you can have students create maps at the beginning, middle, and end of the course, then compare and contrast earlier and later maps, and discuss how their understanding of the course material changed over time. You can also create concept maps yourself to show students how you conceptualize a domain or topic (i.e., an expert knowledge organization).

When asking students to construct concept maps, it's helpful to provide them with a focal question. For example, you could ask students to map their answer to questions such as "What factors precipitated the 2022 Russian invasion of Ukraine?" or "What have been the economic effects of climate change?" For an example of a concept map that visually addresses the question "What are concept maps?" see Figure D.1. For more information on how to create and use concept maps, see Novak (1998).

An online search for "concept mapping tools" will produce a variety of options for tools to help formulate, create, collaborate on, and share concept maps.

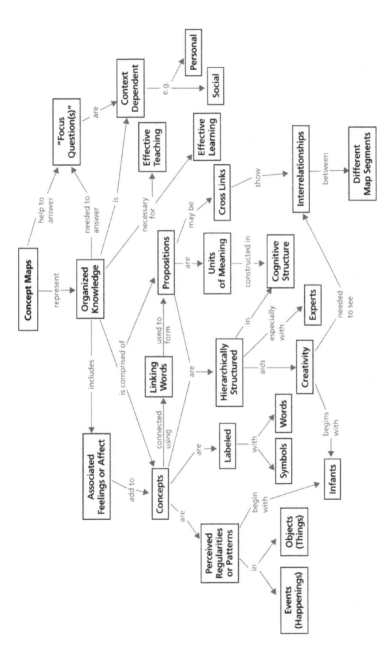

Figure D.1. Sample Concept Map

Source: Reproduced from Novak, J. D., & Cañas, A. J. (2008). The theory underlying concept maps and how to construct them (Technical Report IHMC CmapTools 2006–01 Rev 2008–01). Institute for Human and Machine Cognition. Retrieved March 26, 2009, from http://cmap.ihmc.us/Publications/ResearchPapers/TheoryUnderlyingConceptMaps.pdf

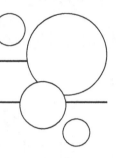

APPENDIX E

What Are Rubrics and How Can We Use Them?

A rubric is a scoring tool that explicitly represents the instructor's performance expectations for an assignment or piece of work. A rubric divides the assigned work into component parts and provides clear descriptions of different levels of quality associated with each component. Rubrics can be used for a wide array of assignments: papers, projects, oral presentations, artistic performances, group projects, and so on. Rubrics can be used as scoring or grading guides and to provide formative feedback to support and guide ongoing learning efforts and skill development.

Using a rubric provides several advantages to both instructors and students. Grading according to an explicit and descriptive set of criteria (designed to reflect the weighted importance of the objectives of the assignment) helps ensure that the instructor's grading standards remain consistent across a given assignment. Furthermore, although they initially take time to develop, rubrics can reduce the time spent grading by reducing uncertainty and by allowing instructors to refer to the rubric description rather than having to write long comments. Finally, grading rubrics are invaluable in large courses that have multiple graders (other instructors, teaching assistants, and so on) because they can help ensure consistency across graders.

Used more formatively, rubrics can help instructors get a clearer picture of the strengths and weaknesses of their students as a group. By recording the component scores and tallying up the number of students scoring below an acceptable level on each component, instructors can identify those skills or concepts that need more instructional time and student effort.

When rubrics are provided to students with the assignment description when the assignment is given, they can help students monitor and assess their progress as they work toward clearly indicated goals. When assignments are scored and returned with the rubric, students can more easily recognize the strengths and weaknesses of their work and direct their efforts accordingly.

For sample rubrics, see Exhibits E.1, E.2, E.3, E.4., and E.5. For detailed information on how to construct a rubric, see Stevens and Levi (2013).

Exhibit E.1. Rubric for Class Participation

	A (Exemplary)	B (Competent)	C (Developing)	D/R
Frequency and Quality	Attends class regularly and *always contributes* to the discussion by raising thoughtful questions, analyzing relevant issues, building on others' ideas, synthesizing across readings and discussions, expanding the class's perspective, and appropriately challenging assumptions and perspectives	Attends class regularly and *sometimes contributes* to the discussion in the aforementioned ways	Attends class regularly but *rarely contributes* to the discussion in the aforementioned ways	Attends class regularly but *never contributes* to the discussion in the aforementioned ways

SOURCE: Eberly Center for Teaching Excellence, Carnegie Mellon University.

Exhibit E.2. Rubric for Oral Exams

Dimensions	A (18–20 points) Exemplary	B (16–17 points) Competent	C (14–15 points) Developing	D/R
Overall Understanding	Shows a deep/robust understanding of the topic with a fully developed argument per the following categories	Shows a limited understanding of the topic, not quite a fully developed argument per the following categories	Shows a superficial understanding of the topic, argument not developed enough per the following categories	Shows no understanding of the topic and no argument per the following categories
Argument	Clearly articulates a position or argument	Articulates a position or argument that is incomplete or limited in scope	Articulates a position or argument that is unfocused or ambiguous	Does not articulate a position or argument
Evidence	Presents evidence that is *relevant* and *accurate* Presents *sufficient* amount of evidence to support argument	Presents evidence that is mostly relevant and/or mostly *accurate* Presents *limited* evidence to support argument	Presents evidence that is *somewhat inaccurate and/or irrelevant*, but corrects when prompted Does *not* present *enough* evidence to support argument, but augments when prompted	Presents *a lot of inaccurate and/or irrelevant evidence* Doesn't present enough evidence to support argument, even when prompted repeatedly

Implications	Fully discusses the major implications of the argument or position	Adequately discusses some of the major implications of the position	Discusses minor implications (missing the major ones) or does not discuss major implications adequately	Doesn't discuss the implications of the argument or position
Structure	Provides a logic in the progression of ideas	Provides a few areas of disjointedness or intermittent lack of logical progression of ideas	Provides ideas that are somewhat disjointed and/or do not always flow logically, making it a bit difficult to follow	Provides ideas that are disjointed and/or do not flow logically, hence argument is very difficult to follow
Prompting	Did not have to prompt with probing questions at all	Prompted minimally (one or two probing questions)	Prompted a lot (a series of probing questions)	

SOURCE: Eberly Center for Teaching Excellence, Carnegie Mellon University.

Exhibit E.3. Rubric for Papers

	Excellent	Competent	Not Yet Competent	Poor
Creativity and Originality	You exceed the parameters of the assignment with original insights or a particularly engaging style.	You meet all the parameters of the assignment.	You meet most of the parameters of the assignment.	You do not meet the parameters of the assignment.
Argument	Your central argument is clear, interesting, and demonstrable (i.e., based on evidence, not opinion). The claims made in the body of your paper clearly and obviously support your central argument. Your arguments and claims reflect a robust and nuanced understanding of key ideas from this course.	Your central argument is clear and demonstrable. The claims made in the body of your paper support your central argument. Your arguments and claims reflect a solid understanding of key ideas from this course.	Your central argument is demonstrable but not entirely clear. A few of the claims made in the body of your paper do not clearly support your central argument. Your arguments and claims reflect some understanding of key ideas from this course.	Your central argument is unclear or it is not demonstrable. The claims made in the body of your paper do not support your central argument. Your arguments and claims reflect little understanding of key ideas from this course.
Evidence	The evidence you use is specific, rich, varied, and unambiguously supports your claims. Quotations and illustrations are framed effectively and explicated appropriately in the text.	The evidence you use supports your claims. Quotations and illustrations are framed reasonably effectively and explicated appropriately in the text.	Some of the evidence you use does not support your claims. Some of the quotations and illustrations are not framed effectively or explicated appropriately in the text.	Little of the evidence you use supports your claims. Few of the quotations and illustrations are framed effectively or explicated appropriately in the text.

Structure	Your ideas are presented in a logical and coherent manner throughout the paper, with strong topic sentences to guide the reader. The reader can effortlessly follow the structure of your argument.	The reader can follow the structure of your argument with very little effort.	The reader cannot always follow the structure of your argument.	The reader cannot follow the structure of your argument.
Clarity	Your sentences are concise and well crafted, and the vocabulary is precise; the reader can effortlessly discern your meaning.	The reader can discern your meaning with very little effort.	The reader cannot always discern your meaning.	The reader cannot discern your meaning.
Mechanics	There are no distracting spelling, punctuation, or grammatical errors, and quotations are all properly cited.	There are few distracting spelling, punctuation, and/or grammatical errors, and quotations are all properly cited.	There are some distracting spelling, punctuation, and/or grammatical errors, and/or some of the quotations are not properly cited.	There are significant and distracting spelling, punctuation, or grammatical errors, and/or the quotations are improperly cited.

SOURCE: Eberly Center for Teaching Excellence, Carnegie Mellon University.

Exhibit E.4. Senior Design Project Rubric

Component	Sophisticated	Competent	Not Yet Competent
Research and Design			
Identifies project objectives based on general description and client requirements	All important major and minor objectives are identified and appropriately prioritized.	All major objectives are identified but one or two minor ones are missing or priorities are not established.	Many major objectives are not identified.
Identifies relevant and valid information to support decision-making	All relevant information is obtained and information sources are valid. Design recommendations are well supported by the information.	Sufficient information is obtained and most sources are valid. Design recommendations are mostly supported by the information.	Insufficient information is obtained and/or sources lack validity. Design recommendations are not supported by information collected.
Generates and analyzes alternatives	Three or more alternatives are considered. Each alternative is appropriately and correctly analyzed for technical feasibility.	At least three alternatives are considered. Appropriate analyses are selected but analyses include some minor procedural errors.	Only one or two alternatives are considered. Inappropriate analyses are selected and/or major procedural and conceptual errors are made.
Identifies relevant constraints (economic, environmental/safety, sustainability, etc.)	All relevant constraints are identified and accurately analyzed.	Most constraints are identified; some are not adequately addressed or accurately analyzed.	Few or no constraints are identified or some constraints are identified but not accurately analyzed.
Generates valid conclusions/decisions	Recommended solution is based on stated criteria, analysis, and constraints.	Solution/decision is reasonable; further analysis of some of the alternatives or constraints may have led to different recommendation.	Only one solution is considered or other solutions were ignored or incompletely analyzed. Many constraints and criteria were ignored.

Communication

Presentation Visual aids	Slides are error-free and logically present the main components of the process and recommendations. Material is readable and the graphics highlight and support the main ideas.	Slides are error-free and logically present the main components of the process and recommendations. Material is mostly readable and graphics reiterate the main ideas.	Slides contain errors and lack a logical progression. Major aspects of the analysis or recommendations are absent. Diagrams or graphics are absent or confuse the audience.
Oral presentation	Speakers are audible and fluent on their topic, and do not rely on notes to present or respond. Speakers respond accurately and appropriately to audience questions and comments.	Speakers are mostly audible and fluent on their topic, and require minimal referral to notes. Speakers respond to most questions accurately and appropriately.	Speakers are often inaudible or hesitant, often speaking in incomplete sentences. Speakers rely heavily on notes. Speakers have difficulty responding clearly and accurately to audience questions.
Body language	Body language, as indicated by appropriate and meaningful gestures (e.g., drawing hands inward to convey contraction, moving arms up to convey lift, etc.), eye contact with audience, and movement, demonstrates a high level of comfort and connection with the audience.	Body language, as indicated by a slight tendency to repetitive and distracting gestures (e.g., tapping a pen, wringing hands, waving arms, clenching fists, etc.) and breaking eye contact with audience, demonstrates a slight discomfort with the audience.	Body language, as indicated by frequent, repetitive, and distracting gestures, little or no audience eye-contact, and/or stiff posture and movement, indicate a high degree of discomfort interacting with audience.

(Continued)

Exhibit E.4. (Continued)

Component	Sophisticated	Competent	Not Yet Competent
Team Work (Based on peer evaluation, observations of group meetings, and presentation)			
Delegation and fulfillment of responsibilities	Responsibilities delegated fairly. Each member contributes in a valuable way to the project. All members always attended meetings and met deadlines for deliverables.	Some minor inequities in the delegation of responsibilities. Some members contribute more heavily than others but all members meet their responsibilities. Members regularly attended meetings with only a few absences, and deadlines for deliverables were met.	Major inequities in delegation of responsibilities. Group has obvious freeloaders who fail to meet their responsibilities or members who dominate and prevent others from contributing. Members would often miss meetings, and/or deadlines were often missed.
Team morale and cohesiveness	Team worked well together to achieve objectives. Members enjoyed interacting with each other and learned from each other. All data sources indicated a high level of mutual respect and collaboration.	Team worked well together most of the time, with only a few occurrences of communication breakdown or failure to collaborate when appropriate. Members were mostly respectful of each other.	Team did not collaborate or communicate well. Some members would work independently, without regard to objectives or priorities. A lack of respect and regard was frequently noted.

Exhibit E.5. Rubric for Online Discussion Post

	Excellent (3)	Good (3)	Fair (1)	Poor (0)
Does post address prompt?	Post *completely* addresses the discussion prompt(s).	Post *partially* addresses the discussion prompt(s).	Post *fails* to address the discussion prompt(s).	No post
Does post use relevant information?	Post *robustly* uses relevant information from readings and class discussions.	Post *partially* uses some relevant information from readings, class discussions.	Post *fails* to use relevant information from readings, class discussions.	No posting
Does post contribute to the discussion?	Post *strongly* contributes to the discussion with questions, attempts to motivate the group discussion, or presentation of relevant application or innovative perspectives.	Post *moderately* contributes to the discussion with some questions, attempts to motivate the group discussion, or presentation of relevant application or innovative perspectives.	Post *minimally* contributes to the discussion with few questions, attempts to motivate the group discussion, or presentation of relevant application or innovative perspectives.	No effort contributed to the discussion
Is the post free of errors?	Writing is free of grammatical, spelling, punctuation, or citation errors.	Writing includes less than 1–2 grammatical, spelling, punctuation, or citation errors.	Writing includes 4–5 grammatical, spelling, punctuation, or citation errors.	Writing includes more than 5 grammatical, spelling, punctuation, or citation errors.
				Total ____ /12

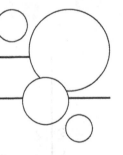

APPENDIX F

What Are Learner Checklists and How Can We Use Them?

Checklists help instructors make their expectations for an activity or assignment explicit to students. This is often quite helpful because students do not always fully understand our expectations, and they may be guided by disciplinary or cultural conventions, or even the expectations of other instructors, that mismatch with what we expect for the current activity or assignment. In addition, checklists raise students' awareness of the required elements of complex tasks and thus can help students develop a more complete appreciation for the steps and sequencing involved in effectively completing a given assignment.

Checklists should be made available upfront on the learning management system or distributed to students in advance of an assignment's due date, and students should be informed that it is their responsibility to fill out the checklist—making changes to their work, as necessary—and then attach the completed checklist to their assignment for submission. This increases the likelihood that certain basic criteria are met and avoids some annoying student tendencies (such as not double spacing when asked to do so). For a sample checklist for a paper assignment, see Exhibit F.1.

Exhibit F.1. Sample Paper Checklist

Name:

Note: Please complete this checklist and include it when you submit your paper for this course.

___ I have addressed all parts of the assignment.

___ My argument would be clear and unambiguous to any reader.

___ My paragraphs are organized logically and help advance my argument.

___ I use a variety of evidence (e.g., quotes, examples, facts, illustrations) to reinforce my argument(s).

___ My conclusion summarizes my argument and explores its implications; it does not simply restate the topic paragraph.

___ I have revised my paper ___ times to improve its organization, argument, sentence structure, and style.

___ I have proofread my paper carefully, not relying on my computer to do it for me.

___ My name is at the top of the paper.

___ The paper is double-spaced.

___ I have not used anyone else's work, ideas, or language without citing them appropriately.

___ All my sources are in my bibliography, which is properly formatted in APA style.

___ I have read the plagiarism statement in the syllabus, understand it, and agree to abide by the definitions and penalties described there.

Student Signature: _____ Date: _____

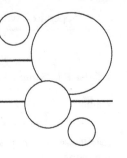

APPENDIX G

What Are Learning Objectives and How Can We Use Them?

Learning objectives articulate the knowledge and skills you want students to acquire by the end of the course or after completing a particular assignment. There are numerous benefits to clearly stating your objectives, for both you and your students. First, learning objectives communicate your intentions to students, and they give students information to better direct their learning efforts and monitor their own progress. Objectives also provide you with a framework for selecting and organizing course content, and they can guide your decisions about appropriate assessment and evaluation methods. Finally, objectives provide a framework for selecting appropriate teaching and learning activities (Miller, 1987).

What makes a learning objective clear and helpful? There are four elements. First, learning objectives should be *student-centered*, for example, stated as "Students should be able to _____." Second, they should *break down the task* and focus on specific cognitive processes. Many activities that faculty members believe require a single skill (e.g., writing or problem-solving) actually involve a synthesis of many component skills. To master these complex skills, students must practice and gain proficiency in the discrete component skills. For example, writing may involve identifying an argument, enlisting appropriate evidence, organizing paragraphs, and so on, whereas problem-solving may require defining the parameters of the problem, choosing appropriate formulas, and so on. Third, clear objectives should *use action verbs* to focus on concrete actions and behaviors that enable us to make student learning explicit and communicate to students the kind of intellectual effort we expect of them. Furthermore, using action verbs reduces ambiguity in what it means to "understand." Finally, clear objectives should be *measurable*. We should be able to easily check (i.e., assess) whether students have mastered a skill (e.g., asking students to *state* a given theorem, *solve* a textbook problem, or *identify* the appropriate principle).

Determining the action verbs for learning objectives is made easier as a result of the work of Benjamin Bloom, who created a taxonomy of educational objectives (1956) that, with slight revision (Anderson et al., 2001), is still used today by educators around the world. This taxonomy represents six levels of intellectual behavior, from the simple recall of facts to the creation of new knowledge. These levels, combined with verbs that represent the intellectual activity at each level, can help faculty members articulate their course objectives and hence focus both their and their students' attention and effort.

For examples of action verbs, see Table G.1, and for sample objectives, see Exhibit G.1.

Table G.1. Sample Verbs for Bloom's Taxonomy

Remember	Understand	Apply	Analyze	Evaluate	Create
Arrange	Associate	Calculate	Break down	Appraise	Assemble
Define	Classify	Construct	Combine	Argue	Build
Describe	Compare	Demonstrate	Compare	Assess	Compose
Duplicate	Contrast	Develop	Contrast	Check	Construct
Identify	Describe	Employ	Debate	Conclude	Design
Label	Differentiate	Estimate	Diagram	Critique	Formulate
List	Discuss	Examine	Examine	Detect	Generate
Locate	Exemplify	Execute	Experiment	Judge	Integrate
Name	Explain	Formulate	Extrapolate	Justify	Produce
Recall	Infer	Implement	Formulate	Monitor	Propose
Recite	Interpret	Modify	Illustrate	Rank	Rearrange
Recognize	Paraphrase	Sketch	Organize	Rate	Set up
Reproduce	Restate	Solve	Predict	Recommend	Transform
Select	Summarize	Use	Question	Select	
State	Translate			Test	
				Weigh	

Exhibit G.1. Sample Learning Objectives

By the end of the course students should be able to

- Articulate and debunk common myths about Mexican immigration (History)
- Discuss features and limitations of various sampling procedures and research methodologies (Statistics)
- Design an experimental study, carry out an appropriate statistical analysis of the data, and properly interpret and communicate the analyses (Decision Sciences)
- Analyze simple circuits that include resistors and capacitors (Engineering)
- Execute different choreographic styles (Dance)
- Sketch and/or prototype scenarios of use to bring opportunity areas to life (Design)
- Analyze any vocal music score and prepare the same score individually for any audition, rehearsal, or performance (Musical Theater)

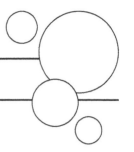

What Are Active Learning Strategies and How Can We Use Them?

A ctive learning strategies require students to engage in more interaction with each other and the instructional material compared to what they might do in a traditional lecture—passively listening and note-taking. Active learning strategies ideally set the stage for most (if not all) students to be engaged in such interactions, rather than the select few who choose to raise their hand with a question or answer. Although some instructors have the false impression that active learning strategies take significant time, the range of options for active learning include many that take five minutes or less. Table H.1 lists a variety of active learning strategies in order of the time they take to implement in class, and it provides a description and some discipline-based examples for each.

Table H.1. Sample Active Learning Strategies

Time	Activity Title	Description	Example(s)
1 min	Minute Paper	Students write on a notecard or sheet of paper for 1–3 minutes in response to an open-ended prompt.	*Mechanical Engineering:* "Today we discussed conductive heat transfer. In one minute, list as many features of this process as you can." *Biology:* "What does the term *biodiversity* mean?"
1 min	Muddiest Point	Students write on a notecard or sheet of paper the concept or idea they are still struggling with the most.	*General:* "On your note card, write the one concept you have the most trouble understanding and/or on which you could use more practice."
1 min	Application Card	Students are asked to apply a concept or skill to a new situation or to generate examples that illustrate a concept in action.	*Psychology:* "Describe an everyday situation that contrasts positive and negative reinforcement."
5 min	Think-Pair-Share	Students individually answer a question posed to the class, then compare their answer with a partner, and synthesize a joint response to share with the class.	*English:* "What is the main point from today's reading? Justify your response with two supporting reasons from the text." *Economics:* "How would the output of this model change if we relaxed the assumption that this market is a monopoly?"
5 min	Set It Up	After providing students with a quantitative problem, ask them to set up the equations they would use to solve it without generating a numerical answer.	*Physics:* "Using the provided circuit diagram, label each component and then set up the equations you would use to calculate the current through the circuit at point A."

10 min	Role-Playing	Students are asked to act out a role or part in a simulated scenario. In doing so, they get a better idea of the concepts and theories being discussed.	*Modern Languages:* "Role 1: You are a traveler who just missed the train to your destination. Role 2: You are a travel agent assisting a customer. Both: Playing your assigned role, discuss in [language] the situation and determine a solution." *Public Policy:* "Each member of the group should adopt the persona of a different stakeholder in our scenario and then discuss the three proposed policies from that person's perspective."
> 15 min	Case Studies	Using real-life stories that describe what happened to a community, family, school, industry, or individual, prompt students to integrate classroom knowledge with real-world situations, actions, and consequences.	*Business:* "Consider the marketing strategies that P&G used to develop its Pringles line of potato chips. Would you consider their marketing strategies successful? Why or why not?"

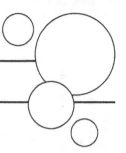

APPENDIX I

What Are Reader Responses/Peer Reviews and How Can We Use Them?

Reader response (often called *peer review*) is a process in which students read and comment on each other's work as a way to improve their peers' (and their own) writing.

Reader response/peer review offers advantages to readers, writers, and instructors alike. The advantage to writers is targeted feedback from several readers that they can use to guide revisions of the paper. The advantage to instructors is that students engage in the revision process before instructors ever see the paper, producing (one hopes) a better final product. Some empirical research has shown that if students get focused feedback from four peers, their revisions are better than those students who received feedback from their professors only. And the expectation for readers/reviewers is that by analyzing others' strengths and weaknesses, they can become better at recognizing and addressing their own weaknesses.

In order for students to be able to engage in this process effectively. . .

- Reviewers need
  - A structure to guide their reading and feedback (see Exhibit I.1 for an example)
  - Sufficient time to write their reviews.
- Writers need
  - Reviews from several readers
  - Sufficient time to implement feedback and revise their work

Because the reader response/peer review process requires the exchange of documents at several different points, instructors must think through the logistics of these hand-offs and offer appropriate tools, such as shared drives. They should also think through the timing of each phase of the process and set interim deadlines for the submission of drafts, reviews, and final products.

Following in Exhibit I.1 is an example of guidelines for peer reviewers that one instructor provides for a basic academic argument paper. Notice that the instructions are geared toward helping reviewers identify the gist of the paper first, then locate the meaningful components of the argument, and then provide feedback. As with any instruments instructors use in their classes, the instructions make the most sense when they are grounded within the course context.

Exhibit I.1. Sample Reader Response/Peer Review Instrument

To the reviewer: The purpose of the peer review is to provide targeted feedback to the writer about what is working in the paper and what is not.

- Please read the paper through the first time without making any markings on it in order to familiarize yourself with the paper.
- During the second read through, please do the following:
  - Underline the main argument of the paper.
  - Put a check mark in the left column next to pieces of evidence that support the argument.
  - Circle the conclusion.
- During the third and final read through, respond briefly to the following questions:
  - Does the first paragraph present the writer's argument and the approach the writer is taking in presenting that argument? If not, which piece is missing, unclear, understated, and so forth?
  - Does the argument progress clearly from one paragraph to the next (e.g., is the sequencing/organization logical)? Does each paragraph add to the argument (i.e., link the evidence to the main purpose of the paper)? If not, where does the structure break down, and/or which paragraph is problematic and why?
  - Does the writer support the argument with evidence? Please indicate where there is a paragraph weak on evidence, evidence not supporting the argument, and so on.
  - Does the conclusion draw together the strands of the argument? If not, what is missing?
  - What is the best part of the paper?
  - Which area(s) of the paper needs most improvement (e.g., the argument, the organization, sentence structure or word choice, evidence)? Be specific so that the writer knows where to focus his or her energy.

251

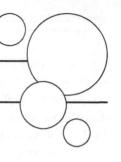

What Are Exam Wrappers and How Can We Use Them?

All too often when students receive back a graded exam, they focus on a single feature—the score they earned. Although this focus on the grade is understandable, it can lead students to miss out on several learning opportunities that an assessment can provide:

- Identifying their own individual areas of strength and weakness to guide further study
- Reflecting on the adequacy of their preparation time and the appropriateness of their study strategies
- Characterizing the nature of their errors to find any recurring patterns that could be addressed

To encourage students to process their graded exams more deeply, instructors can use *exam wrappers*, short reflection assignments in the form of a questionnaire that students complete when an exam is returned to them. Exam wrappers direct students to review and analyze their performance (and the instructor's feedback) with an eye toward adjusting their future learning.

One way to use exam wrappers is to ask students to complete the corresponding questionnaire when they get back their graded exams. This way, students are immediately encouraged to think through *why* they earned the score they did (what kinds of errors they made, how their performance might relate to their approach to studying) and how they might do better next time. Once students complete the exam wrapper, their responses should be collected, both for review by the instructional team and for safe keeping (because students will need to use their responses in preparation for the next exam; see next paragraph). Implementing exam wrappers online—for example, as an online survey—so that instructors can review all responses and students can revisit their own is another convenient approach. Then, the instructor, teaching assistants, or both can skim students' responses to look for patterns in how students analyzed their strengths and weaknesses or in how students described their approach to studying for the exam. These patterns may give the instructor some insights into students' patterns of performance and what advice might facilitate improvements on the next exam. (For example, if students only reread their notes for a problem-oriented exam, the instructor could advise students to solve practice problems from sample exams.)

Then, a week or so before the next exam, students' exam wrapper responses are returned to them, either in a recitation section or in some other setting where there is opportunity for structured discussion. Students can then be asked to reread their responses from the previous exam and reflect on how they might implement their own advice (or the instructor's advice) for trying a better approach to studying for the upcoming exam. A structured class discussion can also be useful at this point to engage students in sharing their more effective study strategies and getting input and encouragement from the instructional team.

For a sample exam wrapper from a physics course, see Exhibit J.1.

Exhibit J.1. Sample Exam Wrapper

Physics Post-Exam Reflection   Name: _____

This activity is designed to give you a chance to reflect on your exam performance and, more importantly, on the effectiveness of your exam preparation. Please answer the questions sincerely. Your responses will be collected to inform the instructional team regarding students' experiences with this exam and how we can best support your learning. We will hand back your completed sheet in advance of the next exam to inform and guide your preparation for that exam.

(Continued)

Exhibit J.1. (Continued)

1. Approximately how much time did you spend preparing for this exam?

   _____

2. What percentage of your test-preparation time was spent in each of these activities?
   a. Reading textbook section(s) for the first time _____
   b. Rereading textbook section(s) _____
   c. Reviewing homework solutions _____
   d. Solving problems for practice _____
   e. Reviewing your own notes _____
   f. Reviewing materials from course website _____(What materials?
      _____)
   g. Other _____(Please specify: _____)

3. Now that you have looked over your graded exam, estimate the percentage of points you lost due to each of the following (make sure the percentages add up to 100):
   a. Trouble with vectors and vector notation _____
   b. Algebra or arithmetic errors _____
   c. Lack of understanding of the concept _____
   d. Not knowing how to approach the problem _____
   e. Careless mistakes _____
   f. Other _____(Please specify: _____)

4. Based on your responses to the previous questions, name at least three things you plan to do differently in preparing for the next exam. For instance, will you just spend more time studying, change a specific study habit or try a new one (if so, name it), make math more automatic so it does not get in the way of physics, try to sharpen some other skill (if so, name it), solve more practice problems, or something else?

5. What can we do to help support your learning and your preparation for the next exam?

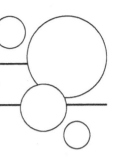

REFERENCES

Ackerman-Barger, K., Boatright, D., Gonzalez-Colaso, R., Orozco, R., & Latimore, D. (2020). Seeking inclusion excellence: Understanding racial microaggressions as experienced by underrepresented medical and nursing students. *Academic Medicine, 95*(5), 758-763.

Adams, M., Bell, L. A., & Griffin, P. (2007). *Teaching for diversity and social justice* (2nd ed.). Routledge.

Ahmed, L. (1993). *Women and gender in Islam: Historical roots of a modern debate.* Yale University Press.

Aleven, V., Stahl, E., Schworm, S., Fischer, F., & Wallace, R. (2003). Help seeking and help design in interactive learning environments. *Review of Educational Research, 73*(3), 277-320.

Alexander, L., Frankiewicz, R. G., & Williams, R. E. (1979). Facilitation of learning and retention of oral instruction using advance and post organizers. *Journal of Educational Psychology, 71,* 701-707.

Alexander, P., Schallert, D., & Hare, V. (1991). Coming to terms: How researchers in learning and literacy talk about knowledge. *Review of Educational Research, 61,* 315-343.

Alibali, M. W. (1999). How children change their minds: Strategy change can be gradual or abrupt. *Developmental Psychology, 35,* 27-145.

Allport, G. (1954). *The nature of prejudice.* Addison-Wesley.

Alvermann, D., Smith, I. C., & Readance, J. E. (1985). Prior knowledge activation and the comprehension of compatible and incompatible text. *Reading Research Quarterly, 20,* 420-436.

Ames, C. (1990). Motivation: What teachers need to know. *Teachers College Record, 91,* 409-472.

Anderson, J. R. (1992). Automaticity and the ACT theory. *American Journal of Psychology, 105,* 165-180.

Anderson, J. R. (2016). *The architecture of cognition.* Psychology Press.

Anderson, J. R., Conrad, F. G., & Corbett, A. T. (1989). Skill acquisition and the LISP tutor. *Cognitive Science, 13*(4), 467–505.

Anderson, J. R., Corbett, A. T., Koedinger, K. R., & Pelletier, R. (1995). Cognitive tutors: Lessons learned. *Journal of the Learning Sciences, 4,* 167–207.

Anderson, L. W., Krathwohl, D. R., & Bloom, B. S. (2001). *A taxonomy for learning, teaching, and assessing: A revision of Bloom's Taxonomy of educational objectives* (Complete ed.). Longman.

Ang, S., Van Dyne, L., & Rockstuhl, T. (2015). Cultural intelligence: Origins, conceptualization, evolution, and methodological diversity. In M. J. Gelfand, C.-Y. Chiu, & Y.-Y. Hong (Eds.), *Handbook of advances in culture and psychology* (Vol. 5, pp. 273–323). Oxford University Press.

Arbaugh, J. B. (2001). How instructor immediacy behaviors affect student satisfaction and learning in web-based courses. *Business Communication Quarterly, 64*(4), 42–54.

Armbruster, P., Patel, M., Johnson, E., & Weiss, M. (2009). Active learning and student-centered pedagogy improve student attitudes and performance in introductory biology. *Cell Biology Education, 8*(3), 203–213.

Aronson, J., Fried, C. B., & Good, C. (2002). Reducing the effects of stereotype threat on African American college students by shaping theories of intelligence. *Journal of Experimental Social Psychology, 38*(2), 113–125.

Association of American Universities. (2020). *Report on the AAU Campus Climate Survey on Sexual Assault and Misconduct.* Retrieved from https://www.aau.edu/sites/default/files/AAU-Files/Key-Issues/Campus-Safety/Revised%20Aggregate%20report%20%20and%20appendices%201-7_(01-16-2020_FINAL).pdf

Astin, A. W. (1993). Diversity and multiculturalism on the campus: How are students affected? *Change, 25*(2), 44–49.

Astin, A. W. (1999). Student involvement: A developmental theory for higher education. *Journal of College Student Development, 40*(5), 518–529.

Atkinson, J. (1964). *An introduction to motivation.* Van Nostrand.

Atkinson, J. W. (1957). Motivational determinants of risk taking behavior. *Psychological Review, 64,* 369–372.

Ausubel, D. P. (1960). The use of advance organizers in the learning and retention of meaningful verbal material. *Journal of Educational Psychology, 51,* 267–272.

Ausubel, D. P. (1978). In defense of advance organizers: A reply to the critics. *Review of Educational Research, 48,* 251–257.

Ausubel, D. P., & Fitzgerald, D. (1962). Organizer, general background, and antecedent learning variables in sequential verbal learning. *Journal of Educational Psychology, 53,* 243–249.

Babcock, L., Peyser, B., Vesterlund, L., & Weingart, L. (2022). *The no club: Putting a stop to women's dead-end work*. Simon & Schuster.

Baddeley, A. D., & Hitch, G. J. (1974). Working memory. In G. A. Bower (Ed.), *Recent advances in learning and motivation* (Vol. 8, pp. 47–89). Academic Press.

Baker-Smith, C., Coca, V., Goldrick-Rab, S., Looker, E., Richardson, B., & Williams, T. (2020). *#RealCollege 2020: Five years of evidence on campus basic needs insecurity*. The Hope Center for College, Community, and Justice. Retrieved from https://hope4college.com/wp-content/uploads/2020/02/2019_RealCollege_Survey_Report.pdf

Baker, C. (2010). The impact of instructor immediacy and presence for online student affective learning, cognition, and motivation. *The Journal of Educators Online, 7*(1), 1–30.

Ballester, E. P. (2013). Verbal and nonverbal teacher immediacy and foreign language anxiety in an EFL university course. *Porta Linguarum, 23*, 9–24. Retrieved from http://www.ugr.es/~portalin/articulos/PL_numero23/1%20%20Elisabet%20Pladevall.pdf

Balzer, W. K., Doherty, M. E., & O'Connor, R. (1989). Effects of cognitive feedback on performance. *Psychological Bulletin, 106*, 410–433.

Bandura, A. (1997). *Self-efficacy: The exercise of control*. W. H. Freeman.

Barnett, S. M., & Ceci, S. J. (2002). When and where do we apply what we learn? A taxonomy for far transfer. *Psychological Bulletin, 128*(4), 612–637.

Barron, K., & Harackiewicz, J. (2001). Achievement goals and optimal motivation: Testing multiple goal models. *Journal of Personality and Social Psychology, 80*, 706–722.

Bartlett, F. C. (1995). *Remembering: A study in experimental and social psychology* (2nd ed.). Cambridge University Press.

Bassok, M. (1990). Transfer of domain-specific problem-solving procedures. *Journal of Experimental Psychology: Learning, Memory, and Cognition, 16*(3), 522–533.

Baxter-Magolda, M. (1992). *Knowing and reasoning in college: Gender-related patterns in students' intellectual development*. Jossey-Bass.

Baxter-Magolda, M. (2001). *Making their own way: Narratives for transforming higher education to promote self-development*. Stylus.

Baxter Magolda, M. B. (2008). Three elements of self-authorship. *Journal of College Student Development, 49*(4), 269–284.

Bear, J. B., & Woolley, A. W. (2011). The role of gender in team collaboration and performance. *Interdisciplinary Science Reviews, 36*(2), 146–153.

Beasley, M. A., & Fischer, M. J. (2012). Why they leave: The impact of stereotype threat on the attrition of women and minorities from science, math and engineering majors. *Social Psychology of Education, 15*(4), 427–448.

Beaufort, A. (2007). *College writing and beyond: A new framework for university writing instruction*. Utah State University Press.

Beemyn, G., & Rankin, S. (2011). *The lives of transgender people*. Columbia University Press.

Beilock, S. L., Wierenga, S. A., & Carr, T. H. (2002). Expertise, attention and memory in sensorimotor skill execution: Impact of novel task constraints on dual-task performance and episodic memory. *The Quarterly Journal of Experimental Psychology A: Human Experimental Psychology, 55A*, 1211–1240.

Belenky, M., Clinchy, B., Goldberger, N., & Tarule, J. (1986). *Women's ways of knowing: The development of self, voice, and mind*. Basic Books.

Belkin, D. (2021, September 6). A generation of American men give up on college: "I just feel lost." *The Wall Street Journal*. Retrieved from https://www.wsj.com/articles/college-university-fall-higher-education-men-women-enrollment-admissions-back-to-school-11630948233

Bellman, R.E. (1957). *Dynamic programming*. Princeton University Press.

Benson, B. (2016). *Cognitive biases*. Retrieved from https://busterbenson.com/piles/cognitive-biases/

Bentrim, E. M., & Henning, G. W. (2022). *The impact of a sense of belonging in college: Implications for student persistence, retention, and success*. Stylus.

Bereiter, C., & Scardamalia, M. (1987). *The psychology of written composition*. Erlbaum.

Bernal, M. E., Gómez, M., & Iodice, R. (2018). Conceptual interaction between critical thinking and metacognition. *Revista Latinoamericana de Estudios Educativos, 15*(1), 193–217.

Berry, D. C., & Broadbent, D. E. (1988). Interactive tasks and the implicit-explicit distinction. *British Journal of Psychology, 79*, 251–272.

Biederman, I., & Shiffrar, M. M. (1987). Sexing day-old chicks: A case study and expert systems analysis of a difficult perceptual-learning task. *Journal of Experimental Psychology: Learning, Memory, and Cognition, 13*(4), 640–645.

Bielaczyc, K., Pirolli, P. L., & Brown, A. L. (1995). Training in self-explanation and self-regulation strategies: Investigating the effects of knowledge acquisition activities on problem solving. *Cognition and Instruction, 13*(2), 221–252.

Binning, K. N., McGreevy, E. M., Fotuhi, O., Chen, S., Marshman, E., Kalender, Z. Y., Limeri, L., Betancur, L., & Singh, C. (2020). Changing social contexts to foster equity in college science courses: An ecological-belonging intervention. *Psychological Science, 31*(9), 1059–1070.

Bjork, R. A., & Bjork, E. L. (2020). Desirable difficulties in theory and practice. *Journal of Applied Research in Memory and Cognition, 9*(4), 475–479.

Black, P., & William, D. (1998). Assessment and classroom learning. *Assessment in Education, 5*, 7–74.

Blessing, S. B., & Anderson, J. R. (1996). How people learn to skip steps. *Journal of Experimental Psychology: Learning, Memory, and Cognition, 22*, 576–598.

Bloom, B. S. (1956). *Taxonomy of educational objectives, handbook I: The cognitive domain.* David McKay.

Bloom, B. S. (1984). The 2-sigma problem: The search for methods of group instruction as effective as one-to-one tutoring. *Educational Researcher, 13*, 4–6.

Blum, L. (2004). Women in computer science: The Carnegie Mellon experience. In D. P. Resnick & D. Scott (Eds.), *The innovative university.* Carnegie Mellon University Press.

Boster, J. S., & Johnson, J. C. (1989). Form or function: A comparison of expert and novice judgments of similarity among fish. *American Anthropologist, 91*, 866–889.

Bower, G. H., Clark, M. C., Lesgold, A. M., & Winzenz, D. (1969). Hierarchical retrieval schemes in recall of categorical word lists. *Journal of Verbal Learning and Verbal Behavior, 8*, 323–343.

Bradshaw, G. L., & Anderson, J. R. (1982). Elaborative encoding as an explanation of levels of processing. *Journal of Verbal Learning and Verbal Behavior, 21*, 165–174.

Bransford, J. D., & Johnson, M. K. (1972). Contextual prerequisites for understanding: Some investigations of comprehension and recall. *Journal of Verbal Learning and Verbal Behavior, 11*, 717–726.

Braxton, J. (2012). *Reworking the student departure puzzle.* Vanderbilt University Press.

Brewer, M. B. (1988). A dual process model of impression formation. In T. K. Srull & R. S. Wyer Jr. (Eds.), *Advances in social cognition* (Vol 1., pp. 1–36). Erlbaum.

Brewer, W. F., & Lambert, B. L. (2001). The theory-ladenness of observation and the theory-ladenness of the rest of the scientific process. *Philosophy of Science, 68*(3), Supplement: *Proceedings of the 2000 Biennial Meeting of the Philosophy of Science Association, Part 1,* S176–S186.

Broda, M., Yun, J., Schneider, B., Yeager, D. S., Walton, G. M., & Diemer, M. (2018). Reducing inequality in academic success for incoming college students: A randomized trial of growth mindset and belonging interventions. *Journal of Research on Educational Effectiveness, 11*(3), 317–338.

Brookfield, S. D., & Preskill, S. (2005). *Discussion as a way of teaching: Tools and techniques for democratic classrooms* (2nd ed.). Jossey-Bass.

Broughton, S. H., Sinatra, G. M., & Reynolds, R. E. (2007). The refutation text effect: Influence on learning and attention. Paper presented at the Annual Meeting of the American Educational Researchers Association, Chicago, IL.

Brown, A. L., Bransford, J. D., Ferrara, R. A., & Campione, J. C. (1983). Learning, remembering, and understanding. In J. H. Flavell, & E. M. Markman (Eds.), *Handbook of child psychology* (Vol. 3, 4th ed., pp. 77–166). Wiley.

Brown, A. L., & Kane, M. J. (1988). Preschool students can learn to transfer. Learning to learn and learning from example. *Cognitive Psychology, 20,* 493–523.

Brown, D. (1992). Using examples to remediate misconceptions in physics: Factors influencing conceptual change. *Journal of Research in Science Teaching, 29,* 17–34.

Brown, D., & Clement, J. (1989). Overcoming misconceptions via analogical reasoning: Factors influencing understanding in a teaching experiment. *Instructional Science, 18,* 237–261.

Brown, L. T. (1983). Some more misconceptions about psychology among introductory psychology students. *Teaching of Psychology, 10,* 207–210.

Burgoyne, A. P., Hambrick, D. Z., & Macnamara, B. N. (2020). How firm are the foundations of mind-set theory? The claims appear stronger than the evidence. *Psychological Science, 31*(3).

Butler, D. (1997). The roles of goal setting and self-monitoring in students self-regulated engagement of tasks. Paper presented at the annual meeting of the American Educational Research Association, Chicago, IL.

Byers, D. S., McInroy, L. B., Craig, S. L., Slates, S., & Kattari, S. K. (2020). Naming and addressing homophobic and transphobic microaggressions in social work classrooms. *Journal of Social Work Education, 56*(3), 484–495.

Canning, E. A., Muenks, K., Green, D. J., & Murphy, M. C. (2019). STEM faculty who believe ability is fixed have larger racial achievement gaps and inspire less student motivation in their classes. *Science Advances, 5*(2), 4734. https://doi.org/10.1126/sciadv.aau4734

Cardelle, M., & Corno, L. (1981). Effects on second language learning of variations in written feedback on homework assignments. *TESOL Quarterly, 15,* 251–261.

Carey, L. J., Flower, L., Hayes, J., Shriver, K. A., & Haas, C. (1989). *Differences in writers' initial task representations* (Technical Report No. 34). Center for the Study of Writing at University of California at Berkeley and Carnegie Mellon University.

Carver, C. S., & Scheier, M. F. (1998). *On the self-regulation of behavior.* Cambridge University Press.

Cass, V. (1979). Homosexual identity formation: A theoretical model. *Journal of Homosexuality, 4,* 219–235.

Catrambone, R. (1995). Aiding subgoal learning: Effects on transfer. *Journal of Educational Psychology, 87,* 5–17.

Catrambone, R. (1998). The subgoal learning model: Creating better examples so that students can solve novel problems. *Journal of Experimental Psychology: General, 127*, 355-376.

Catrambone, R., & Holyoak, K. J. (1989). Overcoming contextual limitations on problem solving transfer. *Journal of Experimental Psychology, 15*(6), 1147-1156.

Cavanagh, S. R. (2016). *The spark of learning: Energizing the college classroom with the science of emotion.* West Virginia University Press.

Center for Urban Education. (2021). *Equity mindedness.* Retrieved from https://cue.usc.edu/equity/equity-mindedness/

Chase, W. G., & Ericsson, K. A. (1982). Skill and working memory. In G. H. Bower (Ed.), *The psychology of learning and motivation* (Vol. 16, pp. 1-58). Academic Press.

Chase, W. G., & Simon, H. A. (1973a). The mind's eye in chess. In W. G. Chase (Ed.), *Visual information processing.* Academic Press.

Chase, W. G., & Simon, H. A. (1973b). Perception in chess. *Cognitive Psychology, 1*, 31-81.

Chen, X. (2013). *STEM attrition: College students' paths into and out of STEM fields.* National Center for Education Statistics.

Chi, M.T.H. (2008). Three types of conceptual change: Belief revision, mental model transformation, and categorical shift. In S. Vosniadou (Ed.), *Handbook of research on conceptual change* (pp. 61-82). Erlbaum.

Chi, M.T.H., Bassok, M., Lewis, M. W., Reimann, P., & Glaser, R. (1989). Self-explanations: How students study and use examples in learning to solve problems. *Cognitive Science, 13*, 145-182.

Chi, M.T.H., DeLeeuw, N., Chiu, M.-H., & LaVancher, C. (1994). Eliciting self-explanations improves understanding. *Cognitive Science, 18*, 439-477.

Chi, M.T.H., Feltovich, P. J., & Glaser, R. (1981). Categorization and representation of physics problems by experts and novices. *Cognitive Science, 5*, 121-152.

Chi, M.T.H., & Roscoe, R. D. (2002). The processes and challenges of conceptual change. In M. Limon & L. Mason (Eds.), *Reconsidering conceptual change: Issues in theory and practice* (pp. 3-27). Kluwer.

Chi, M.T.H., & VanLehn, K. (1991). The content of physics self-explanations. *Journal of the Learning Sciences, 1*, 69-105.

Chi, M.T.H., & Wylie, R. (2014). The ICAP framework: Linking cognitive engagement to active learning outcomes. *Educational Psychologist, 49*(4), 219-243.

Chickering, A. (1969). *Education and identity.* Jossey-Bass.

Chinn, C. A., & Malhotra, B. A. (2002). Children's responses to anomalous scientific data: How is conceptual change impeded? *Journal of Educational Psychology, 94*, 327-343.

Cho, M. K., & Kim, M. Y. (2022). Factors affecting the global health and cultural competencies of nursing students. *International Journal of Environmental Research and Public Health, 19*(7), 4109.

Choney, S. K., Berryhill-Paapke, E., & Robbins, R. R. (1995). The acculturation of American Indians: Developing frameworks for research and practice. In J. G. Ponterotto, J. M. Casas, L. A. Suzuki, & C. M. Alexander (Eds.), *Handbook of multicultural counseling* (pp. 73–92). Sage.

Christophel, D. M., & Gorham, J. (1995). A test-retest analysis of student motivation, teacher immediacy, and perceived sources of motivation and demotivation in college classes. *Communication Education, 44*(4), 292–306.

Clark, R. C., & Mayer, R. E. (2016). *e-Learning and the science of instruction: Proven guidelines for consumers and designers of multimedia learning* (4th ed.). Wiley.

Clarke, T. A., Ayres, P. L., & Sweller, J. (2005). The impact of sequencing and prior knowledge on learning mathematics through spreadsheet applications. *Educational Technology Research and Development, 53*, 15–24.

Claro, S., Paunesku, D., & Dweck, C. S. (2016). Growth mindset tempers the effects of poverty on academic achievement. *Proceedings of the National Academy of Sciences of the United States of America, 113*(31), 8664–8668.

Clement, J. (1993). Using bridging analogies and anchoring intuitions to deal with students' misconceptions in physics. *Journal of Research in Science Teaching, 30*, 1241–1257.

Clement, J. J. (1982). Students' preconceptions in introductory mechanics. *American Journal of Physics, 50*, 66–71.

Cognition and Technology Group at Vanderbilt. (1994). From visual word problems to learning communities: Changing conceptions of cognitive research. In K. McGilly (Ed.), *Classroom lessons: Integrating cognitive theory and classroom practice* (pp. 157–200). MIT Press/Bradford Books.

Cohen, G. L., Garcia, J., & Purdie-Vaughns, V. (2012). An identity threat perspective on intervention. In M. Inzlicht & T. Schmader (Eds.), *Stereotype threat: Theory, process, and application*. Oxford University Press.

Cohen, G. L., Garcia, J., Purdie-Vaughns, V., Apfel, N., & Brzustoski, P. (2009). Recursive processes in self-affirmation: Intervening to close the minority achievement gap. *Science, 324*(5925), 400–403.

Cohen, G. L., & Sherman, D. K. (2014). The psychology of change: Self-affirmation and social psychological intervention. *Annual Review of Psychology, 65*(1), 333–371.

Cohen, G. L., & Steele, C. M. (2002). A barrier of mistrust: How stereotypes affect cross-race mentoring. In J. Aronson (Ed.), *Improving academic achievement: Impact of psychological factors on education* (pp. 305–331). Academic Press.

Collins, C. (2018). What is white privilege, really? *Teaching Tolerance, 60*, 1–11.

Confrey, J. (1990). A review of the research on student conceptions in mathematics, science, and programming. In C. B. Cazden (Ed.), *Review of research in education*. American Educational Research Association.

Cook, J. E., Purdie-Vaughns, V., Garcia, J., & Cohen, G. L. (2012). Chronic threat and contingent belonging: Protective benefits of values affirmation on identity development. *Journal of Personality and Social Psychology, 102*(3), 479–496.

Cooper, G., & Sweller, J. (1987). The effects of schema acquisition and rule automation on mathematical problem-solving transfer. *Journal of Educational Psychology, 79*, 347–362.

Coutinho, M.V.C., Thomas J., Fredricks-Lowman, I., & Bondaruk, M. V. (2020). The Dunning-Kruger effect in Emirati college students: Evidence for generalizability across cultures. *International Journal of Psychology & Psychological Therapy, 20*(1), 29–36.

Cowan, N. (2008). What are the differences between long-term, short-term, and working memory? *Progress in Brain Research, 169*, 323–338.

Creasey, G., Jarvis, P., & Gadke, D. (2009). Student attachment stances, instructor immediacy, and student-instructor relationships as predictors of achievement expectancies in college students. *Journal of College Student Development, 50*(4), 353–372.

Crenshaw, K. (1989). Demarginalizing the intersection of race and sex: A Black feminist critique of antidiscrimination doctrine, feminist theory, and antiracist politics. *University of Chicago Legal Forum, 1989*(1), 139–167.

Croizet, J. C., & Claire, T. (1998). Extending the concept of stereotype threat to social class: The intellectual underperformance of students from low socio-economic backgrounds. *Personality and Social Psychology Bulletin, 24*, 588–594.

Cross, W. (1995). The psychology of nigrescence: Revisiting the cross model. In J. Ponterotto, J. Casas, L. Suzuki, & C. Alexander (Eds.), *Handbook of multicultural counseling* (pp. 93–122). Sage.

Csikszentmihalyi, M. (1991). *Flow: The psychology of optimal experience*. Harper Collins.

Cury, F., Elliot, A. J., Da Fonseca, D., & Moller, A. C. (2006). The social-cognitive model of achievement motivation and the 2 × 2 achievement framework. *Journal of Personality and Social Psychology, 90*(4), 666–679.

D'Agustino, S. (2016). *Creating teacher immediacy in online learning environments*. Information Science Reference.

D'Augelli, A. R. (1994). Identity development and sexual orientation: Toward a model of lesbian, gay, and bisexual development. In E. Trickett, R. Watts, & D. Birman (Eds.), *Human diversity: Perspectives on people in context* (pp. 312–333). Jossey-Bass.

Dean, R. S., & Enemoh, P.A.C. (1983). Pictorial organization in prose learning. *Contemporary Educational Psychology, 8*, 20–27.

Deci, E. L. (1971). Effects of externally mediated rewards on intrinsic motivation. *Journal of Personality and Social Psychology, 18*, 105–115.

DeGroot, A. (1965). *Thought and choice in chess.* Mouton.

DeJong, T., & Ferguson-Hessler, M. (1996). Types and qualities of knowledge. *Educational Psychologist, 31*, 105–113.

Del Mas, R. C., & Liu, Y. (2007). Students' conceptual understanding of the standard deviation. In M. C. Lovett & P. Shah (Eds.), *Thinking with data* (pp. 87–116). Erlbaum.

Denton, A. W., & Velaso, J. (2017). Changes in syllabus tone affect warmth (but not competence) ratings of both male and female instructors. *Social Psychology of Education, 21*, 173–187.

Derek Bok Center for Teaching and Learning. (2007). *Race in the classroom: The multiplicity of experiences* (DVD). Anker Publishing.

Deslauriers, L., McCarty, L. S., Miller, K., & Kestin, G. (2019). Measuring actual learning versus feeling of learning in response to being actively engaged in the classroom. *Proceedings of the National Academy of Sciences of the United States of America, 116*(39), 19251–19257.

Deslauriers, L., Schelew, E., & Wieman, C. (2011). Improved learning in a large-enrollment physics class. *Science, 332*, 862–864.

DeSurra, C., & Church, K. A. (1994). Unlocking the classroom closet: Privileging the marginalized voices of gay/lesbian college students. Paper presented at the Annual Meeting of the Speech Communication Association.

Díaz-García, C., González-Moreno, A., & Sáez-Martínez, F. J. (2013). Gender diversity within R&D teams: Its impact on radicalness of innovation. *Innovation, 15*(2), 149–160.

DiPietro, M. (2007). *Checklist of assumptions that can impact motivation, learning, and performance.* Eberly Center for Teaching Excellence. Retrieved from https://www.cmu.edu/teaching/resources/Teaching/CourseDesign/InstructionalStrategies/checklist-assumptions.doc

DiPietro, M. (2012). Applying the seven learning principles to creating LGBT-inclusive classrooms. *Diversity and Democracy, 15*(1), 5–7.

DiSessa, A. A. (1982). Unlearning Aristotelian physics: A study of knowledge-based learning. *Cognitive Science, 6*, 37–75.

Dooling, D. J., & Lachman, R. (1971). Effects of comprehension on retention of prose. *Journal of Experimental Psychology, 88*, 216–222.

Dunbar, K. N., Fugelsang, J. A., & Stein, C. (2007). Do naïve theories ever go away? Using brain and behavior to understand changes in concepts. In M. C. Lovett & P. Shah (Eds.), *Thinking with data.* Erlbaum.

Dunning, D. (2007). *Self-insight: Roadblocks and detours on the path to knowing thyself.* Taylor & Francis.

Dweck, C., & Leggett, E. (1988). A social-cognitive approach to motivation and personality. *Psychological Review, 95*, 256-273.

Egan, D. E., & Schwartz, B. J. (1979). Chunking in recall of symbolic drawings. *Memory & Cognition, 7*, 149-158.

Eisenberg, D., Golberstein, E., & Hunt, J. (2009). Mental health and academic success in college. *The B.E. Journal of Economic Analysis & Policy, 9*(1).

El Guindi, F. (1999). *Veil: Modesty, privacy, and resistance.* Berg Publishers.

Elliot, A. J. (1999). Approach and avoidance motivation and achievement goals. *Educational Psychologist, 34*, 169-189.

Elliot, A. J., & Fryer, J. W. (2008). The goal construct in psychology. In J. Y. Shah & W. L. Gardner (Eds.), *Handbook of motivation science* (pp. 235-250). Guilford Press.

Elliot, A. J., & McGregor, H. A. (2001). A 2 × 2 achievement goal framework. *Journal of Personality and Social Psychology, 80*(3), 501-519.

Ericsson, K. A., & Charness, N. (1994). Expert performance: Its structure and acquisition. *American Psychologist, 49*, 725-747.

Ericsson, K. A., Chase, W. G., & Faloon, S. (1980). Acquisition of a memory skill. *Science, 208*, 1181-1182.

Ericsson, K. A., Krampe, R. T., & Tescher-Romer, C. (2003). The role of deliberate practice in the acquisition of expert performance. *Psychological Review, 100*, 363-406.

Ericsson, K. A., & Lehmann, A. C. (1996). Expert and exceptional performance: Evidence on maximal adaptations on task constraints. *Annual Review of Psychology, 47*, 273-305.

Ericsson, K. A., & Smith, J. (1991). *Toward a general theory of expertise: Prospects and limits.* Cambridge University Press.

Ericsson, K. A., & Staszewski, J. J. (1989). Skilled memory and expertise: Mechanisms of exceptional performance (pp. 235-267). In D. Klahr, & K. Kotovsky (Eds.), *Complex information processing: The impact of Herbert A. Simon.* Erlbaum.

Erikson, E., & Erikson, J. (1997). *The life cycle completed: Extended version.* W. W. Norton.

Eylon, B., & Reif, F. (1984). Effects of knowledge organization on task performance. *Cognition and Instruction, 1*, 5-44.

Feldblum, M., Hubbard, S., Lim, A., Penichet-Paul, C., & Siegel, H. (2020). Undocumented students in higher education: How many students are in U.S. colleges and universities, and who are they? *New American Economy.* Retrieved from https://research.newamericaneconomy.org/wp-content/uploads/sites/2/2021/03/Undocumented_brief_V3.pdf

Festinger, L. (1957). *A theory of cognitive dissonance.* Stanford University Press.

Finucane, M. L., Alhakami, A., Slovic, P., & Johnson, S. M. (2000). The affect heuristic in judgments of risks and benefits. *Journal of Behavioral Decision Making, 13*, 1-17.

265

Fiske, S. T., & Taylor, S. E. (2017). *Social cognition* (3rd ed.). Sage.

Fletcher-Wood, H. (2022). Is growth mindset real? New evidence, new conclusions. *Improving Teaching*, March 6. Retrieved from https://improvingteaching.co.uk/2022/03/06/is-growth-mindset-real-new-evidence-new-conclusions/

Forber-Pratt, A. J., & Aragon, S. R. (2013). A model of social and psychosocial identity development for postsecondary students with physical disabilities. In M. Wappett & K. Arndt (Eds.), *Emerging perspectives on disability studies*. Palgrave Macmillan.

Ford, M. E. (1992). *Motivating humans: Goals, emotions and personal agency beliefs*. Sage.

Forrest-Bank, S. S., & Cuellar, M. J. (2018). The mediating effects of ethnic identity on the relationships between racial microaggression and psychological well-being. *Social Work Research, 42*(1), 44–56.

Fowler, J. (1981). *Stages of faith: The psychology of human development and the quest for meaning*. Harper & Row.

Freeman, S., Eddy, S. L., McDonough, M., Smith, M. K., Okoroafor, N., Jordt, H., & Wenderoth, M. P. (2014). Active learning increases student performance in science, engineering, and mathematics. *Proceedings of the National Academy of Sciences of the United States of America, 111*(23), 8410–8415.

Freire, P. (2000) *Pedagogy of the oppressed* (30th anniv. ed.). Continuum.

Fries-Britt, S. (2000). Identity development of high-ability black collegians. In M. Baxter-Magolda (Ed.), *Teaching to promote intellectual and personal maturity: Incorporating students' worldviews and identities into the learning process* (Vol. 82). Jossey-Bass.

Fu, W. T., & Gray, W. D. (2004). Resolving the paradox of the active user: Stable suboptimal performance in interactive tasks. *Cognitive Science, 28*(6), 901–935.

Gallegos, P., & Ferdman, B. (2012). Latina and Latino ethnoracial identity orientations: A dynamic and developmental perspective. In C. Wijeyesinghe & B. Jackson (Eds.), *New perspectives on racial identity development: Integrating emerging frameworks* (2nd ed., pp. 51–80). New York University Press.

Gardner, R. M., & Dalsing, S. (1986). Misconceptions about psychology among college students. *Teaching of Psychology, 13*, 32–34.

Garfield, J., del Mas, R. C., & Chance, B. (2007). Using students' informal notions of variability to develop an understanding of formal measures of variability. In M. C. Lovett & P. Shah (Eds.), *Thinking with data* (pp. 117–147). Erlbaum.

Garrison, D. R., Anderson, T., & Archer, W. (1999). Critical inquiry in a text-based environment: Computer conferencing in higher education. *The Internet and Higher Education, 2*(2), 87–105.

Gentner, D., Holyoak, K. J., & Kokinov, B. N. (2001). *The analogical mind*. MIT Press.

Gentner, D., Loewenstein, J., & Thompson, L. (2003). Learning and transfer: A general role for analogical encoding. *Journal of Educational Psychology, 95*, 393–405.

Gibson, J. (2006). Disability and clinical competency: An introduction. *The California Psychologist, 39*, 6-10.

Gibson, J., Pousson, J. M., Laux, S., & Myers, K. (2018). Disability identity development of people who have low vision or are blind. *Journal of Education and Human Development, 7*(3), 18-27.

Gick, M. L., & Holyoak, K. J. (1980). Analogical problem solving. *Cognitive Psychology, 12*, 306-355.

Gick, M. L., & Holyoak, K. J. (1983). Schema induction and analogical transfer. *Cognitive Psychology, 15*, 1-38.

Gilligan, C. (1977). In a different voice: Women's conception of self and morality. *Harvard Educational Review, 47*, 481-517.

Gobet, F., & Charness, N. (2006). Expertise in chess. In K. A. Ericsson et al. (Eds.), *The Cambridge handbook of expertise and expert performance* (pp. 523-538). Cambridge University Press.

Gómez, J.P.P., & Arenas, Y. (2019). Development of bisexual identity. *Ciencia & saude coletiva, 24*, 1669-1678.

Gonyea, R., & Moore III, J. (2007). Gay, lesbian, bisexual and transgender students and their engagement in educationally purposeful activities in college. Paper presented at the annual meeting of the Association for the Study of Higher Education, Louisville, KY.

Gonzales, P. M., Blanton, H., & Williams, K. J. (2002). The effects of stereotype threat and double-minority status on the test performance of Latino women. *Personality and Social Psychology Bulletin, 28*(5), 659-670.

Good, C. Aronson, J., & Inzlicht, M. (2003). Improving adolescents' standardized test performance: An intervention to reduce the effects of stereotype threat. *Journal of Applied Developmental Psychology, 24*(6), 645-662.

Good, C., Rattan, A., & Dweck, C. S. (2012). Why do women opt out? Sense of belonging and women's representation in mathematics. *Journal of Personality and Social Psychology, 102*(4), 700-717.

Goodrich Andrade, H. (2001). The effects of instructional rubrics on learning to write. *Current Issues in Education, 4*(4).

Griskevica, I., & Iltners, M. (2021). Relationship between academic self-efficacy and cognitive load for students in distance learning. *Education. Innovation. Diversity, 1*(2), 31-40.

Gutman, A. (1979). Misconceptions of psychology and performance in the introductory course. *Teaching of Psychology, 6*, 159-161.

Guzetti, B. J., Snyder, T. E., Glass, G. V., & Gamas, W. S. (1993). Meta-analysis of instructional interventions from reading education and science education to promote conceptual change in science. *Reading Research Quarterly, 28*, 116-161.

Hacker, D. J., Bol, L., Horgan, D. D., & Rakow, E. A. (2000). Test prediction and performance in a classroom context. *Journal of Educational Psychology, 92*, 160–170.

Hall, R., & Sandler, B. (1984). *Out of the classroom: A chilly campus climate for women.* Association of American Colleges.

Hall, R. M., & Sandler, B. R. (1982). *The classroom climate: A chilly one for women?* Association of American Colleges. Retrieved from https://files.eric.ed.gov/fulltext/ED215628.pdf

Hansen, D. (1989). Lesson evading and dissembling: Ego strategies in the classroom. *American Journal of Education, 97*, 184–208.

Harackiewicz, J., Barron, K., Taucer, J., Carter, S., & Elliot, A. (2000). Short-term and long-term consequences of achievement goals: Predicting interest and performance over time. *Journal of Educational Psychology, 92*, 316–330.

Hardiman, R., & Jackson, B. (1992). Racial identity development: Understanding racial dynamics in college classrooms and on campus. In M. Adams (Ed.), *Promoting diversity in college classrooms: Innovative responses for the curriculum, faculty and institutions* (Vol. 52, pp. 21–37). Jossey-Bass.

Harnish, R. J., & Bridges, K. R. (2011). Effect of syllabus tone: Students' perceptions of instructor and course. *Social Psychology of Education: An International Journal, 14*(3), 319–330.

Hattie, J., & Timperley, H. (2007). The power of feedback. *Review of Educational Research, 77*, 81–112.

Hayes, J. R., & Flower, L. S. (1986). Writing research and the writer. *American Psychologist Special Issue: Psychological Science and Education, 41*, 1106–1113.

Healy, A. F., Clawson, D. M., & McNamara, D. S. (1993). The long-term retention of knowledge and skills. In D. L. Medin (Ed.), *The psychology of learning and motivation* (pp. 135–164). Academic Press.

Hecht, C. A., Yeager, D. S., Dweck, C. S., & Murphy, M. C. (2021). Beliefs, affordances, and adolescent development: Lessons from a decade of growth mindset interventions. *Advances in Child Development and Behavior, 61*, 169–197.

Helms, J. (1993). Toward a model of White racial identity development. In J. Helms (Ed.), *Black and White racial identity: Theory, research and practice.* Praeger.

Henderson, V. L., & Dweck, C. S. (1990). Motivation and achievement. In S. S. Feldman & G. R. Elliott (Eds.), *At the threshold: The developing adolescent* (pp. 308–329). Harvard University Press.

Hidi, S., & Renninger, K. A. (2006). The four-phase model of interest development. *Educational Psychologist, 41*(2), 111–127.

Hinds, P. J. (1999). The curse of expertise: The effects of expertise and debiasing methods on predictions of novice performance. *Journal of Experimental Psychology: Applied, 5*(2), 205–221.

Hinsley, D. A., Hayes, J. R., & Simon, H. A. (1977). From words to equations: Meaning and representation in algebra word problems. In M. A. Just & P. S. Carpenter (Eds.), *Cognitive processes in comprehension*. Erlbaum.

Holyoak, K. J., & Koh, K. (1987). Surface and structural similarity in analogical transfer. *Memory & Cognition, 15*, 332–340.

Hong, L., & Page, S. (2004). Groups of diverse problem solvers can outperform groups of high-ability problem solvers. *PNAS, 101*(46), 16385–16389.

Hulleman, C. S., Barron, K. E., Kosovich, J. J., & Lazowski, R. A. (2016). Student motivation: Current theories, constructs, and interventions within an expectancy-value framework. In A. A. Lipnevich, F. Preckel, & R. D. Roberts (Eds.), *Psychosocial skills and school systems in the 21st century: Theory, research, and practice* (pp. 241–278). Springer International Publishing.

Hulleman, C. S., & Happel, J. (2018). *Help students navigate life's transitions with a mindset GPS. Motivate Lab Blog*.

Hurtado, S., Milem, J., Clayton-Pedersen, A., & Allen, W. (1999). *Enacting diverse learning environments: Improving the climate for racial/ethnic diversity in higher education*. The George Washington University.

Immordino-Yang, M. H. (2016). *Emotions, learning, and the brain: Exploring the educational implications of affective neuroscience*. W. W. Norton.

Inzlicht, M., & Ben-Zeev, T. (2000). A threatening intellectual environment: Why females are susceptible to experience problem-solving deficits in the presence of males. *Psychological Science, 11*(5), 365–371.

Inzlicht, M., & Schmader, T. (2011). *Stereotype threat: Theory, process, and application*. Oxford University Press.

Ishiyama, J., & Hartlaub, S. (2002). Does the wording of syllabi affect student course assessment in introductory political science classes? *Political Science and Politics, 35*(03), 567–570.

Joksimović, S., Gašević, D., Kovanović, V., Riecke, B. E., & Hatala, M. (2015). Social presence in online discussions as a process predictor of academic performance. *Journal of Computer Assisted Learning, 31*(6), 638–654.

Judd, C. H. (1908). The relation of special training to general intelligence. *Educational Review, 36*, 28–42.

Kahnemann, D., & Frederick, S. (2002). Representativeness revisited: Attribute substitution in intuitive judgment. In T. Gilovich, D. Griffin, & D. Kahnemann (Eds.), *Heuristics and biases: The psychology of intuitive judgment*. Cambridge University Press.

Kaiser, M. K., McCloskey, M., & Proffitt, D. R. (1986). Development of intuitive theories of motion: Curvilinear motion in the absence of external forces. *Developmental Psychology, 22*, 67–71.

Kalyuga, S. (2011). Cognitive load theory: How many types of load does it really need? *Educational Psychology Review, 23*(1), 1–19.

Kalyuga, S., Ayres, P., Chandler, P., & Sweller, J. (2003). Expertise reversal effect. *Educational Psychologist, 38*, 23–31.

Kandel, A. (1986). *Processes of Jewish American identity development: Perceptions of conservative Jewish women.* Unpublished Doctoral Dissertation, University of Massachusetts at Amherst.

Kaplan, J., Fisher, D., & Rogness, N. (2009). Lexical ambiguity in statistics: What do students know about the words: Association, average, confidence, random and spread? *Journal of Statistics Education, 17*(3).

Kim, J. (2012). Asian American racial identity development theory. In C. Wijeyesinghe & B. Jackson (Eds.), *New perspectives on racial identity development: Integrating emerging frameworks* (2nd ed., pp. 138–160). New York University Press.

Klahr, D., & Carver, S. M. (1988). Cognitive objectives in a LOGO debugging curriculum: Instruction, learning, and transfer. *Cognitive Psychology, 20*, 362–404.

Klebig, B., Goldonowicz, J., Mendes, E., Miller, A. N., & Katt, J. (2016). The combined effects of instructor communicative behaviors, instructor credibility, and student personality traits on incivility in the college classroom. *Communication Research Reports, 33*(2), 152–158.

Klintman, M. (2019). *Knowledge resistance: How we avoid insight from others.* Manchester University Press.

Knowles, M. S. (1984). *Andragogy in action: Applying modern principles of adult education.* Jossey Bass.

Koedinger, K. R., & Anderson, J. R. (1990). Abstract planning and perceptual chunks: Elements of expertise in geometry. *Cognitive Science, 14*(4), 511–550.

Koedinger, K. R., & Anderson, J. R. (1993). Reifying implicit planning in geometry: Guidelines for model-based intelligent tutoring system design. In S. Lajoie & S. Derry (Eds.), *Computers as cognitive tools.* Erlbaum.

Koedinger, K. R., Kim, J., Jia, J. Z., McLaughlin, E. A., & Bier, N. L. (2015). Learning is not a spectator sport: Doing is better than watching for learning from a MOOC. *Proceedings of the Second ACM Conference on Learning @ Scale* (pp. 111–120). Association for Computing Machinery.

Kohlberg, L. (1976). Moral stages and moralization: The cognitive-developmental approach. In T. Lickona (Ed.), *Moral development and behavior: Theory, research, and social issues* (pp. 31–53). Holt, Rinehart & Winston.

Kole, J. A., & Healy, A. (2007). Using prior knowledge to minimize interference when learning large amounts of information. *Memory & Cognition, 35*, 124–137.

Kornell, N., & Bjork, R. A. (2008). Learning concepts and categories: Is spacing the "enemy of induction"? *Psychological Science, 19*(6), 585–592.

Krugman, P. (2020) *Arguing with zombies: Economics, politics, and the fight for a better future.* W. W. Norton.

Lamburg, W. (1980). Self-provided and peer-provided feedback. *College Composition and Communication, 31*(1), 63–69.

Lansdown, T. C. (2002). Individual differences during driver secondary task performance: Verbal protocol and visual allocation findings. *Accident Analysis & Prevention, 23*, 655–662.

Larkin, J., McDermott, J., Simon, D. P., & Simon, H. (1980). Expert and novice performance in solving physics problems. *Science, 208*(4450), 1335–1342.

Lehman, R. M., & Conceição, S.C.O. (2010). *Creating a sense of presence in online teaching: How to "be there" for distance learners.* Jossey-Bass.

Lesgold, A., Rubinson, H., Feltovich, P. J., Glaser, R., Klopfer, D., & Wang Y. (1988). Expertise in a complex skill: Diagnosing x-ray pictures. In M.T.H. Chi & R. Glaser (Eds.), *The nature of expertise* (pp. 311–342). Erlbaum.

Levi-Strauss, C. (1969). *The elementary structures of kinship.* Beacon Press.

Levy, B. (1996). Improving memory in old age through implicit self-stereotyping. *Journal of Personality and Social Psychology, 71*(6), 1092–1107.

Li, Y., & Bates, T. C. (2019). You can't change your basic ability, but you work at things, and that's how we get hard things done: Testing the role of growth mindset on response to setbacks, educational attainment, and cognitive ability. *Journal of Experimental Psychology: General, 148*(9), 1640–1655.

Loes, C. N., Culver, K. C., & Trolian, T. L. (2018). How collaborative learning enhances students' openness to diversity. *The Journal of Higher Education, 89*(6), 935–960.

Loewenstein, J., Thompson, L., & Gentner, D. (2003). Analogical learning in negotiation teams: Comparing cases promotes learning and transfer. *Academy of Management Learning and Education, 2*(2), 119–127.

Loh, E. K. (2019). What we know about expectancy-value theory, and how it helps to design a sustained motivating learning environment. *System, 86*, 102119.

Lovett, M. C. (2001). A collaborative convergence on studying reasoning processes: A case study in statistics. In S. Carver & D. Klahr (Eds.), *Cognition and instruction: Twenty-five years of progress* (pp. 347–384). Erlbaum.

Lyle, K. B., & Crawford, N. A. (2011). Retrieving essential material at the end of lectures improves performance on statistics exams. *Teaching of Psychology, 38*, 94–97.

Macnamara, B. (2018). Schools are buying "growth mindset" interventions despite scant evidence that they work well. *The Conversation.* Retrieved June 26, 2018, from https://theconversation.com/schools-are-buying-growth-mindset-interventions-despite-scant-evidence-that-they-work-well-96001

Maehr, M., & Meyer, H. (1997). Understanding motivation and schooling: Where we've been, where we are, and where we need to go. *Educational Psychology Review, 9*, 371–409.

Major, B., Spencer, S., Schmader, T., Wolfe, C., & Crocker, J. (1998). Coping with negative stereotypes about intellectual performance: The role of psychological disengagement. *Personality and Social Psychology Bulletin, 24*(1), 34–50.

Malott, K. M., Hall, K. H., Sheely-Moore, A., Krell, M. M., & Cardaciotto, L. (2014). Evidence-based teaching in higher education: Application to counselor education. *Counselor Education and Supervision, 53*(4), 294–305.

Mandernach, B. J., Gonzales, R. M., & Garrett, A. L. (2006). An examination of online instructor presence via threaded discussion participation. *Journal of Online Learning and Teaching, 2*(4), 248–260.

Marchesani, L., & Adams, M. (1992). Dynamics of diversity in the teaching-learning process: A faculty development model for analysis and action. In M. Adams (Ed.), *Promoting diversity in college classrooms: Innovative responses for the curriculum, faculty, and institutions* (Vol. 52, pp. 9–20). Jossey-Bass.

Marcia, J. (1966). Development and validation of ego identity status. *Journal of Personality and Social Psychology, 5*, 551–558.

Martin, F., Klein, J. D., & Sullivan, H. (2007). The impact of instructional elements in computer-based instruction. *British Journal of Educational Technology, 38*, 623–636.

Martin, V. L., & Pressley, M. (1991). Elaborative-interrogation effects depend on the nature of the question. *Journal of Educational Psychology, 83*, 113–119.

Mason Spencer, R., & Weisberg, R. W. (1986). Context-dependent effects on analogical transfer. *Memory and Cognition, 14*(5), 442–449.

Mathan, S. A., & Koedinger, K. R. (2005). Fostering the intelligent novice: Learning from errors with metacognitive tutoring. *Educational Psychologist, 40*(4), 257–265.

Maton, K., Beason, T., Godsay, S., Domingo, M., Bailey, T., Sun, S., & Hrabowski, F. (2016). Outcomes and processes in the Meyerhoff Scholars Program: STEM PhD completion, sense of community, perceived program benefit, science identity, and research self-efficacy. *CBE—Life Sciences Education, 15*(48), 1–11.

Mayer, R. E. (2001). *Multimedia learning.* Cambridge University Press.

Mayer, R. E. (2002). *The promise of educational psychology, Volume 2: Teaching for meaningful learning.* Merrill Prentice Hall.

Mayer, R. E., Griffith, E., Jurkowitz, I. T., & Rothman, D. (2008). Increased interestingness of extraneous details in a multimedia science presentation leads to decreased learning. *Journal of Experimental Psychology: Applied, 14*, 329–339.

Mayer, R. E., & Moreno, R. (1998). A split-attention effect in multimedia learning: Evidence for dual coding hypothesis. *Journal of Educational Psychology, 83*, 484–490.

Mayhew, M. J., Rockenbach, A. B., Bowman, N. A., Seifert, T. A., & Wolniak, G. C. (2016). *How college affects students: 21st century evidence that higher education works.* Jossey-Bass.

Mazur, E. (1996). *Peer instruction: A user's manual.* Addison-Wesley.

McCloskey, M. (1983). Naïve theories of motion. In D. Gentner & A. Stevens (Eds.), *Mental models* (pp. 289-324). Erlbaum.

McCloskey, M., Caramazza, A., & Green, B. (1980). Curvilinear motion in the absence of external forces: Naïve beliefs about the motion of objects. *Science, 210,* 1139-1141.

McClusky, H. Y. (1963). The course of the adult life span. In W. C. Hallenbeck (Ed.), *Psychology of adults.* Adult Education Association of the U.S.A.

McDaniel, M. A., Agarwal, P. K., Huelser, B. J., McDermott, K. B., & Roediger, H. L. (2011). Test-enhanced learning in a middle school science classroom: The effects of quiz frequency and placement. *Journal of Educational Psychology, 103,* 399-414.

McDaniel, M. A., & Donnelly, C. M. (1996). Learning with analogy and elaborative interrogation. *Journal of Educational Psychology, 88,* 508-519.

McGregor, H., & Elliot, A. (2002). Achievement goals as predictors of achievement-relevant processes prior to task engagement. *Journal of Educational Psychology, 94,* 381-395.

McIntosh, P. (2003). White privilege: Unpacking the invisible knapsack. In S. Plous (Ed.), *Understanding prejudice and discrimination* (pp. 191-196). McGraw-Hill.

McKendree, J. (1990). Effective feedback content for tutoring complex skills. *Human-Computer Interaction, 5*(4), 381-413.

McKeough, A., Lupart, J., & Marini, A. (1995). *Teaching for transfer: Fostering generalization in learning.* Erlbaum.

McNair, T. B., Bensimon, E. M, & Malcom-Piqueux, L. (2020). *From equity talk to equity walk: Expanding practitioner knowledge for racial justice in higher education.* Jossey-Bass.

Meece, J., & Holt, K. (1993). A pattern analysis of student's achievement goals. *Journal of Educational Psychology, 85,* 582-590.

Merrill, D. C., Reiser, B. J., Ranney, M., & Trafton, G. J. (1992). Effective tutoring techniques: A comparison of human tutors and intelligent tutoring systems. *Journal of the Learning Sciences, 2*(3), 277-305.

Miller, A. H. (1987). *Course design for university lecturers.* Nichols Publishing.

Miller, A. N., Katt, J. A., Brown, T., & Sivo, S. A. (2014). The relationship of instructor self-disclosure, nonverbal immediacy, and credibility to student incivility in the college classroom. *Communication Education, 63*(1), 1-16.

Miller, R., Greene, B., Montalvo, G., Ravindran, B., & Nichols, J. (1996). Engagement in academic work: The role of learning goals, future consequences, pleasing others and perceived ability. *Contemporary Educational Psychology, 21,* 388-422.

273

Minstrell, J. (1992). Facets of students' knowledge and relevant instruction. In R. Duit, F. Goldberg, & H. Niedderer (Eds.), *Research in physics learning: Theoretical issues and empirical studies* (pp. 110–128). Institut für die Pädagogik der Naturwissenschaften.

Minstrell, J. A. (1989). Teaching science for understanding. In L. B. Resnick & L. E. Klopfer (Eds.), *Toward the thinking curriculum: Current cognitive research*. ASCD Books.

Mitchell, T. R. (1982). Motivation: New directions for theory, research, and practice. *Academy of Management Review, 7*, 80–88.

Miyake, A., Kost-Smith, L. E., Finkelstein, N. D., Pollock, S. J., Cohen, G. L., & Ito, T. A. (2010). Reducing the gender achievement gap in college science: A classroom study of values affirmation. *Science, 330*(6008), 1234–1237.

Monteith, M. J., & Mark, A. Y. (2005). Changing one's prejudiced ways: Awareness, affect, and self-regulation. *European Review of Social Psychology, 16*, 113–154.

Monteith, M. J., Sherman, J. W., & Devine, P. G. (1998). Suppression as a stereotype control strategy. *Personality and Social Psychology Review, 2*, 63–82.

Morris, P. E., Gruneberg, M. M., Sykes, R. N., & Merrick, A. (1981). Football knowledge and the acquisition of new results. *British Journal of Psychology, 72*, 479–483.

Morris, T. L, Gorham, J., Cohen, S. H., & Huffman, D. (1996). Fashion in the classroom: Effects of attire on student perceptions of instructors in college classes. *Communication Education, 45*, 135–148.

Munro, G. (2010) The scientific impotence excuse: Discounting belief-threatening scientific abstracts. *Journal of Applied Social Psychology, 40*(3), 579–600.

Nathan, M., & Lee, N. (2013). Cultural diversity, innovation, and entrepreneurship: Firm-level evidence from London. *Economic Geography, 89*(4), 367–394.

Nathan, M. J., & Koedinger, K. R. (2000). An investigation of teachers' beliefs of students' algebra development. *Journal of Cognition and Instruction, 18*(2), 209–237.

Nathan, M. J., & Petrosino, A. (2003). Expert blind spot among preservice teachers. *American Educational Research Journal, 40*(4), 905–928.

National Academies of Sciences, Engineering, and Medicine (NASEM). (2016). *Barriers and opportunities for 2-Year and 4-Year STEM degrees: Systemic change to support students' diverse pathways*. The National Academies Press.

National Center for Education Statistics. (2019). *Status and trends in the education of racial and ethnic groups*. Indicator 19: College Participation Rates. Retrieved from https://nces .ed.gov/programs/raceindicators/index.asp

National Center for Education Statistics. (2020). *Characteristics of postsecondary students*. Retrieved from https://nces.ed.gov/programs/coe/pdf/coe_csb.pdf

National Center for Education Statistics. (2021). *Digest of education statistics, 2019*. Retrieved from https://nces.ed.gov/fastfacts/display.asp?id=60

National Center for Mental Health Checkups (NCMHC). (1999). *Youth mental health and academic achievement.* US Department of Health and Human Services.

National Research Council. (2000). *How people learn: Brain, mind, experience, and school.* National Academies Press.

National Research Council. (2001). *Knowing what students know: The science and design of educational assessment.* National Academies Press.

Navon, D., & Gopher, D. (1979). On the economy of the human-processing system. *Psychological Review, 86,* 214–255.

Naylor, J. C., & Briggs, G. E. (1963). Effects of task complexity and task organization on the relative efficiency of part and whole training methods. *Journal of Experimental Psychology, 65*(2), 217–224.

Neider, M. B., Gaspar, J. G., McCarley, J. S., Crowell, J. A., Kaczmarski, H., & Kramer, A. F. (2011). Walking and talking: Dual-task effects on street crossing behavior in older adults. *Psychology and Aging, 26*(2), 260–268.

Nelson, J. (1990). "This was an easy assignment": Examining how students interpret academic writing tasks. *Research in the Teaching of English, 24*(4), 362–396.

Nickerson, R. (1999). How we know—and sometimes misjudge—what others know: Imputing one's own knowledge to others. *Psychological Bulletin, 125*(6), 737–759.

Nielsen, M. W., Alegria, S., Börjeson, L., Etzkowitz, H., Falk-Krzesinski, H. J., Joshi, A., Leahey, E., Smith-Doerr, L., Woolley, A. W., & Schiebinger, L. (2017). Gender diversity leads to better science. *PNAS, 114*(8), 1740–1742.

Niemiec, C. P., & Ryan, R. M. (2009). Autonomy, competence, and relatedness in the classroom: Applying self-determination theory to educational practice. *Theory and Research in Education, 7*(2), 133–144.

Novak, J. (1998). *Learning, creating, and using knowledge: Concept maps as facilitative tools in schools and corporations.* Erlbaum.

Novak, J. D., & Cañas, A. J. (2008). *The theory underlying concept maps and how to construct them* (Technical Report IHMC CmapTools 2006-01 Rev 2008-01). Institute for Human and Machine *Cognition*. Retrieved March 26, 2009, from http://cmap.ihmc.us/Publications/ResearchPapers/TheoryUnderlyingConceptMaps.pdf

Nyhan, B. (2021). Why the backfire effect does not explain the durability of political misperceptions. *Proceedings of the National Academy of Sciences of the United States of America, 118*(15), e1912440117.

Nyhan, B., & Reifler, J. (2010). When corrections fail: The persistence of political misperceptions. *Political Behavior, 32,* 303–330.

Oh, C. S., Bailenson, J. N., & Welch, G. F. (2018). A systematic review of social presence: Definition, antecedents, and implications. *Frontiers in Robotics and AI, 5*(14), 1–35.

Ong, A. D., Burrow, A. L., Fuller-Rowell, T. E., Ja, N. M., & Sue, D. W. (2013). Racial micro-aggressions and daily well-being among Asian Americans. *Journal of Counseling Psychology, 60*(2), 188–199.

Osborn, T. L., Wasil, A. R., Venturo-Conerly, K. E., Schleider, J. L., & Weisz, J. R. (2020). Group intervention for adolescent anxiety and depression: Outcomes of a randomized trial with adolescents in Kenya. *Behavior Therapy, 51*(4), 601–615.

Paas, F., Renkl, A., & Sweller, J. (2003). Cognitive load theory and instructional design: Recent developments. *Educational Psychologist, 38*(1), 1–4.

Paas, F., Renkl, A., & Sweller, J. (2004). Cognitive load theory: Instructional implications of the interaction between information structures and cognitive architecture. *Instructional Science, 32*, 1–8.

Paas, F., & van Merrienboer, J. (1994). Variability of worked examples and transfer of geometrical problem solving skills: A cognitive-load approach. *Journal of Educational Psychology, 86*, 122–133.

Page, S. (2008). *The difference: How the power of diversity creates better groups, firms, schools, and societies*. Princeton University Press.

Palinscar, A. S., & Brown, A. L. (1984). Reciprocal teaching of comprehension-fostering and comprehension-monitoring activities. *Cognition & Instruction, 1*, 117–175.

Palmer, P. (2017). *The courage to teach: Exploring the inner landscape of a teacher's life, 20th Anniversary Edition*. Jossey-Bass.

Pascarella, E., & Terenzini, P. (1977). Patterns of student-faculty informal interaction beyond the classroom and voluntary freshman attrition. *Journal of Higher Education, 5*, 540–552.

Pascarella, E., & Terenzini, P. (1991). *How college affects students: Findings and insights from twenty years of research*. Jossey-Bass.

Pascarella, E., & Terenzini, P. T. (2005). *How college affects students: A third decade of research*. Jossey-Bass.

Pascarella, E., Whitt, E., Edison, M., & Nora, A. (1997). Women's perceptions of a "chilly climate" and their cognitive outcomes during the first year of college. *Journal of College Student Development, 38*(2), 109–124.

Pashler, H. (1994). Dual-task interference in simple tasks: Data and theory. *Psychological Bulletin, 116*(2), 220–244.

Pashler, H., Bain, P., Bottge, B., Graesser, A., Koedinger, K., McDaniel, M., & Metcalfe, J. (2007). *Organizing instruction and study to improve student learning* (NCER 2007-2004). Washington, DC: National Center for Education Research, Institute of Education Sciences, US Department of Education. Retrieved from https://files.eric.ed.gov/fulltext/ED498555.pdf

Pashler, H., McDaniel, M., Rohrer, D., & Bjork, R. (2008). Learning styles: Concepts and evidence. *Psychological Science in the Public Interest, 9*(3), 105-119.

Patton, L., Renn, K., Guido, F., and Quaye, S. J. (2016) *Student development in college: Theory, research, and practice* (3rd ed.). Jossey-Bass.

Patton, L. D., Harper, S. R., & Harris, J. (2015). Using critical race theory to (re)interpret widely studied topics related to students in US higher education. In A. M. Martinez-Aleman, B. Pusser, & E.M. Bensimon (Eds.), *Critical approaches to the study of higher education: A practical introduction* (pp. 193-219). Johns Hopkins University Press.

Peeck, J., Van Den Bosch, A. B., & Kruepeling, W. (1982). The effect of mobilizing prior knowledge on learning from text. *Journal of Educational Psychology, 74,* 771-777.

Peek, L. (2005). Becoming Muslim: The development of a religious identity. *Sociology of Religion, 66(3),* 215-242.

Perfetto, G. A., Bransford, J. D., & Franks, J. J. (1983). Constraints on access in a problem-solving context. *Memory and Cognition, 11,* 24-31.

Perry, W. (1968). *Forms of intellectual and ethical development in the college years: A scheme.* Holt, Rinehart & Winston.

Phillips, K. W., Liljenquist, K. A., Neale, M. A. (2008). Is the pain worth the gain? The advantages and liabilities of agreeing with socially distinct newcomers. *Personality & Social Psychology Bulletin, 35*(3), 336-350.

Pintrich, P. R. (2000). The role of goal orientation in self-regulated learning. In M. Boekaerts, P. R. Pintrich, & M. Zeider (Eds.), *Handbook of self-regulation* (pp. 451-502). Academic Press.

Pittsburgh Science of Learning Center. (2009). *Instructional principles and hypotheses.* Retrieved December 4, 2022, from https://learnlab.org/research/wiki/index.php/Instructional_Principles_and_Hypotheses

Poore-Pariseau, C. (2021). Support pronoun disclosure when students are ready. *The National Teaching & Learning Forum, 30*(3), 7-8.

Ram, A., Nersessian, N. J., & Keil, F. C. (1997). Special issue: Conceptual change. *The Journal of the Learning Sciences, 6,* 1-91.

Rankin, S. (2003). *Campus climate for gay, lesbian, bisexual, and transgender people: A national perspective.* The National Gay and Lesbian Task Force Policy Institute.

Rankin, S., Blumenfeld, W., Weber, G., & Frazer, S. (2010). *State of higher education for LGBT people: Campus Pride 2010 National College Climate Survey.* Campus Pride.

Rawson, K. A., & Kintsch, W. (2005). Rereading effects depend on time of test. *Journal of Educational Psychology, 97*(1), 70-80.

Read, J. P., Ouimette, P., White, J., Colder, C., & Farrow, S. (2011). Rates of DSM-IV-TR trauma exposure and posttraumatic stress disorder among newly matriculated college students. *Psychological Trauma: Theory, Research, Practice and Policy, 3*(2), 148–156.

Reardon, S. F. (2011). The widening achievement gap between the rich and the poor: New evidence and possible explanations. In G. J. Duncan & R. J. Murnane (Eds.), *Whither opportunity?* (pp. 91–115). Russell Sage Foundation.

Reber, P. J., & Kotovsky, K. (1997). Implicit learning in problem solving: The role of working memory capacity. *Journal of Experimental Psychology: General, 126,* 178–203.

Reder, L. M., & Anderson, J. R. (1980). A partial resolution of the paradox of interference: The role of integrating knowledge. *Cognitive Psychology, 12,* 447–472.

Reed, S. K., Ernst, G. W., & Banerji, R. (1974). The role of analogy in transfer between similar problem states. *Cognitive Psychology, 6,* 436–450.

Rege, M., Hanselman, P., Solli, I. F., Dweck, C. S., Ludvigsen, S., Bettinger, E., Crosnoe, R., Muller, C., Walton, G., Duckworth, A., & Yeager, D. S. (2020). How can we inspire nations of learners? An investigation of growth mindset and challenge-seeking in two countries. *American Psychologist, 76*(5), 755–767.

Resnick, L. B. (1976). Task analysis in instructional design: Some cases from mathematics. In D. Klahr (Ed.), *Cognition and instruction* (pp. 51–80). Erlbaum.

Resnick, L. B. (1983). Mathematics and science learning. *Science, 220,* 477–478.

Richardson, J., & Swan, K. (2003). Examining social presence in online courses in relation to students' perceived learning and satisfaction. *Journal of Asynchronous Learning Networks, 7,* 68–88.

Ritter, S., Anderson, J. R., Koedinger, K. R., & Corbett, A. (2007). Cognitive tutor: Applied research in mathematics education. *Psychonomic Bulletin & Review, 14*(2), 249–255.

Roberts, A., & Friedman, D. (2013). The impact of teacher immediacy on student participation: An objective cross-disciplinary examination. *International Journal of Teaching and Learning in Higher Education, 25*(1), 38–46.

Roediger, H. L., & Karpicke, J. D. (2006a). The power of testing memory: Basic research and implications for educational practice. *Perspectives on Psychological Science, 1,* 181–210.

Roediger, H. L., & Karpicke, J. D. (2006b). Test-enhanced learning: Taking memory tests improves long-term retention. *Psychological Science, 17,* 249–255.

Rohrer, D., & Taylor, K. (2007). The shuffling of mathematics problems improves learning. *Instructional Science, 35*(6), 481–498.

Rosch, E. H. (1973). Natural categories. *Cognitive Psychology, 4*(3), 328–350.

Rosenthal, R., & Jacobson, L. (1992). *Pygmalion in the classroom: Teacher expectation and pupils' intellectual development.* Irvington Publishers.

Ross, B. H. (1987). This is like that: The use of earlier problems and the separation of similarity effects. *Journal of Experimental Psychology: Learning, Memory, and Cognition, 13*, 629–639.

Ross, B. H. (1989). Distinguishing types of superficial similarity: Different effects on the access and use of earlier problems. *Journal of Experimental Psychology: Learning, Memory, and Cognition, 15*, 456–468.

Rothkopf, E. Z., & Billington, M. J. (1979). Goal-guided learning from text: Inferring a descriptive processing model from inspection times and eye movements. *Journal of Educational Psychology, 71*, 310–327.

RTI International. (2019). *First-generation college students: Demographic characteristics and postsecondary enrollment.* NASPA. Retrieved from https://firstgen.naspa.org/files/dmfile/FactSheet-01.pdf

Rubin, S. (1985). Professors, students, and the syllabus. (1985, August 7). *The Chronicle of Higher Education.*

Ryan, A. M., Pintrich, P. R., & Midgley, C. (2001). Avoiding seeking help in the classroom: Who and why? *Educational Psychology Review, 13*, 93–114.

Ryan, R. M., & Deci, E. L. (2000). Self-determination theory and the facilitation of intrinsic motivation, social development, and well-being. *American Psychologist, 55*, 68–78.

Ryan, R. M., & Deci, E. L. (2017). *Self-determination theory: Basic psychological needs in motivation, development, and wellness.* Guilford Press. Retrieved from https://doi.org/10.1521/978.14625/28806

Ryan, T. A. (1970). *Intentional behavior.* Ronal Press.

Salden, R.J.C. M., Paas, F., & van Merrienboer, J.J.G. (2006). A comparison of approaches to learning task selection in the training of complex cognitive skills. *Computers in Human Behavior, 22*, 321–333.

Sandler, B., & Hall, R. (1986). *The campus climate revisited: Chilly for women faculty, administrators, and graduate students.* Association of American Colleges.

Santilli, V., Miller, A. N., & Katt, J. (2011). A comparison of the relationship between instructor nonverbal immediacy and teacher credibility in Brazilian and U.S. classrooms. *Communication Research Reports, 28*(3), 266–274.

Schoenfeld, A. H. (1987). What's all the fuss about metacognition? In A. H. Schoenfeld (Ed.), *Cognitive science and mathematics education* (pp. 189–215). Erlbaum.

Schommer, M. (1994). An emerging conceptualization of epistemological beliefs and their role in learning. In R. Barner & P. Alexander (Eds.), *Beliefs about text and instruction with text* (pp. 25–40). Erlbaum.

279

Schrodt, P., & Witt, P. L. (2006). Students' attributions of instructor credibility as a function of students' expectations of instructional technology use and nonverbal immediacy. *Communication Education, 55*(1), 1-20.

Schutt, M., Brock S. A., & Laumakis, M. A. (2009). The effects of instructor immediacy behaviors in online learning environments. *Quarterly Review of Distance Education, 10*(2), 135-148.

Schwartz, D. L., & Bransford, J. D. (1998). A time for telling. *Cognition and Instruction, 16*, 475-522.

Schwartz, D. L., Lin, X., Brophy, S., & Bransford, J. D. (1999). Toward the development of flexibly adaptive instructional designs. In C. M. Reigelut (Ed.), *Instructional design theories and models: Volume 2*. Erlbaum.

Sensoy, Ö., & DiAngelo, R. (2014). Respect differences? Challenging the common guidelines in social justice education. *Democracy & Education, 22*(2), 1-10.

Seymour, E., & Hewitt, N. (1997). *Talking about leaving: Why undergraduates leave the sciences*. Westview Press.

Shih, M., Pittinsky, T., & Ambady, N. (1999). Stereotype susceptibility: Identity salience and shifts in quantitative performance. *Psychological Science, 10*, 80-83.

Shnabel, R., Purdie-Vaughns, V., Cook, J. E., Garcia, J., & Cohen, G. L. (2013). Demystifying values-affirmation interventions: Writing about social belonging is a key to buffering against identity threat. *Personality & Social Psychology Bulletin, 39*(5), 663-676.

Shuman, R. E. (1979). How to grade student writing. In G. Stanford (Ed.), *Classroom practices in teaching English 1979–1980: How to handle the paper load*. National Council of Teachers of English.

Singley, M. K. (1995). Promoting transfer through model tracing. In A. McKeough, J. Lupart, & A. Marini (Eds.), *Teaching for transfer* (pp. 69-92). Erlbaum.

Singley, M. K., & Anderson, J. R. (1989). *The transfer of cognitive skill*. Harvard University Press.

Skulmowski, A., & Xu, M. (2021). Understanding cognitive load in digital and online learning: A new perspective on extraneous cognitive load. *Educational Psychology Review, 34*(1), 171-196.

Smith, E. E., Adams, N., & Schorr, D. (1978). Fact retrieval and the paradox of interference. *Cognitive Psychology, 10*, 438-464.

Smith, J. L., Cech, E., Metz, A., Huntoon, M., & Moyer, C. (2014). Giving back or giving up: Native American student experiences in science and engineering. *Cultural Diversity & Ethnic Minority Psychology, 20*(3), 413-429.

Smith, J. M. (2011). Becoming an atheist in America: Constructing identity and meaning from the rejection of theism. *Sociology of Religion, 72*(2), 215-237.

Smith, M. D., & Chamberlin, C. J. (1992). Effect of adding cognitively demanding tasks on soccer skill performance. *Perceptual and Motor Skills, 75*, 955-961.

Solorzano, D., Ceja, M., & Yosso, T. (2000). Critical race theory, racial microaggressions, and campus racial climate: The experiences of African American college students. *The Journal of Negro Education, 69*(1/2), 60-73.

Soloway, E., Adelson, B., & Ehrlich, K. (1988). Knowledge and processes in the comprehension of computer programs. In M.T.H. Chi & R. Glaser (Eds.), *The nature of expertise* (pp. 129-152). Erlbaum.

Somuncuoglu, Y., & Yildirim, A. (1999). Relationship between achievement goal orientations and use of learning strategies. *Journal of Educational Research, 92*, 267-277.

Soria, K. M. (2018). *Evaluating campus climate at US research universities opportunities for diversity and inclusion.* Springer International Publishing.

Spiro, R. J., Feltovich, P. J., Coulson, R. L., & Anderson, D. K. (1989). Multiple analogies for complex concepts: Antidotes for analogy-induced misconception in advanced knowledge acquisition. In S. Vosniadou & A. Ortony (Eds.), *Similarity and analogical reasoning* (pp. 498-531). Cambridge University Press.

Sprague, J., & Stuart, D. (2000). *The speaker's handbook.* Harcourt College Publishers.

Stahl, S. A. (1999). Different strokes for different folks: A critique of learning styles. *American Educator, 23(3)*, 27-31.

Steele, C. (2010) *Whistling Vivaldi: How stereotypes affect us and what we can do.* W. W. Norton.

Steele, C. M., & Aronson, J. R. (1995). Stereotype threat and the intellectual test performance of African Americans. *Journal of Personality and Social Psychology, 69*(5), 797-811.

Stevens, D. D., & Levi, A. J. (2013). *Introduction to rubrics: An assessment tool to save grading time, convey effective feedback and promote student learning* (2nd ed). Stylus.

Stewart, D. L. (2018). Ideologies of absence: Anti-Blackness and inclusion rhetoric in student affairs practice. *Journal of Student Affairs, 28*, 15-30.

Stone, L. (2000). *Kinship and gender: An introduction.* Westview Press.

Strayer, D. L., & Johnston, W. A. (2001). Driven to distraction: Dual-task studies of simulated driving and conversing on a cellular telephone. *Psychological Science, 12*(6), 462-466.

Sun, R., Merrill, E., & Peterson, T. (2001). From implicit skills to explicit knowledge: A bottom-up model of skill learning. *Cognitive Science, 25*, 203-244.

Sweller, J. (2010). Element interactivity and intrinsic, extraneous, and germane cognitive load. *Educational Psychology Review, 22*(2), 123-138.

Sweller, J., & Cooper, G. A. (1985). The use of worked examples as a substitute for problem-solving in learning algebra. *Cognition and Instruction, 2*, 59-89.

Tajfel, H. (1978). The achievement of inter-group differentiation. In H. Tajfel (Ed.), *Differentiation between social groups* (pp. 77–100). Academic Press.

Tatum, B. D. (2017). *Why are all the Black kids sitting together in the cafeteria? And other conversations about race*. Basic Books.

Taylor, A. K., & Kowalski, P. (2004). Naïve psychological science: The prevalence, strength, and sources of misconceptions. *The Psychological Record, 54*, 15–25.

Teague, R. C., Gittelman, S. S., & Park, O.-C. (1994). *A review of the literature on part-task and whole-task training and context dependency* (Report No. 1010). Army Research Institute for the Behavioral and Social Sciences.

Terry, J. M., Hendrick, R., Evangelou, E., & Smith, R. L. (2010). Variable dialect switching among African American children: Inferences about working memory. *Lingua, 120*(10), 2463–2475.

Theobald, E. J., Hill, M. J., Tran, E., Agrawal, S., Arroyo, E. N., Behling, S. J., Chambwe, N., Cintrón, D. L., Cooper, J. D., Dunster, G. P., Grummer, J. A., Hennessey, K., Hsiao, J. C., Iranon, N. N., Jones, L. N., Jordt, H., Keller, M., Lacey, M. E., Littlefield, C. E., … Freeman, S. (2020). Active learning narrows achievement gaps for underrepresented students in undergraduate science, technology, engineering, and math. *Proceedings of the National Academy of Sciences of the United States of America, 117*, 6476–6483.

Thonis, E. (2005). Reading instruction for language minority students. In C. Leyba (Ed.), *Schooling and language minority students: A theoretical framework* (3rd ed). Evaluation, Dissemination and Assessment Center, California State University.

Thorndike, E. L., & Woodworth, R. S. (1901). The influence of improvement in one mental function upon the efficiency of other functions. *Psychological Review, 8*(3), 247–261.

Tinto, V. (2012). *Completing college: Rethinking institutional action*. University of Chicago Press.

Trad, L., Katt, J., & Miller, A. H. (2014). The effect of face threat mitigation on instructor credibility and student motivation in the absence of instructor nonverbal immediacy. *Communication Education, 63*(2), 136–148.

Traxler, M. J., & Gernsbacher, M. A. (1992). Improving written communication through minimal feedback. *Language and Cognitive Processes, 7*, 1–22.

Treisman, U. (1992). Studying students studying calculus: A look at the lives of minority mathematics students in college. *The College Mathematics Journal, 23*(5), 362–372.

University of Michigan. (2022). *Social identity wheel*. Retrieved from https://sites.lsa.umich.edu/inclusive-teaching/social-identity-wheel/

University System of Georgia (USG). (2011). *The University System of Georgia's African-American Male Initiative*. Retrieved from https://www.usg.edu/aami/assets/aami/files/AAMI_Brochure_2011.pdf

282

Valle, A., Cabanach, R., Nunez, J., Gonzales-Pienda, J., Rodriguez, S., & Piñeiro, I. (2003). Multiple goals, motivation and academic learning. *British Journal of Educational Psychology, 73*, 71-87.

Van Merriënboer, J.J.G., & Ayres, P. (2005). Research on cognitive load theory and its design implications for e-Learning. *Educational Technology Research and Development, 53*(3), 5-13.

Violanti, M. T., Kelly, S. E., Garland, M. E., & Christen, S. (2018). Instructor clarity, humor, immediacy, and student learning: Replication and extension. *Communication Studies, 69*(3), 251-262.

Vosniadou, S., & Brewer, W. F. (1987). Theories of knowledge restructuring in development. *Review of Educational Research, 57*, 51-67.

Vygotsky, L. S. (1978). *Mind in society: The development of the higher psychological processes.* The Harvard University Press. (Originally published 1930 Oxford University Press.)

Wall, V. A., & Evans, N. J. (1999). *Toward acceptance: Sexual orientation issues on campus.* University Press of America.

Walton, G. M., & Cohen, G. L. (2007). A question of belonging: Race, social fit, and achievement. *Journal of Personality and Social Psychology, 92*(1), 82-96.

Walton, G. M., & Cohen, G. L. (2011). A brief social-belonging intervention improves academic and health outcomes of minority students. *Science, 331*(6023), 1447-1451.

Wason, P. C. (1960). On the failure to eliminate hypotheses in a conceptual task. *Quarterly Journal of Experimental Psychology, 12*, 129-140.

Watson, L. W., Terrell, M. C., & Wright, D. J. (2002). *How minority students experience college: Implications for planning and policy.* Stylus.

Weick, K. (1995). *Sensemaking in organisations.* Sage.

Weiner, B. (1986). *An attributional theory of motivation and emotion.* Springer-Verlag.

White, B. Y., & Frederickson, J. R. (1990). Causal models progressions as a foundation for intelligent learning environments. *Artificial Intelligence, 42*, 99-157.

Whitt, E., Nora, A., Edison, M., Terenzini, P., & Pascarella, E. (1999). Women's perceptions of a "chilly climate" and cognitive outcomes in college: Additional evidence. *Journal of College Student Development, 40*(2), 163-177.

Wickens, C. D. (1991). Processing resources and attention. In D. L. Damos (Ed.), *Multiple task performance* (pp. 3-34). Taylor & Francis.

Wigfield, A., & Cambria, J. (2010). Students' achievement values, goal orientations, and interest: Definitions, development, and relations to achievement outcomes. *Developmental Review, 30*, 1-35.

Wigfield, A., & Eccles, J. (1992). The development of achievement task values: A theoretical analysis. *Developmental Review, 12*, 265-310.

Wigfield, A., & Eccles, J. (2000). Expectancy-value theory of achievement motivation. *Contemporary Educational Psychology, 25*, 68–81.

Wigfield, A., & Eccles, J. S. (2020). 35 years of research on students' subjective task values and motivation: A look back and a look forward. In A. J. Elliot (Ed.), *Advances in motivation science* (pp. 161–198). Elsevier Academic Press.

Wightman, D. C., & Lintern, G. (1985). Part-task training for tracking and manual control. *Human Factors, 27*(3), 267–283.

Wikan, U. (1982). *Behind the veil in Arabia: Women in Oman*. University of Chicago Press.

Wilson, T. D., & Linville, P. W. (1985). Improving the performance of college freshmen with attributional techniques. *Journal of Personality and Social Psychology, 49*(1), 287–293.

Winkelmes, M., Bernacki, M., Butler, J., Zochowski, M., Golanics, J., & Weevil, K. H. (2016). A teaching intervention that increases underserved college students' success. *Peer Review, 18*(1/2), 31–36.

Winne, P. H., & Hadwin, A. F. (1998). Studying as self-regulated learning. In D. Hacker, J. Dunlosky, & A. Graesser (Eds.), *Metacognition in educational theory and practice*. Erlbaum.

Witt, P. L., Wheeless, L. R., & Allen, M. (2004). A meta-analytic review of the relationship between teacher immediacy and student learning. *Communication Monographs, 71*(2), 184–207.

Woloshyn, V. E., Paivio, A., & Pressley, M. (1994). Use of elaborative interrogation to help students acquire information consistent with prior knowledge and information inconsistent with prior knowledge. *Journal of Educational Psychology, 86*, 79–89.

Woolley, A., & Malone, T. (2011). What makes a team smarter? More women. *Harvard Business Review, 89*(6), 32–33.

Wu, Z., Spreckelsen, T. F., & Cohen, G. L. (2021). A meta-analysis of the effect of values affirmation on academic achievement. *Journal of Social Issues, 77*(3), 702–750.

Yeager, D. S. (2019). *The National Study of Learning Mindsets*, [United States], 2015–2016. Inter-university Consortium for Political and Social Research.

Yeager, D. S., & Dweck, C. S. (2020). What can be learned from growth mindset controversies? *The American Psychologist, 75*(9), 1269–1284.

Yeager, D. S., Hanselman, P., Walton, G. M., Murray, J. S., Crosnoe, R., Muller, C., Tipton, E., Schneider, B., Hulleman, C. S., Hinojosa, C. P., Paunesku, D., Romero, C., Flint, K., Roberts, A., Trott, J., Iachan, R., Buontempo, J., Yang, S. M., Carvalho, C. M., ... Dweck, C. S. (2019). A national experiment reveals where a growth mindset improves achievement. *Nature, 573*(7774), 364–369.

Zhou, X., Chai, C. S., Jong, M. S.-Y., & Xiong, X. B. (2021). Does relatedness matter for online self-regulated learning to promote perceived learning gains and satisfaction? *The Asia-Pacific Education Researcher, 30*, 205–215.

Zhu P., Garcia I., & Alonzo E. (2019). An independent evaluation of growth mindset intervention. MDRC. Retrieved from https://files.eric.ed.gov/fulltext/ED594493.pdf

Zimmerman, B. J. (2001). Theories of self-regulated learning and academic achievement: An overview and analysis. In B. J. Zimmerman & D. H. Schunk (Eds.), *Self-regulated learning and academic achievement* (2nd ed., pp. 1–38). Erlbaum.

INDEX OF NAMES

INDEX

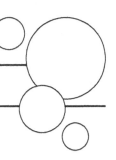

299